IMPORTANCE OF MEDICINAL PLANTS

IMPORTANCE OF MEDICINAL PLANTS

By

Dr. Noor Ahmed Khan

M.Phil., Ph.D.

Saifia Science College

Barkatullah University

Bhopal (India)

&

Dr. Syed Aftab Iqbal

M.Sc. , Ph.D., FICS

FICC, FIAEM, MNASc.

Professor

Department of Chemistry

Saifia Science College

Barkatullah University

Bhopal (India)

DISCOVERY PUBLISHING HOUSE PVT. LTD.

NEW DELHI-110 002

Published by:
Tilak Wasan
DISCOVERY PUBLISHING HOUSE PVT. LTD.
4831/24, Ansari Road, Prahlad Street
Darya Ganj, New Delhi-110002 (India)
Phone: +91-11-23279245, 43764432
Fax: +91-11-23253475
E-mail: parul.wasan@gmail.com
discoverypublishinghouse@gmail.com
info@discoverypublishinggroup.com
web: www.discoverypublishinggroup.com
First Edition: 2011.
Reprint: 2017
ISBN: 978-81-8356-775-6

Importance of Medicinal Plants

Printed at:
Shree Balaji Art Press
Delhi

PREFACE

Herbs are staging a comeback and herbal 'renaissance' is happening all over the globe. The herbal products today symbolise safety in contrast to the synthetics that are regarded as unsafe to human and environment. Although herbs had been priced for their medicinal, flavouring and aromatic qualities for centuries, the synthetic products of the modern age surpassed their importance, for a while. However, the blind dependence on synthetics is over and people are returning to the naturals with hope of safety and security.

It has been estimated that in developed countries such as United States, plant drugs constitute as much as 25% of the total drugs, while in fast developing countries such as China and India, the contribution is as much as 80%. Thus, the economic importance of medicinal plants is much more to countries such as India than to rest of the world. These countries provide two third of the plants used in modern system of medicine and the health care system of rural population depend on indigenous systems of medicine.

Traditional systems of medicine continue to be widely practised on many accounts. Population rise, inadequate supply of drugs, prohibitive cost of treatments, side effects of several allopathic drugs and development of resistance to currently used drugs for infectious diseases have led to increased emphasis on the use of plant materials as a source of medicines for a wide variety of human ailments. Global estimates indicate that 80% of about four billion population can not afford the products of the Western Pharmaceutical Industry and have to rely upon the use of traditional medicines which are mainly derived from plant material. This fact is well documented in the inventory of medicinal plants, listing over 20,000 species. In spite of the overwhelming influences and our dependence on modern medicine and tremendous advances in synthetic drugs, a large segment of the world population still like drugs from plants. In many of the developing countries the use of plant drugs is increasing because modern life saving drugs are beyond the reach of three quarters of the third world's population although many such countries spend 40-50% of their total wealth on drugs and health care. As a part of the strategy to reduce the financial burden on developing countries, it is obvious that an increased use of plant drugs will be followed in the future.

Author

CONTENTS

1 INTRODUCTION

Herbs are staging a comeback and herbal 'renaissance' is happening all over the globe. The herbal products today symbolise safety in contrast to the synthetics that are regarded as unsafe to human and environment. Although herbs had been priced for their medicinal, flavouring and aromatic qualities for centuries, the synthetic products of the modern age surpassed their importance, for a while. However, the blind dependence on synthetics is over and people are returning to the naturals with hope of safety and security.

Over three-quarters of the world population relies mainly on plants and plant extracts for health care. More than 30% of the entire plant species, at one time or other, were used for medicinal purposes. It is estimated that world market for plant derived drugs may account for about Rs. 2,00,000 crores. Presently, Indian contribution is less than Rs. 2000 crores. Indian export of raw drugs has steadily grown at 26% to Rs. 165 crores in 1994-95 from Rs. 130 crores in 1991-92. The annual production of medicinal and aromatic plant's raw material is worth about Rs. 200 crores. This is likely to touch US $1150 by the year 2000 and US $5 trillion by 2050.

It has been estimated that in developed countries such as United States, plant drugs constitute as much as 25% of the total drugs, while in fast developing countries such as China and India, the contribution is as much as 80%. Thus, the economic importance of medicinal plants is much more to countries such as India than to rest of the world. These countries provide two third of the plants used in modern system of medicine and the health care system of rural population depend on indigenous systems of medicine.

Of the 2,50,000 higher plant species on earth, more than 80,000 are medicinal. India is one of the world's 12 biodiversity centres with the presence of over 45000 different plant species. India's diversity is unmatched due to the presence of 16 different agro-climatic zones, 10 vegetation zones, 25 biotic provinces and 426 biomes (habitats of specific species). Of these, about 15,000-20,000 plants have good medicinal value. However, only 7,000-7,500 species are used for their medicinal values by traditional communities. In India, drugs of herbal origin have been used in traditional systems of medicines such as *Unani, Siddha* and *Ayurveda* etc. since ancient times. The *Ayurveda* system of medicine uses about 700 species, *Unani* 700, *Siddha* 600, *Amchi* 600 and modern medicine around 30 species. The drugs are derived either from the whole plant or from different organs, like leaves, stem, bark, root, flower, seed, etc. Some drugs are prepared from excretory plant product such as gum, resins and latex. Even the Allopathic system of medicine has adopted a number of plant-derived drugs which form an important segment of the modern pharmacopoeia. Some important chemical intermediates needed for manufacturing the modern drugs are also obtained from plants (eg. diosgenin, solasodine, b-ionone). Not only, that plant-derived drug offers a stable market world wide, but also plants continue to be an important source for new drugs.

Traditional systems of medicine continue to be widely practised on many accounts. Population rise, inadequate supply of drugs, prohibitive cost of treatments, side effects of several allopathic drugs and development of resistance to currently used drugs for infectious diseases have led to increased emphasis on the use of plant materials as a source of medicines for a wide variety of human ailments. Global estimates indicate that 80% of about four billion population can not afford the products of the Western Pharmaceutical Industry and have to rely upon the use of traditional medicines which are mainly derived from plant material. This fact is well documented in the inventory of medicinal plants, listing over 20,000 species. In spite of the overwhelming influences and our dependence on modern medicine and tremendous advances in synthetic drugs, a large segment of the world population still like drugs from plants. In many of the developing countries the use of plant drugs is increasing because modern life saving drugs are beyond the reach of three quarters of the third world's population although many such countries spend 40-50% of their total wealth on drugs and health care. As a part of the strategy to reduce the financial burden on developing countries, it is obvious that an increased use of plant drugs will be followed in the future.

Among ancient civilisations, India has been known to be rich repository of medicinal plants. The forest in India is the principal repository of large number of medicinal and aromatic plants, which are largely collected as raw materials for manufacture of drugs and perfumery products. About 8,000 herbal remedies have been codified in Ayurveda. The *Rigveda* (5000 BC) has recorded 67 medicinal plants, *Yajurveda* 81 species, *Atharvaveda* (4500-2500 BC) 290 species, *Charak Samhita* (700 BC) and *Sushrut Samhita* (200 BC) had described properties and uses of 1100 and 1270 species respectively, in compounding of drugs and these are still used in the classical formulations, in the Ayurvedic system of medicine. Unfortunately, much of the ancient knowledge and many valuable plants are being lost at an alarming rate. With the rapid depletion of forests, impairing the availability of raw drugs, *Ayurveda*, like other systems of herbal medicines has reached a very critical phase. About 50% of the tropical forests, the treasure house of plant and animal diversity have already been destroyed. In India, forest cover is disappearing at an annual rate 1.5m ha/yr. What is left at present is only 8% as against a mandatory 33% of the geographical area. Many valuable medicinal plants are under the verge of extinction. The *Red Data Book of India* has 427 entries of endangered species of which 28 are considered extinct, 124 endangered, 81 vulnerable, 100 rare and 34 insufficiently known species.

Ayurveda, *Siddha*, *Unani* and folk (tribal) medicines are the major systems of indigenous medicines. Among these systems, *Ayurveda* is most developed and widely practised in India. *Ayurveda* dating back to 1500-800 BC has been an integral part of Indian culture. The term comes from the Sanskrit root *Au* (life) and *Veda* (knowledge). As the name implies it is not only the science of treatment of the ill but covers the whole gamut of happy human life involving the physical, metaphysical and the spiritual aspects. *Ayurveda* recognises that besides a balance of body elements one has to have an enlightened state of consciousness, sense organs and mind if one has to be perfectly healthy. *Ayurveda* by and large is an experience with nature and unlike in Western medicine, many of the concepts elude scientific explanation. *Ayurveda* is gaining prominence as the natural system of health care all over the world. Today this system of medicine is being practised in countries like Nepal, Bhutan, Sri Lanka, Bangladesh and Pakistan, while the traditional system of medicine in the other countries like Tibet, Mongolia and Thailand appear to be derived from Ayurveda. Phytomedicines are also being used increasingly in Western Europe. Recently the US Government has established the "Office of Alternative Medicine" at the

National Institute of Health at Bethesda and its support to alternative medicine includes basic and applied research in traditional systems of medicines such as Chinese, Ayurvedic, etc. with a view to assess the possible integration of effective treatments with modern medicines.

The development of systematic pharmacopoeias dates back to 3000 BC, when the Chinese were already using over 350 herbal remedies. *Ayurveda*, a system of herbal medicine in India, Sri Lanka and South-East Asia has more than 8000 plant remedies and using around 35,000-70,000 plant species. China has demonstrated the best use of traditional medicine in providing the health care. China has pharmacologically validated and improved many traditional herbal medicines and eventually integrated them in formal health care system.

Green plants synthesise and preserve a variety of biochemical products, many of which are extractable and used as chemical feed stocks or as raw material for various scientific investigations. Many secondary metabolites of plant are commercially important and find use in a number of pharmaceutical compounds. However, a sustained supply of the source material often becomes difficult due to the factors like environmental changes, cultural practices, diverse geographical distribution, labour cost, selection of the superior plant stock and over exploitation by pharmaceutical industry.

Plants, especially used in *Ayurveda* can provide biologically active molecules and lead structures for the development of modified derivatives with enhanced activity and/or reduced toxicity. The small fraction of flowering plants that have so far been investigated have yielded about 120 therapeutic agents of known structure from about 90 species of plants. Some of the useful plant drugs include vinblastine, vincristine, taxol, podophyllotoxin, camptothecin, digitoxigenin, gitoxigenin, digoxigenin, tubocurarine, morphine, codeine, aspirin, atropine, pilocarpine, capscicine, allicin, curcumin, artemesinin and ephedrine among others. In some cases, the crude extract of medicinal plants may be used as medicaments. On the other hand, the isolation and identification of the active principles and elucidation of the mechanism of action of a drug is of paramount importance. Hence, works in both mixture of traditional medicine and single active compounds are very important. Where the active molecule cannot be synthesised economically, the product must be obtained from the cultivation of plant material. About 121 (45 tropical and 76 sub-tropical) major plant drugs have been identified for which no synthetic one is currently available. The scientific study of traditional medicines, derivation of drugs through bioprospecting and systematic conservation of the concerned medicinal plants are thus of great importance.

Tropical countries are a treasure house of a wide variety of medicinal plants. Some species are found wild, while a number of species have been domesticated by the farmers. Many species have been grown in homesteads and become part of traditional home remedies. A limited number of species are commercially cultivated though a few more have potential for large-scale production. The important tropical and subtropical medicinal plants are discussed here highlighting the importance, medicinal and other uses, distribution, botany, agrotechnology, chemical constituents and activity.

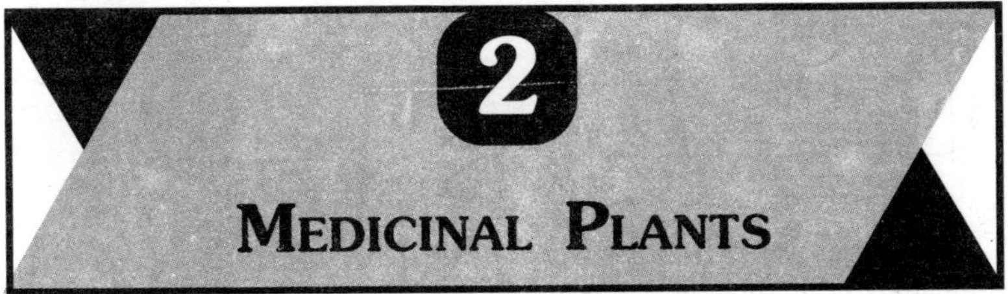

2
MEDICINAL PLANTS

ALOE VERA

Aloe vera also called "the elixir of youth" by the Russians, "the herb of immortality" by the old Egyptians or the "harmonious remedy" by the Chinese, *Aloe vera* is without a doubt the medicinal herb most widely known for its noticeable impacts on health and at the same time the ingredient most widely used in the cosmetic industry. Not one study conducted so far was fully able to explain the wonders which lie within this herb and how its compounds work together in a miraculous way to bring about the treatment or the alleviation of some of the most serious illnesses such as cancer or AIDS.

Description

Aloe vera or "*Aloe barbadensis*" is a plant which originated in North Africa and spread to the fertile lands with mild climate. Its physical aspect is similar to that of the cactus; the thick rind hides a succulent core formed mostly of water.

Fig. 2.1: Aloe Vera

The afore-mentioned herb gained worldwide recognition and has been intensively used from the oldest of times due to its extraordinary features. A clear proof of this fact is a clay plank found in the antic city of Nippur, Babilon (the Irak from today) dating from year 2200 b.c. From Greek physicians like Celsius and Dioscorides to Romanians (Pylni the Great) and Arabs (Al-Kindi) to C.E. Collins, the one who published the first modern medical thesis in United States (1934), "aloe vera" has always been an issue with a long history behind it. Just about every important civilization used it for its benefical effects over health and beauty. Egyptians would mix aloe with other herbs while preparing remedies for internal and external anomalies. After the Second World War, aloe vera was introduced in treating the victims of the catastrophies from Nagasaki and Hiroshima because of its ability of mitigating the pain of the patients and renewing skin tissues.

Proprieties

The most oftenly used substance from this herb is the aloe gel, a thick viscid liquid found in the interior of the leaves. The leaves are used in the treatment of burns and the aloine - a bitter milky yellowish liquid is used as a laxative. The herb contains: 20 minerals (Calcium, Magnesium, Zinc, Chromium , Selenium), 12 vitamins (A, B, C, E, folic acid), 20 aminoacids from the 22 which are necessary to the human body, over 200 active components including enzymes and polysaccharides. All the active substances enumerated before contribute to the therapeutical value of the herb. We shall move on to presenting the main effects that the herb has over the human body: it toughens up the immune system owing to the 23 peptides contained by the aloe vera, it accelerates and regulates the methabolism, purifies the human body from toxins, bringing about a feeling of calm. Moreover, aloe vera has an antiseptic effect (by distroying the bacterias, viruses and fungi), disinfectant capabilities and can also stimulate the cell-renewing process. Aloe vera nourishes and supports the digesting of aliments. Cutting across the human organism, aloe vera manages to bring the human body to a general balanced state.

Treatments

Aloe vera has proved its efficiency from the simplest allergies to the treatment of wounds and skin infections and even to its usage in alleviating more serious afflictions. With the help of this herb a wide variety of internal and external afflictions are controlled, like: asthma, virosis, arthritis, arthrosis, gingivitis, bronchitis, pharyngitis, intestinal inflamations, constipations, obesity, sprains, muscle strains, cutaneous inflamations. The efficiency of the herb was also proven in the cases of anemia, deficiency illnesses, insomnia and depressions and the B-sisterole from the Aloe vera brings about the lowering of the cholesterol level. Also, this herb is used for controlling the side effects of chemotherapy and radiation therapy, diabetes, hepatitis and pancreatitis and multiple sclerosis.

Mixtures

A wide array of products with curative and therapeutic effects is obtained from aloe vera. This herb is one of the

Fig. 2.2: Aloe Vera

main attractions of the pharma-ceutical and cos-metic industries and also the most widely used ingredient - starting from vitamins and laxatives to face creams and body care lotions. Aloe vera gel contains B-sisterole, power-ful anti-inflammatory and anti-cholesterol formulas and lupeol - a strong anti-septic tranquilizer. The aloebased lotions and gels are used as protections against the powerful sunlight and as a remedy against sunburns. Oint-ments having aloe as a main ingredient moist the skin and protect it against bug stings and scratches. Furthermore, the aloe-based ointment is efficient in treating acne. Owing to its proprieties, Aloe vera was incorporated in the composition of deodorants.

What should be noted is the fact that this herb can be also administrated internally due to its high nourishing influence. When mixed with other fruits, aloe vera can be ingested as an excellent natural beverage rich in vitamins and minerals. Also, it is recommended that it is ingested during travels to prevent dehydration.

Cultivation

Because it is not a pretentious herb, aloe vera can be easily tended for. This herb requires a great amount of light (even if it is artificial - 16 hours a day) and a little bit of water (especially in the cold season).

ANISE (*Pimpinella anisum*)

It is a herbal, aromatic plant, which is cultivated. It grows as high as 40-70 cm in the light, in rich soils and it needs moderate humidity.

Parts used: the bulb, the leaves, the seeds and the roots.

The therapeutic virtues of the anise have been known since the ancient times. Pythagoras claimed that the anise enhanced man's strength, cured insomnia, stimulated appetite, made men more fertile and facilitated digestion.

Main constituents known: The vitamins, the B complex (B_1, B_2), C, calcium, phosphorus, potassium, sulphur, iron, aromatic essences.

Pharmacologic Action

Carminative, antispasmodic, expectorant, a pancreatic stimulant. As food, the anise is used for cooking sweet and spicy dishes. It has been used as an aphrodisiac since the Greeks' time. The medical tests have confirmed that anise seeds intensified lust.

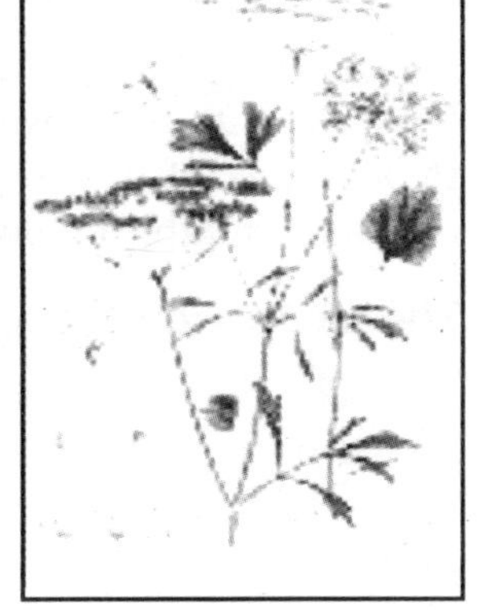

Fig. 2.3: Anise

The anise fruit have got a nice taste and are used in the phytotherapy. As a ripe fruit or as juice, it is recommended for curing asthenia and for stimulating suckling mothers' lactation. Synthetically speaking, one may say about the anise that it is a medicine plant recommended for curing nervous asthenia, migraines, vertigos, rheumatism, cough, bronchial asthma, gastric pains, and slow digestion.

Natural Treatments and Application Procedures

The Anise Fruit Infusion

The infusion is made from half a tea-spoon of mashed anise fruit scalded in 250 ml of boiling water. The tea should be left for 10-15 minutes in order to become an infusion. It should be drunk in fractions: half a mug before a main meal. *Caution:* The tea must only be kept for a short time before its consuming. As for sucklings, an infusion from 5-6 anise fruit scalded in 250 ml of boiling water is to be made. It treats flatulence and children's colics.

The tea for Eliminating Helminths

The infusion is made from 10 grams of mashed fruit scalded in 100 ml of boiling water. The tea should be drunk in the morning on an empty stomach.

The Tea from Anise Seeds

The infusion is made from one tea-spoon of anise seeds boiled in 250 ml of water for 30 seconds. One mug of tea is to be drunk after the main meals. This tea treats bronchial asthma, cough, a slow digestion.

The Decoction from Anise Roots

The decoction is made from 30 gr of broken up roots boiled in one litre of water for 20-30 minutes. One mug of tea is to be drunk after the main meals. This tea treats painful menses.

The Anise Ether Oil

It is used for curing stomach and intestine disorders, flatulence and colds.

APPLES

The apple, as a fruit, contains between 83 and 93% water.

Nutritional Information about the Apple.

Apple is also known to contain free and combined organic acids , pectin's, proteins, Ca, Na, Fe, K, P and in small quantities Si, Al, S, Co etc.

Apples also contain Vitamins A, B, C and PP in the exterior part of the fruit. Very important is the fact that the skin of the apple contains two times the quantity of Pentatonic acids and vitamin C than in the pulp.

Fig. 2.4: Apples

Therapeutic Recommendations

Internal

- Because of its moderate acidity it helps the digestive system, provoking trough reflex act an important growth of saliva and gastric secretions.
- Apple eaten with its skin is a little bit laxative, absorbing the toxins and microorganisms from the intestine level.
- Apple without the skin represents an important treatment for children in acute and chronic diarrhoea.
- The diuretic action is evident but more important is the massive elimination of uric acid.
- They also have a favorable action in high blood pressure which, combined with its properties to reduce cholesterol make from apple a good recommendation in atherosclerosis.

- Apples are also good in diets against obesity.
- Doctors also noted favorable results in infantile diabetic treatment with apples and tomatoes diets.
- At the nervous system level they have a calming action, being known the fact that an apple eaten before bed helps and eases the sleep.

External

Traditional medicine recommends warm covering of boiled fruits in ear pains.

Cosmetic

Apple juice helps invigorate tissues. You can use the juice to massage cheeks and breasts for a relaxing effect.

Apple Cider Vinegar and his Health Benefits

As borsch, apple cider vinegar take over the qualities of base from witch it was obtain, in this case from apples, fruits very rich in potassium, essential mineral for normal function of important system from our body (nervous, cardiovascular). Apple vinegar contains all the important minerals, like potassium, magnesium, calcium, phosphor, sulfur and iron. Apple vinegar diet is recommended to those who have a low potassium level, an often seen thing at in cases of hyper protein diets that is a diet based, in principle, on meat. Let's see, how we can fix these problems.

Health Benefits of Apple Vinegar

To putt weight we can make a simple treatment with a higher efficiency: every morning, when we wake up, will drink a glass of water on an empty stomach, with two tea spoons of apple vinegar. Then, over day, after each meal, will drink half a glass of water with a single tea spoon of apple vinegar and two tea spoons of honey.

Big appetite it's held under control with a simple diet, but with powerful effects: before each meal, eat two cloves of garlic and drink a spoon of apple vinegar and same water.

You should remember that this diet, pretty tough for digestive system, it can be made no more then seven days, followed by a seven days pause.

Difficult digestion take, before and after meal, a quarter of a glass, diluted with a spoon of apple vinegar. Vinegar stimulates saliva, gastric juice secretion. Also, it improves lipids metabolism, substances witch are very hard to digest.

Headaches especially those which appear as a consequence of food excess, it's treated with two tea spoons of apple vinegar. Externally, it's recommended rubbing the temples with apple vinegar.

External Applications with Apple Vinegar

Fatigue after long periods with no sleep, you can refresh yourself with an apple vinegar massage of shoulders, nape and forehead zone. This treatment it will be no longer then thirty minutes and it will be followed by a shower.

ARNICA

Description

Arnica montana is a herb which has been used from the oldest of times to cure wounds. Starting in the 16th century this herb has been used in North America, Germany and Russia due to its anti-inflammatory and calming effects. It should not be confused with *Arnica chamissonis*, which is not a medicinal herb, but a decorative one.

Fig. 2.5: Arnica

The active compounds contained by arnica are its volatile oil, carotenoids, flavornoids, and triterpenic alcohol.

Its roots contain volatile oil (0.5-1.5%), caffeic acid, inuline, thymol, and saccharose.

Arnica has antiseptic, anti-inflammatory, anti-bacterial, decongestive and antifungal properties. It also stimulates the forming the granular tissues and thus accelerating the healing process. It eliminates micro-organisms and keeps bacteria and pathogenic funguses from multiplying.

The arnica flowers are used for treating the pale face skin complexion, wounds, bruises and burns. It should be noted however that the arnica flowers are not harmless because the arnica tincture can be an irritant when applied locally on skin or even internally in small doses can provoke gastro-enteritis or the paralysis of central nerve system. Other medicinal uses of this herb involve the treatment of bruises, dislocations, bacterial infections, skin cancer, bronchitis, tonsillitis, pharyngitis, flu, lung virosis, cystitis, nephritis, kidney infections, coronary insufficiencies, hypertension, breastplate angina, cerebral trauma, headaches, paresis, semiparesis, insomnia, heart palpitations, nightmares, night terrors, moral depressions, neurosis, hysteria etc.

The mixtures from arnica are as follows:

Tincture

Tincture recommended in cases of trauma, sprains, and wounds by applying a dab on the affected area. Internally, the arnica tincture is administrated in 3-4 doses daily. The usual dose consists of one spoon diluted in approximately 100 ml of water. It is also recommended in treating breathing disorders by completing the antibiotic effect recommended by the physician. Many satisfactory results are obtained in cases of poor health conditions and also in treating urinary renal illnesses. In treating throat infections, gargling with arnica is recommended. One to two spoons of arnica are dissolved in half a glass of water and caution should be employed as to not swallow the mixture.

The tincture can also be used by the individuals highly sensitive to cold to energetically rub their feet numb with cold or the chest. A salve of chamomile is usually applied on the rubbed spots. Warning! Arnica tincture is toxic if more than 30 drops are administrated in the same day. Over dosage of arnica is very dangerous, leading to digestion problems, nausea and even diarrhoea. For children younger than 7-year old arnica can only be administrated under medical surveillance.

Oil

It is prepared in the following way: one handful of arnica flowers are grinded and then put into a jar, on top of which 200 ml of pumpkin or soybean oil is poured. For two weeks the mixture is left to heat in the sun and after that it gets strained.

Powder

It is obtained from dry arnica flower by grinding them with an electrical grinder and then strained to obtain the white powder. From this a white powder giving off a strong perfumed smell is obtained from which only a really small quantity is administered four times a day.

Ointments

Ointments based on arnica and black bryony - have the same usages as the other products containing arnica. Arnica creams are renowned for their ability of treating acne.

ARTICHOKE (Cynara scolymus)

Originating from Carthage and from the Mediterranean regions, the artichoke has been cultivated since the ancient times for its exceptional qualities. At present days this vegetable and medicine plant is being used in all regions of the planet. The artichoke is a two metre high, strongly ramified biannual culture plant.

Pharmacologic Action

It stimulates the metabolization of the cholesterol in the liver; it is diuretic, tonic, depurative, hypoglycaemic. Young artichokes consumed in their raw condition are indicated in chronic diarrhoeas.

Phytotherapy uses the artichoke leaves.

The preparations made from the artichoke (teas, powder, tincture) have got exceptional therapeutic qualities in case of the disorders of the blood circulation, of the hepatic and renal ones.

The artichoke powder, made from dried up leaves, is given to the patients in 2-4 grams a day quantities, in several steps and the recommendation is that it should be kept under the tongue for a few minutes and then swallowed with water.

Synthetically speaking, artichoke preparations may be used for treating cardio-vascular, liver, kidney disorders, eczemas, diabetes, podagra, hemorrhoids and for regenerating hepatic cells.

Fig. 2.6: Artichoke

Natural Treatments and Application Procedures

The Artichoke Juice

One small glass of artichoke juice is recommended to be drunk before breakfast and lunch. It is a treatment indicated for constipated people and for those with dramatic weight enhancement. It is a draining treatment in case of constipation without however aggressing the liver.

The Artichoke Tea

The infusion is made from one spoon of mashed artichoke leaves scalded in 500 ml of water. The tea should be left for 15-20 minutes in order to become an infusion. The former mug of tea should be drunk in the morning on an empty stomach. The latter mug is to be drunk in 2 stages, namely one half of mug before breakfast and then before dinner. The treatment is to be made in 21-30 days cures with 30 day breaks.

The Artichoke Tincture

It is made from 20 grams of mashed artichoke leaves macerated in 100 ml of 70 degree alcohol for 15 days. 5-15 drops should be taken 3 times a day. The tincture shall be diluted with water or with tea whenever taken.

ASPARAGUS

Asparagus (Asparagus Officinalis), also known as sparrow grass, is a vegetable which has been grown from early times in ancient Egypt and in the Roman Empire. Because it is rare and pretentious to both growing and cooking conditions, the plant is considered to be a delicacy.

Description

Asparagus is a plant which grows spontaneously in hay fields. It is cultivated in different varieties. In the earth it has a strong rhizome. The leaves are scale shaped, and the fruits are actually linear ramifications of the stems. The flowers are small, of a whitish-green colour. The fruits are of red color.

Properties

The vegetable contains phosphate and vitamin B, which gives it remineralizing and stimulating properties.

Also, it has rare nutrients: copper, iron, zinc, manganese, chrome, calcium, sodium, potassium, which give it depurative, and laxative properties and make it a hepatic and renal drainer.

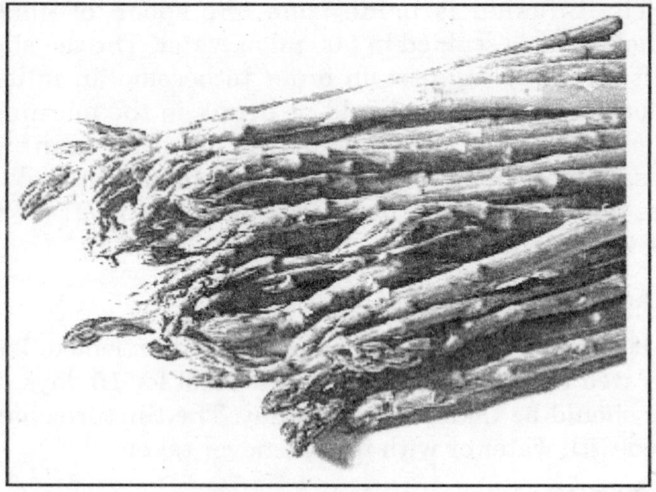

Fig. 2.7: Asparagus

Treatments

Next to its qualities of being a refined vegetable, asparagus is also used in natural medicine. It is used to control some stomach affections, clean the liver, lungs and intestines of their wastes and toxins. Apart from its depurative effects, the vegetable also has a protecting action on the arteries. Consumed regularly, it prevents the development of arteriosclerosis and cleans the blood.

For cases of physical or intellectual asthenia, anemia and convalescence, the asparagus diet is recommended, consumed in its raw state.

Also, for treating cardio-vascular erythrism, the raw asparagus diet is recommended. Consuming this vegetable stimulates the decrease of glycosuria and increases diuresis, a reason why it is recommended to diabetics.

The asparagus stem has the property of eliminating toxins from the digestive trap. The pulp of the asparagus stem is used, its exterior side being first cleaned.

The asparagus root, boiled in vinegar, is used in treating paradontosis. The asparagus tea is used for its diuretic actions.

Mixtures

In order for it to be consumed, the asparagus has to be very fresh. Most often it is consumed in the form of a salad. A way of preparing this salad is: the asparagus is cleaned of fibrous threads, is washed, cut into pieces having lengths of about 4-5cm and boiled in salt water for about 20 minutes. In a bowl, the sauce formed of vinegar, oil, mustard, pepper and salt is mixed. After that the asparagus is drained and mixed with the sauce. The asparagus juice is consumed along with carrot juice, having a diuretic action.

Warning

Asparagus is not recommended to those with affections of the urinary system - cystitis, prostatitis, and gonorrhea - and neither in cases of acute articulacy rheumatism, because of its high content of purines.

BANANA (*Musa paradisiaca*)

The banana, a plant originating in South Africa, is considered to have been the first fruit to appear on the Earth, having been mentioned in writings that date back to the beginning of mankind. Today it is the favorite fruit of many people, being rich in vitamins and minerals.

Description

The banana plant is a herbaceous plant of the family Musaceae, which because of its size and structure, is on many occasions confused with a tree. The plant is grown for its fruit, being of southeastern Asian origin.

Bananas that are destined for human consumption do not contain seeds. The plant produces two stems at the same time: a bigger one for the immediate obtaining of the fruit, and a smaller one, which produces the fruit 6-8 months later. The lifespan of a banana plant plantation is at least 25 years.

Fig. 2.8: Banana

Properties

Bananas are true sources of energy. A banana contains potassium, proteins, fibres, carbohydrates and an association of vitamins: A, B, B_6, C and E; it is rich in calcium, magnesium, iron, zinc and folic acid. These facts being taken into consideration, the banana is one of the healthiest fruits. It also contains serotonin or the substance of happiness, having an anti-stress role.

Other properties of bananas: especially helpful in anti-fat treatments, being very dense, it offers a sensation of satisfaction.

Treatments

Being rich in iron, the bananas stimulate the production of hemoglobin in the blood, thus helping in cases of anemia. Because of its high potassium, but low salt content, it is indicated for those having problems with arterial pressure.

Being an aliment that is rich in fibres, the banana helps with constipation, through the regaining of the intestines' normal activity. Containing a type of protein, which the body transforms into serotonin, the fruit is indicated in treatments against depression, leading to an improved affective state. The banana is also indicated for calming of nerves, being used in treatments for the regulating of intestinal traffic. Having a fine and soft texture, it is also used in treating ulcer.

The fruit has the power of growing its concentration capacity. The potassium contained in bananas helps regulating heartbeats, brings oxygen to the brain and maintains the water quantity in the body at a constant level.

At moments of stress, the metabolism is accelerated and the level of potassium decreases, a situation in which the consumption of bananas is recommended.

The fruit is also useful against smoking, helping the body regenerate after the effects of lack of nicotine.

Many cultures see the banana as a refreshing fruit, which can decrease the physical and emotional temperature of pregnant women.

Against hangovers, a milkshake can be prepared, sweetened with honey. The banana calms the body and rebuilds the sugar level in the body, while the milk calms and hydrates the body.

Mosquito bites can be treated if the affected area is rubbed with the interior part of a banana peal. Bananas are used in cosmetics for treating dried complexions, limp skin and itches. In cases of solar burns or numbness from cold, a crushed banana can be applied on the face to calm pain and reduce inflammations.

Mixtures

It is recommended that bananas be consumed when they have only a few spots of brownish color because that is when it is richest in minerals and vitamins.

Creams based on bananas, used in cosmetics for treating dried complexions, are prepared from crushed bananas, a teaspoon of liquid honey is added and the mixture is stirred well. It is applied on the face under the form of a mask. It is kept that way for 15 minutes, and then washed away with mineral water. Another mask against itching is prepared of a crushed banana mixed with yogurt. It is applied on the face and kept for ten minutes before washing it away.

Facial lotion, for dried complexions is obtained like this: a very ripe banana is taken, crushed in the mixer, added to a glass of milk and a teaspoon of olive or sweet almond oil.

Recommendations

In the moment of the fruit's consumption, its colour has to be taken into account. It should not be eaten while it is of a pale yellow or green color because at such a time it contains starch, which is hard to digest.

Being rich in calories, it is recommended that those who are holding anti-fat treatments and who suffer from diabetes consume it moderately. It is not indicated for use in a severe anti-cholesterol diet. Bananas do not bear temperatures lower than 12 degrees and they should never be kept in refrigerators.

BARBERRY

Barberry is one of the oldest medicinees. Not too long ago thousands of lives were being saved with the help of mixtures prepared from barberry root. Those mixtures would diminish fever, control common cold and lung infections.

Description

Barberry, named scientifically as "*Berberis vulgaris*", is a thorny shrub with yellow flowers, small red fruits and leaves which are narrow at the base and narrow and serrated on the edges; it grows along with other shrubs at the edge of fields or the outskirts of forests. It's a decorative herb through its nicely colored flowers and fruits which last throughout the year including winter time and through its leaves that change color during the autumn season. Barberry is often cultivated as a hedge in parks and gardens. It is also planted around houses where because of its thorny aspect that keeps away any unwanted guests. However, barberry is a propitious host for "Puccinia graminis" (stem rust of wheat), and for that reason it's forbidden for the barberry to be cultivated in certain areas like the agricultural ones.

The herb has been used throughout the time for its medicineal characteristics. In the traditional Chinese medicine, barberry was mentioned more than 3000 years ago.

Proprieties

In the chemical composition of the herb there are a considerable number of active substances. The bark contains a large number of alkaloids (berberine, berbamine, oxyacantha) and tanines. Barberry fruits contain glucose, fructose, malic acid, pectine, vitamin C. The active substances from the herb bring about the following effects: haemostatic, diuretic, vasodilator, hypertensive, antibacterial (kills bacteria and parasites), and anti-inflammatory. Berberine, the potent agent has numerous usages in controlling different illnesses (stimulates digestion and reduces the gastrointestinal pains) and at the same time it toughens the immune system.

Treatments

Among the most recommended usages of barberry are those against diarrhoea (and in its more serious forms - cholera), against fever, anemia and also against hangovers. It's also efficient against a considerable number of infections

- malaria or the lung infections, while controlling the secretions of the mucous membrane. It has a strong sedative effect, decreases the blood pressure and is also a uterine stimulant. Barberry can be administrated to help correct the growth of the spleen.

Preparations

Barberry can be ingested as an aliment due to its generous supply of vitamin C. Its fruits are used for making juice, syrup and jam.

Fig. 2.9: Barberry

Only the dry crust from the roots and stem is being used in medicinal purposes. Barbarry can be found on the market under the forms of tea, tincture, pills and ointment. Usually the percentage of berberine from those products is between 8 and 12 per cent.

Following is the shortened version on how to prepare the barberry decoct: ½ of powdered barberry crust is boiled in a cup of water for 5 minutes, after which it is let to cool down and then is strained. The final mixture gets poured in a cup (2 a day at the most), almost half an hour before dinner. For gargling (against sore throats) the decoct is prepared from one spoon of powdered barberry crust mixed with 0.5 litres of water.

As for the tincture, it should be consumed three times a day in doses of 1.2 ml.

As a remedy against kidney problems it's recommended that the next recipe based on barberry crust to be put into use: Finely cut bits of barberry get added in a bottle half filled with plum brandy at 35-40° Celsius until the bottle is filled to the brim. It gets covered with a cork and is let to sit for about 20-30 minutes in a heated place, after which it gets strained. This mixture lasts for five years and is considered a true miracle in fighting the kidney illnesses. It is administrated 2-3 times a day by using a spoon.

Against conjunctivitis the use of cataplasms with powdered barberry crust is recommended.

Warning

Exceding the recommended doses leads to the occurance of side efects (nausea, vomit, dizziness, convulsions) and can also lead to nosebleeds, kidney failure, swells of skin and eyes, blood sugar decrease. The mixturees made from crust of barberry are forbidden to children, pregnant women or women in lactation period. In cases of interaction between this herb with other medicinee to avoid side effects, the advice of the physician should be asked for.

BARLEY (*Hordeum Vulgare*)

One of the seven sacred cereals, barley comes from the eastern Balkans. From an esoteric point of view, barley is considered a mild nourishing force which stimulates the heart and is used for easing the emotional tension of a person.

Description

Barley is a type of cereal which can reach heights of around 0.7 to 1.2 metres. The plant's fruit is ear shaped. This way there are a number of types of barley, depending on the number of granules on the ear: summer and winter barley. The winter barley is used for feeding animals because of the inferior quality of its granules. Barley develops well especially in flat, moist areas, but they can adapt to more unfavorable conditions as well.

Properties

Fig. 2.10: Barley

When it reaches a height of 20-30 cm, barley contains the most nutritive resources necessary for the human body. Thus, barley leafs contain vitamins B (B_1, B_2, B_6, and B_{12}), vitamins E and C, a great amount of iron, calcium, manganese, magnesium, molybdenum, germanium, zinc, copper, lithium, biofla-vonoid, polysaccharides, and poly-peptides.

The green stem of barley, apart from containing vita-mins, minerals and enzymes, also contains natural hor-mones and chlorophyll. These nutritive substances give barley antioxidant, anti-inflammatory, anti-cancer and antiviral properties.

Treatments

Green barley contains the most valuable elements necessary for the human body and it is also a product with excellent therapeutic effects.

Barley diet is indicated for eliminating toxins from the body, including the blood, for immune stimulation, cicatrisation and regeneration. Barley helps regulate arterial pressure, eliminates the excess of weight, hydrates the teguments and increases virility. This diet is recommended to be held for a minimum period of two weeks. For chronic diseases it can last for a month.

In cases of high fever, barley extract helps reduce the patient's fever. Green barley contains an active proteic enzyme, which has a powerful effect in curing diseases, revitalizing the body and slowing the aging process. This enzyme intervenes in the deactivation of free radicals.

Barley helps improve memory, bringing clarity in thought. Also, it eases stomach pains, heals ulcers, and lessens arthritic pains and inflammations. In obesity it helps eliminate weight excess. Green barley juice has an anti-inflammatory effect, revitalizing the tegument and curing it of its dryness. The plant shows visible results in the fight against collagen and leukemia, also neutralizing the toxic effects of tobacco.

Other diseases in which the treatment with barley is utilized: anorexia, anemia, stomatitis, pancreatitis, miocardic arrest, bronchic asthma, arthritis, and epilepsy. Barley stimulates the drainage and regeneration of the liver, activates the immune system helping in the fight against the hepatic virus.

Mixtures

Barley juice is obtained from mixing a handful of green stems with water. They are mixed until a paste is obtained, which is filtered with a colander or with some gauze. The juice has to be consumed only a few moments after it was prepared.

Green barley powder is obtained through the dehydration of the fresh green barley juice, at small temperatures, thus allowing the enzymes to remain active.

Out of crushed green barley sprouts, mixed with honey and fruit, a delicious desert can be made which has exceptional invigorating properties. Barley can also be consumed in the form of a salad, crushed into small pieces and combined with other unripe elements or with honey.

Warning

It is recommended that people who can't stand gluten do not consume beer which is based on barley.

BASIL (*Ocimum basilicum*)

The basil is a herbaceous annual culture plant, ramified from the ground, 20-60 cm tall with hairy stems, round-oval leaves and white or reddish flowers.

The basil has been known since ancient times and is a holy plant in India, very much appreciated by Egyptians, too; bouquets of basil were found in the Egyptian pyramids.

An aromatic plant, the basil is used in the culinary art as a seasoning for diverse meat and sauce dishes. Traditional medicine uses basil as a remedy for chronic gastritis and stomach aches.

Pharmacological actions: sedative, diuretic, antiseptic.

Starting from the essential oil content of the basil, as related to the other active elements, basil is recommended in the treatment of gastro-intestinal and renal affections, bronchitis and fever.

The use of basil leaf tea is recommended in nervous system fatigue, insomnia and painful menstruation. To avoid the unpleasant effects of insect stings rub the wounded spot with fresh basil leaves or with the juice from fresh basil plants.

Health Benefits of Basil and applying techniques

Basil Tea

The infusion is prepared of 1-2 spoonfuls of basil leaves, shredded, boiled in 250 ml of water. The tea is left to infuse two minutes. Drink 2-3 cups a day. It is recommended to drink a cup after every meal. This tea treats distention and intestinal colics, gastric ulcer, anorexia, urinary infections, diarrhoea.

In case of diabetes, the tea should be consumed unsweetened, but in all the other cases can be sweetened with bee honey. The tea for throat wash will be prepared like a decoction with 2 spoonfuls of shredded leaves at 100 ml of water. It will be used to treat mouth lesion, inflammation and erosion.

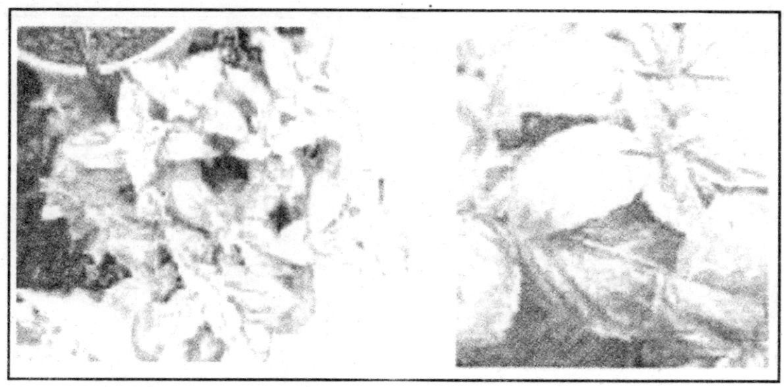

Fig. 2.11: Basil

Tonic Basil Wine

It is prepared of 2 handfuls of basil leaves, well-washed and dried, minced and deposited in a bottle. Over the leaves will be poured one litre of red wine and a spoonful of honey. It is left to macerate 5-7 days. To extract most efficiently the active elements from the leaves shake the bottle 4-5 times a day. After filtration the obtained tonic wine will be put in a well-sealed bottle. It is an excellent natural medicine for stimulating the appetite. Drink it 15-30 minutes before every meal. Children should be administered a spoonful of wine 2-3 times a day and adults should drink 100 ml, 3 times a day.

Basil Tincture

Twenty gram of minced basil plants are left to macerate in 100 ml 70° alcohol. The macerating process lasts 15 days. After macerating, it is filtered and put in a well sealed bottle. For internal use is administered to children 3-5 drops in 100 ml of water 3 times a day. Adults take a spoonful of tincture in 100 ml of water, 3 times a day. For external use the tincture will be diluted in water in a ratio of 1/5 and can go to 1/10 for more sensible patients. In case of insect stings, wounds, eczema, tampon with tincture or apply compresses.

BEAN

Because of its nutritive qualities, the common bean can successfully replace meat. Its rich containment of proteins (approximately 70% of the necessary amino acids which can be found in meat, carbohydrates and the lack of toxins, it is best recommended for its benefiting effects on health.

Fig. 2.12: Bean

Description

Bean (*Phaseolus vulgaris*) is a herba-ceous plant from the Legumnosae family. From what is known, this is one of the vegetabls earliest used in alimentation, having been known for 4000 years. There are a number of hypothesis concerning the origin of the common bean: some are convinced that it originated in Central America (there are traces of beans in prehistoric tombs) while others declare that beans originate in Latin America and more precisely, Peru, from where it was brought to Europe after the discovery of America. Because of its nutritional qualities, beans can successfully replace meat. Its rich containment of proteins (approximately 70% of the necessary amino acids which can be found in meat), carbohydrates and the lack of toxins, it is best recommended for its beneficial effects on health. Moreover, beans also have the property of reducing cholesterol. Studies about this were made and they have revealed that including beans in daily alimentation leads to the drop in the value of cholesterol with 20% and 30% in best cases. Nowadays, the majority of nutritionists say that the consumption of beans is important for maintaining health of the nervous system, liver, kidneys, pancreas and bones.

Properties

Besides its proteic content, bean also contains organic and mineral substances (sodium, potassium, calcium, magnesium, silicium, nickel, copper, and cobalt), vitamins (A_1, B_1, B_2, B_5, B_6, C, E, and P_1) bean also contains fibres (soluble and insoluble) with an important role in the body: it reduces the level of cholesterol, prevents constipation and colon cancer. Vitamin B_2 helps prevent cardiovascular diseases while pro-vitamin B_5 helps prevent cancer and blocks the growth of tumors. Bean also benefits the immune system through its anti-infectious effect which facilitates the growing of the number of leucocytes, destroying injurious microorganisms in the body. This effect is present because of chromium - a substance present in beans with the ròle of stimulating lymphatic ganglions.

A special species of beans in which case the pods produce no seeds (named Fructus phaseolii sine seminibus) contains arginine, asparagine, tizoline and tipofan - aminoacids with a diuretic and antidiabetic role.

Treatments and Mixtures

Bean Pod Tea

For preparing tea, one tablespoon of bean pods is boiled in 250 ml of water for a period of 15 to 20 minutes. From this dietetic and anti-rheumatic tea, one or two cups are drunk per day. The tea thus prepared is good for states of hydropsy (water accumulation in the tissues), heart, kidney, and urinary bladder diseases, such as cystitis. At the same time, bean pod tea helps calm spasms, normalize urination and increasing the quantity of urine, remove the excess of water from the body. As a direct consequence of this action, the body loses a great amount of toxins - an important result for the amelioration of rheumatic states. For those suffering from hyperglycemia, the consumption of dried been pod tea is recommended. Because of the specifics of this disease, the tea will not be sweetened with sugar but only with saccharin. Furthermore, in skin diseases such as acne, beans added in the daily alimentation, or consumed as a tea, contribute to the rapid removal of these problems.

Been Flour

Bean pods are rich in salicic acid, which is why they are recommended as energizers for the body. For this reason, flour obtained from beans leads to the removal of unpleasant sensations caused by eczemas, acne or other skin diseases. Manner of utilization: affected areas will be covered with cataplasms containing bean flour.

Beans in Alimentation

It is important to know the fact that this vegetable plays an important part in preventing the development of diabetes. Researches have proved that the number of people suffering from insulin-dependent diabetes is surprisingly small in the case of those who have even just slightly added beans to their daily nutrition. Also, in cases of osteoporosis (atrophy of the bones), caused by a loss of calcium and metals and vitamins, or by metabolic imbalances, it has been observed that these are very rare in the cases of those who consume beans. This consequence is tied to the fact that the bean contains a series of vitamins (B_5, P, B_6 etc.) which prevents the loss of calcium from the body.

BILBERRY BUSH (*Vaccinium myrtillus*)

The bilberry bush is a well ramified bush with a 10-15 cm height. The parts used in phytotherapy: the leaves and the fruit.

Fig. 2.13

Pharmacologic action: hypoglycaemic, diuretic and disinfectant for the urinary tubule, anti-diarrhoea, anti-hemorrhagic.

The bilberry bush is generally a bush that grows in the wild and the attempts of cultivating it that have been undertaken for its remarkable qualities have not taken the shape of vast plantations due to profitability reasons.

The active principle, that is myrtilline, also called vegetal insulin, makes sugar decrease from the blood. In order to enhance the efficiency of the tea, bilberry leaves may be associated bean pods and mulberry tree leaves. Our recommendation is that the tea should be drunk sugar-free or saccharin sweetened.

Diabetes treatment is not possible without this plant!

The compositional structure of the bilberries provides them with anti-infectious properties. They are recommended for curing enteritis, cystitis and the circulatory disorders. They are anti-diabetic and have got effects upon the visual acuity.

The tannin content provides an astringent action and rushes the proteins contained in the cells of the digestive tract mucus; it rushes even the proteins of the pathogen flora, thus diminishing the action of the toxic and irritating substances.

- Jams, fine jams, wine; liquor can be made from bilberries in the house pharmacy, as they are both food and medicines.
- the jams and the marmalades for curing chronic diarrhoea. The recommended administration is one tea-spoon three times a day. Bilberries are also recommended to children in order to get rid of rickets.
- the bilberry wine? one tea-spoon shall be given to children and one small glass to grown-ups three times a day. It should be taken before the main meals.

As for convalescent people, a minimum 10 day cure with fresh bilberries or with any of the available fruit preparations is recommended.

As for low immunity individuals, a 20 day cure with bilberry fruit or with a tincture from its leaves is recommended.

As far as pulmonary tuberculosis is concerned, consuming 150-200 grams of bilberry fruit three times a day within a 30 day cure will help for a quick recovery, as this cure is associated to the drug treatment.

Synthetically speaking one may say that the bilberry bush as a medicine plant is useful and efficient in treating the following illnesses: diabetes, oral pharyngeal diseases, anorexia, burns, bronchitis, diarrhoea, eczemas, oedemas, and podagra.

Natural Treatments and Application Procedures

The Bilberry Leaves Tea

The infusion is made from one tea-spoon of bilberry leaves scalded in 250 ml of boiling water. two-three mugs a day should be drunk. The tea must not be sweetened in case of diabetes people.

The Tea Made from Bilberry Fruit

It is an anti-diarrhoea tea, being made from 2 tea-spoons of dry fruit boiled in 250 ml of water for 5 minutes.

The tea should be left for 10-15 minutes in order to become an infusion. 2-3 teas a day should be drunk.

The Bilberry Tincture

100 grams of bilberries shall be macerated in 1000 ml of alcohol for 15 days. One tea-spoon of tincture diluted in a small glass of water should be taken before each main meal. It is recommended for treating diarrhoea and scorbutus.

The Tincture Made from Bilberry Leaves

This one is recommended to diabetes people. It is made from 20 grams of broken up and mashed bilberry leaves, which shall then be macerated in 100 ml of 70 degree alcohol.

The Powder Made from Dry Leaves

It is made from ground dried up fruit. One knife pitch should be taken 3 times a day. It should be kept under the tongue for a while and then swallowed with a bit of water.

The Tea Used in External Treatments

It is made from a handful of bilberries boiled in one litre of water until its volume drops to half of it. This tea is recommended for rinsing one?s mouth in case of pharyngitis, stomatitis and aphtae, for washing eczemas, in compresses for treating hemorrhoids.

The Wine

It is made from 1 litre of wine where 50 grams of mashed bilberries will have been macerated for 8 days. The recommended treatment is to have it before the main meals.

BINDWEED

Bindweed, a species of polygonum, also known as morning glory, is a common herb, used in treating various affections.

Description

A perennial plant, with a voluble stem, stretched out on the ground, the bindweed's leaves are alternately arranged. The root is thin, long and white coloured. The leaves are oval. The flowers are funnel shaped, white coloured with pink stripe and have a pleasant smell. Bindweed blooms starting with June till August. It grows on infields, gardens and near roads.

Fig. 2.14: Bindweed

Properties

The plant contains resins, tanoids, vitamin C and mineral substances. Therefore it has purgative, choleric and cholagogue properties.

Bindweed is used to increase the size of the bile. It has a purgative action, due to the resins that it contains, also being far less irritating. For this purpose an infusion of bindweed leafs is prepared.

For external use it is utilized for furuncles and abscesses. The leaves applied on wounds can stop the bleeding. It is also used in diets based on losing weight, combined with herbs such as dandelion, corn silk, birch or elder.

Mixtures

- Bindweed tincture is prepared from 25g of dried plant added to 120ml of alcohol of 75°, and it is then left to macerate for 12 days. Two to three spoonfuls of this mixture are consumed daily, mixed with syrup or honey to mask the bitter taste. One teaspoon is taken each morning on an empty stomach.
- Bindweed decoct is obtained from a spoonful of herb mixed in a cup of water. It is consumed 2 times a day.
- Bindweed infusion is obtained from 2 teaspoons of herb added to 200ml of boiling water. It is consumed on an empty stomach.
- Bindweed tea mixed with other herbs: celandine, milfoil, all-saints'-wort, buckthorn bark, dandelion roots, mint, eglantine, and corn silk, is boiled for 5 minutes, kept to infuse for another 15, partially sweetened with honey and consumed in a quantity of 2-3 teacups per day, 30 minutes before the most important meals.

BIRCH TREE

A leafy forest (*Betula*) tree, known from ancient times as the medicinal plant used in treating many diseases, the birch tree is also known as the "tree of life".

Description

The birch tree, belonging to the *Betulaceae* family, is a tree or a shrub of small size, with white bark, marked with fine, horizontal lines. It prefers a temperate Nordic climate, growing on hills and mountainsides up to an altitude of 1500 m. The bark is smooth, silverfish-white coloured, with blackish cracks when it grows old. The branches are thin and hang down. The leaves have a rhombus shape, or the shape of a sharp triangle. Their edges are dentated and have a dark green color and a lighter shade on the outer side. The flowers have an elongated shape.

The leaves, buds, bark and sap are used from the birch tree.

Properties

The leaves contain saponin, a bitter substance, mucilage, procatechinic tannin, essential oil, betulin, saccharose, resins. These substances offer the following properties to the birch leaves: diuretic, detoxifying, cicatrizing, anti-rheumatic, astringent, antiulcer, choleretic, slightly hypertensive, anti-fever.

The buds also have a diuretic and antibiotic role. The bark is diuretic, digestive and anti-fever.

Treatments

Appreciated for its properties, birch tree is renowned for being a good diuretic, without forcing the kidneys. It has the capacity to produce perspiration and to help in treating rheumatism and inflammations of the urinary bladder.

Fig. 2.15: Birch Tree

Birch eliminates cholesterol from the blood, and disinfects the body. It is also efficient against liver diseases, ascitis, diarrhoea, constipation or intestinal parasites. Cardiac edemas, originating in circulatory insufficiency, arterial hypertension, and atherosclerosis are also treated with the help of brews based on birch. It is also recommended in treating the flu, fevers, colds and chronic sinusitis. Also in internal use, it is used for easing headaches produced by hyperzotomy, dizziness, allergies and for tonifying the nervous system.

Through diuresis, it eliminates the excess of uric acid, toxins and water from the tissues, having an important role in eliminating cellulite and obesity. Birch leaf baths help strengthen hair roots, prevent the forming of dandruff and contribute to the healing of skin irritations.

The juice squeezed out of fresh leaves is used in treating infections and inflammations of the urinary tract, renal calculosis and edemas. The birch wood coal is chewed immediately after the manifestation of intoxication.

Externally, it is used for treating affections of the skin - dermatitis, eczema, and furunculous.

The bark, rich in betulin and betulinic acid is used in the pharmaceutical industry. Ripped into bands and moistened in hot water, it can be used for immobilizing articulations or fractured arms.

Mixtures

The infusion of birch leaves is prepared out of 20 g of leaves cut into small fine pieces and 200 ml boiling water. It is then covered and left until it cools down to 40° C, sodium bicarbonate is then added with the tip of a knife, which lessens the diuretic action of birch leaves and neutralizes the betuilnic acid. After 6 hours the liquid is passed through a sieve and consumed in two portions with a pause of 4 hours between them. This infusion can also be used externally for strengthening hair roots.

A decoct is obtained out of 200 buds which are boiled in one litre of water until the volume of the liquid is diminished to half. It is consumed in one day, in 4 portions, having an influence in obesity, cellulite and edemas, renal and cardiac hydropisis, rheumatism.

Birch bark decoct is obtained according to the following recipe: two teaspoons of dried and cut bark, which is boiled for 5 minutes in 200 ml of water, it is infused for 10 minutes, kept macerating for 6 hours, then it is filtered, sweetened and drunk in portions of three cups per day, before meals, having digestive, depurative, anti-ulcer effects, with applications in gastric ulcer and skin diseases.

Birch sap stems are recommended in early spring, especially during the months of March through April. After extracting it, it is kept in the refrigerator, not in a freezer, and daily a quantity of 200-400 ml is consumed, in three portions. This has energetic, nutritive, mineralizing, tonifying, depurative properties. Because of its taste, it is also recommended in small doses for children suffering from intense weakness.

The birch sap wine is prepared out of 25 litres of sap with 3 kg of sugar. The mixture is stirred until its volume decreases to half of its initial one. The foam is removed; the liquid is passed through a sieve and poured into a wicker bottle, adding a little beer yeast to it. It is kept to ferment, adding 5 litres of quality wine and 4 lemons cut into slices and with their seeds removed. After the stop of the fermentation, the wicker bottle is plugged with a cork and kept that way for 30 days after which the wine is placed in bottles without filling them completely.

Tincture of buds is obtained from adding 100 g birch buds to a litre of alcohol of 40°. It is macerated for 10-14 days, being stirred daily. It is used to massage the skin on the head for stimulating hair growth.

BLACK CURRANT

The black currant (*Ribes nigrum*) is very appreciated for the alimentary and therapeutic value of its fruits, which contain an important complex of vitamins. The list of therapeutic properties of the black currant fruits was presented in the 18th century by the abbot Bailley de Montaran, from the monastery of Dijon. He underlined their wonderful tonic qualities, considering the currant as being an elixir of youth.

Fig. 2.16: Black Currant

Description

The currant is a fruit bearing shrub, originating from Tibet, extended and cultivated in Europe, dating 400 years back. It can reach the height of 1.5 m. Its leaves are divided into 3-5 triangular lobes, with tooth-like margins, slightly hairy on their interior side. The flowers are small, yellowish-green colored on the outside and red on the inside, sorted into 5-10 hanging groups. The fruits are round, with a diametre of around 0.5-1 cm, black, perfumed, with a pleasant, aromatic, slightly sour taste.

It grows spontaneously in woods, frequent in hilly areas, having a strong resistance towards cold weather. In its wild state, it can be found in more temperate, wet and cool zones, averted from strong winds. The parts used from the black currant are its leaves and fruits, harvested immediately after the complete maturing of the fruits.

Properties

Containing tannin, vitamin C, potassium salts, and essential oil, the black currant is a good diuretic, anti-sclerotic, pectoral, sudorific, stomachic, anti-diaretic, anti-colitic, anti-stringent, hypotensive, and anti-rheumatic. Its leaves have a great diuretic capacity; they have anti-rheumatic effects, favoring the elimination of uric acids.

Treatments

The fruits, leaves and buds of the black currant have multiple effects in treating and preventing various diseases. Because it contains vitamin C, the black currant is used in treating cardiovascular diseases, preventing cardiac insufficiency and vascular accidents, it increases the resistance of fragile sanguine capillaries, reduces arterial hypertension. Also, it intensifies weak peripheral circulation caused by menopause, cleans the blood of toxins, wastes and cholesterol.

The black currant diet is useful against rheumatism, arthritis and gout. The plant stimulates digestion, stimulates the functioning of the liver, pancreas, spleen and kidneys. Because of its diuretic qualities, the plant is useful for people suffering from oliguria.

Being astringent, this fruit is useful against diarrhoea and dysentery. Black currants are also useful against tiredness and overwork. The diet with these fruits is also recommended to plethoric and lymphatic people and to women who suffer from circulation disorders due to menopause.

Black currant is recommended as a systemic anti-inflammatory agent with actions similar to those of natural cortisone, in cutaneous, acute and chronic allergies, bronchial asthma, allergic rhinitis, and diabetic retinopathy. In external use, the mixtures from black currant fruits are used for treating abcess, dermatosis, eczemas, insect stings or hits. The mixtures from buds are used in urticaria.

Mixtures

The black currant tea is prepared from two teaspoons of leaves cut into small pieces, soaked in 250 ml of boiled water. It is consumed three cups per day, between meals, in long diets of 5-6 months.

Natural currant juice is obtained from 400 fruits and 4 big leaves. It can be consumed simply or diluted in 200-500ml water, 3-4 times a day. It has benefic effects against digestive inflammations and febrile states. Throat washes can be made with it more times a day for treating inflamed tonsils and throat aches.

Black currant cream is prepared out of fresh fruits. In a glass bottle or jar, layers of fruit and sugar are alternately added. This is done until the receptacle is filled. It is then closed hermetically and kept macerating for a period of four months. It is agitated once per day. At the end of the four months it is filtered.

The fruit decoct is obtained from a teaspoon of dried fruit to 250 ml of cold water. The composition is boiled with slight bubbling, left to infuse for 30 minutes, then filtered, after which the entire content is consumed during the day in 3 or 4 stages.

Infusion of leaves is made from 10 grams to a litre of boiled water, it is consumed daily in the morning and evening, before going to sleep.

Decoct made from fresh or dried leaves is prepared from 30 grams of leaves to a litre of cold water. It is boiled on a weak fire to the first bubbling; it is then infused for 10 minutes and consumed in 3-4 cups a day. Combined with cataplasms of fresh crushed leaves, it is applied as an external dressing against wounds and other ulcerations.

Currant syrup is obtained through cold pressing of fruit, being consumed daily in doses of 4-6 tablespoons at intervals of 2 hours. It has energizing effects, assures the general fortification of the body, is good for children, senior citizens and ill persons in recovery.

Black currant fruits can also be consumed in form of syrup, jelly, jam, fruit jelly, marmalade or liqueur.

BLACK LOCUST

Recommended in hyperacid gastritis, gastric ulcer, convulsive and asthmatic coughing, insomnia and headaches, this herb has proved its therapeutic qualities. At the same time, black locust is a wood of strong essence, resistant to moisture, used for the production of parquetry fillets or furniture.

Fig. 2.17: Black Locust

Description

The scientific name for black locust is *Robinia pseudo-acacia* - a melliferous tree originating in North America, with a trunk that can reach 30m tall and leaves that can reach lengths of 20-30cm. Its inflorescence has the form of a grape and the fruit is a brown-reddish flattened pod. Its blossom period lasts from May until June. Black locust is a species that grows spontaneously on almost any kind of soil and most especially in level areas with sandy sails. Owing to the fact that black locust is a tree with a strong essence, and very resistant to moisture, it is used in various types of construction, from naval industry to the production of parquetry. Being well-known for their therapeutic properties, only black locust flowers or leaves are used in natural pharmacy. These are picked and dried separately. After being dried, black locust can keep its curative properties for up to two years.

Treatments and Mixtures

Dried black locust leaves help heal wounds produced by burns. Crushed flowers applied directly on the affected skin for two hours promote an aesthetical healing of the skin. The calming effect eases pains caused by light and medium burns.

Excepting its direct use, various brews can be obtained, as those we shall describe later on. The flowers can be dried artificially at high temperatures (35-50 degrees C) or by depositing them in thin layers in airy rooms.

Black Locust Infusion

It is prepared with the help of one spoon of flowers for a cup of water. Two or three cups a day are administered, recommended mostly after the important meals. Because of its properties of calming stomach burns, it is recommended to those who suffer from hyperacid gastritis, distensions, or in the case of consuming aliments that are hard on the stomach. The infusion is also good for eliminating coughs and hoarseness. In these cases, the tea should be consumed as hot as possible, up to one litre a day for cough. It can be sweetened with honey. By having emollient, anti-irritating and expectorant properties, tea is a miraculous remedy against asthma and bronchitis. For headaches (and especially those that appeared as a consequence to mental fatigue) a course of treatment can be followed based on black locust infusion. The best results can be accomplished by combining, in equal shares, black locust flowers with lime flowers. Thus, the prepared infusion has a relaxing effect on the nervous system. The oral and digestive candidosis can be fought with infusions prepared from black locust leaves and flowers.

For external use, the infusion can be added to baths for young children who suffer from insomnia. In this case, the infusion will be very concentrated - prepared from ten spoons of black locust flowers to a litre of water. The sedating and calming effect produces sleep. Also for external use, black locust infusions pulverized on dry and tired complexions have revitalizing effects.

The Decoct of the Black Locust Bark

Due to the fact that the bark of the black locust contains certain plant toxins, the recommended dosage in preparing decocts is not to be exceeded. The mixture is obtained from 30g of black locust bark, boiled in one litre of water. The resulting liquid has to be consumed before meals two times a day and it helps in disinfecting intestines.

Black Locust Flower Powder

The black locust flowers are cut into small pieces until they become a fine powder and are then to be administered on an empty stomach five or six times a day in treating gastritis, gastric ulcer or duodenal. The treatment lasts a month and it can be resumed whenever needed. In case of constipation, honey is added to three spoons of black locust flower powder. This treatment has powerful results and is mild and recommended to women and children.

Tonic Lotion

Black locust also has properties that are very well appreciated in cosmetics, as the emollient, calming and tonic ones. When preparing the tonic lotion, approximately 200g of black locust flowers are added to 200ml of alcohol. For a period between a month and a month and a half it is left to macerate in a dark and cool place. After filtering the liquid, it is supplemented with distilled water until the lotion has an alcohol concentration of 20%.

Warning

Black locust causes allergies to some individuals.

THE BRIER (*Rosa canina*) of Rosaceae family

The brier is a thorny shrub that reaches 2-3 metres, with branches arching out. It appears as a variation of the wild rose. It is a medicinal plant known since ancient times, used as a remedy against rabies. The brier is spread in Europe, Western and Northern Asia.

Fig. 2.18

In medicinal purposes are used the fruit harvested in the months August-September, when the hips have turned dark red.The hips are, from a botanical point of view, false fruit, the real fruit being those small, hairy achenes inside.

In the old times the brier was used as an alimentary tea. In the traditional medicine of yesterday and today it is known that the brier tea increases the body immunity. It is recommended in case of cold, gingivitis and toothaches.

The active elements in hips are the vitamins A, B_1, B2, C, P, K and E. Because of the large quantity of vitamin C it contains (500-100 milligrams for 100 grams of hips) other vitamins and mineral salts, the brier is the most efficient, sure and fast remedy against fatigue and fever. Pharmacological actions: vitamin tonic, normalizes peripheral circulation, diuretic, vermifuge.

The seeds contained by the hips have a diuretic effect. The tea made of these seeds helps treating and curing kidney and bladder affections. The tonic effect of the hips tea shows that it is a wonder medicine for the anemic and even for the asthenic and moreover it is recommended for weight loss, as it is an excellent uric acid and toxin eliminator.

Natural Treatments and Applying Techniques

Hips Tea

The decoction is prepared of two spoonfuls of crushed hips, boiled 5-10 minutes in 500 ml of water. The fruit is put in the water when it is boiling, to avoid the loss of vitamin C. Drink two cups during a day.

Major recommendations: fatigue, anemia, fever, headaches.

Minor recommendations: hepatic pain, intestinal worms.

Hips Cold Maceration

It is prepared of 100 grams of crushed hips, macerated in a litre of cold water for 12 hours. This remedy can be consumed as a refreshing drink if 100 grams of sugar are added and if after the filtration is supplemented with water until it reaches a litre. The maceration is recommended in treating anemia, mental and physical weariness, headaches.

Hips Syrup

The syrup is prepared of 200 grams of shredded hips pulp, over which are poured 1.5 litres of boiling water. It is left to macerate 12 hours and 500 grams of sugar are added. It is boiled until it reaches the consistency of syrup. It is recommended for anemia, convalescence.

Diuretic Seeds Decoction

The decoction is obtained of 1-2 spoonfuls of seeds boiled 10-12 minutes in 250 millilitres of water. Drink 3-4 cups of tea a day.

BUCKTHORN

Description

Buckthorn is a bush (*Rhamnus*) that can be found in everglades, forests and groves.

Fig. 2.19: Buckthron

Only the buckthorn bark is used for medicinal purposes. The external surface is covered with irregular longitudinal cracks. The internal part is finely striated longitudinally. On a section it can be seen that the cut is smooth towards the exterior and fibrous towards the interior. The maxim thickness of the bark is 2 mm and the color differs from the exterior, where it is brown to the interior, where it is light-orange or yellow-brown. If the external surface is scratched a red layer appears immediately inside. The taste is first mucilaginous, then bitter and astringent, giving off a weak smell.

Properties

The bark contains a mixture of anthraquinone derivatives (anthranoids) of which the majority is present as glycosides. The maxim amount of substances is accumulated during springtime. The total content of anthranoids is 2 to 6 per cent. It also contains glycosides of emodin such as glucofrangulin A and B and frangulin A and B. The free aglycones emodin, chrysophanol and physcion are also present in varying concentrations.

It has the advantage that it can be used for a long time without causing dependence. Buckthorn has also choleretic effects over the bile. It can relax the intestinal mussels and it has vermifuge properties. The fruits contain vitamins, mineral substances and fat acids and they have an antioxidant, protective and regenerator action.

Treatments

Known from the 14th century, buckthorn is especially administrated as a laxative or purgative. It is also a good cholagogus and choleretic. Its laxative action manifests within 10 hours from the moment of administration by stimulating mobility of the large intestine.

The chronic and acute constipations can be treated by administrating buckthorn powder (1 - 3g during 24 hours) or worm tea before bedtime. The dose can be repeated in the morning, on the empty stomach, if the problems persist. The quantity used depends on the constipation level, but it should always be low at the beginning of the cure.

Buckthorn is also recommended for liver insufficiency in association with other herbs like dandelion. It is used in the treatment of liver disorders and especially for the treatment of constipations caused by bile insufficiency.

In cases of obesity, the administration of buckthorn powder each morning can produce very good results.

The buckthorn bark can increase bile secretion. It is recommended to combine it with chicory or dandelion in order to increase its effect.

Other afflictions that can be treated with buckthorn are: Giardia, rheumatism, headaches followed by constipation, allergies and hepatitis. It can also be used for intestinal worms.

Used as compresses, buckthorn helps in the treatment of skin dis-eases associated with constipation (acne, all-ergic eczema, psoriasis, infections).

Mixtures

Buckthorn tea is prepared out of one spoon of mashed bark soaked in boiling water (250g) for 15 minutes of water and then boiled for 30 minutes. It must be filtered while it is hot and it must be drunk before bedtime.

The powder must be administrated in the mornings, on the empty stomach. 2-3g of powder sweetened with honey for 5-7 times a week during 3 months make up the cure that must be followed.

The decoct can be prepared from one spoon of bark boiled in 250ml of water. The vessel must be covered for 15 minutes and then boiled for another 15 minutes. The dose depends on the person; the increase must be progressive with 2-3 spoons.

The buckthorn tincture, obtained from 20g of bark macerated for 10 days in 100ml of 70o alcohol, must be consumed in the morning, on the empty stomach. 2 or 4 spoons of tincture mixed with 2 or 4 spoons of honey represent the dose that must be administrated.

Caution

Buckthorn should be consumed in small doses, because otherwise it can cause colics and diarrhoea. Fresh herb must not be digested because it can cause nausea; the herb must be used only after one year from picking.

BUCKWHEAT

Buckwheat is the fruit seed of a plant originally from Asia and is known for driving the evil away from homes. It is also very attractive for bees which can produce a special kind of honey, dark colored and strong flavored. In ancient times witches would use buckwheat to draw circles in aid of their rituals. For this reason in Eastern cultures, buckwheat is a symbol of propriety and a defender of it.

Description

Buckwheat is part of the *Polygonaceae* family. Scientifically it is named bitter buckwheat, and is both an aliment and a herb with healing characteristics.

Fig. 2.20: Buckwheat

Proprieties

Buckwheat contains linoleic acid, vitamins (B_1, B_2, B_3, B_5, E, P), essential amino acids, minerals - chromium, copper, manganese, folic acid - and is an excellent source of magnesium. These proprieties recommend buckwheat as having a pronounced Yang feature. It has anti-tumor and tonic effects.

Treatments

Due to the presence of inosit, buckwheat adjusts metabolism, fat and the lipo-soluble vitamins. It also helps the liver in processing hormones, medicines, and glucoses, with a protective hepatic effect.

Buckwheat provides the necessary amount of proteins necessary for the body because it contains essential amino acids which the body cannot synthesize and who need to be taken from one's daily nutrition.

Buckwheat decreases the cholesterol level by eliminating fat and assuring protection against arthrosclerosis. It prevents the developing of biliary lithiasis by optimizing the synthesizing of biliary acids and eliminating neutral and acid fat.

Owing to the quantity of magnesium contained, buckwheat has a relaxing effect over blood vessels, improving circulation and decreasing blood pressure.

Because it contains plenty of vitamins with B complex, buckwheat is recommended in cases of liver disorders and sugary diabetes, illnesses where it is unadvisable to increase the quantity of sugary substances consumed each day. Due to the fact that it lacks sugary substances makes buckwheat ideal for those who need to keep a restrictive diet.

This herb offers protection against breast cancer as well as against other forms of cancer dependent on hormones. Through the contained antioxidants buckwheat is an antidote for X ray irradiations or other forms of irradiation.

Mixtures

Before consumption, it is essential that the herb be thoroughly washed.

Buckwheat macerate is made from 2 spoonfuls of buckwheat flour left to macerate for 6 to 8 hours in 300 ml clear or mineral water. It is consumed on an empty stomach half an hour before meals.

Poultices are obtained from buckwheat flour mixed in warm water until it becomes solid paste. It is then applied for 2 to 4 hours in the evening or night over the painful areas.

In cooking, buckwheat is left to sit in water for 24 hours, often replacing the water with fresh water. The mixture is then boiled and then left to cool down for 20 minutes. It can be used as an alternative in case of rice or preparing puddings. Buckwheat flour has to be kept in the fridge and should be consumed in several months.

Buckwheat milk from buckwheat flour is obtained by mixing 2 spoonfuls of buckwheat flour with 250 ml of warm water of 38 degrees Celsius. It is then mixed rapidly with a fork for about 5 minutes after which it gets filtered and consumed with sugar.

BUTTERBUR

Butterbur is used today in controlling the headaches, asthma and serious cases of cough. During the Middle Ages it was used to treat the plague known as the "black death". Recent studies show that this herb can be used successfully to keep the common cold under control.

Fig. 2.21: Butterbur

Description

Bearing the latin name of *Petasites officinalis* and more commonly known under the names of langwort or butterbur this herb is of perennial type and grows on the fields of Europe, Asia and North America. It can reach considerable sizes; only one leaf can grow as wide as an umbrella. It blooms at the end of April and the roots bearing a finger-like thickness are entwined in an underground net. In Europe, the butterbur has long been known as a medicinal herb. For centuries the herb has been considered as an effective remedy against fever and spasm. The Greek physician Dioscurides - who described the medicinal propreties of over six hundred herbs and over a thousand types of narcotics - used the butterbur leaves in treating the skin illnesses. Later in the 14th century the butterbur was used for relieving the effects of the "black death" plague and fever. Native Americans applied butterbur as a remedy for headaches and inflamations. The main usage of the butterbur today is mostly linked to controlling headaches, *asthma* and allergies. Extracts from the butterbur root are used in the treatment of stomach ulcer, infections and congestions.

Proprieties

The main active components are: the petasin and the isopetasin. The highest concentration of the two substances is found in the root of the herb and they play a very important part in the decrease of spasm, muscle relaxant and the soothing of the inflamed nasal membrane. The anti-spasmodical and anti-inflammatory proprieties of the herb have an important role in adjusting the calcium flow in the human body.

Mixtures and Treatments

The butterbur herb is found on the market under different aspects like extracts from the root of the herb and leaves, powder, tincture or medicin and pills. In the United States the easiest to come accross is the extract of butterbur for relieving of headaches and *asthma*, but it's not as effective at it as the extract from the butterbur leaves is, though the latter is not so oftenly found. It is known that the deep butterbur roots can protect against lung infections and body toxins. Also the butterbur root adjusts the blood pressure and is recommended in the cases of high and low blood pressure. In case of oscillating blood pressure it is recommended to have a spoon of butterbur powder on an empty stomach three times a day. Moreover, the powdered root of butterbur combined with an equal measure of Agrimony (*Agrimonia eupatoria*) make up a year long treatment effective against Basedow.

Usage: one spoon a day on an empty stomach, three times a day. Simultaneously a strict diet with hawthorn (*Crataegus oxyacantha*) mixed with Silver linden (*Tilia tomentosa*) is recommended.

Butterbur leaves have a strong sweet parfume to them which bear a calming effect, driving nightmares away, and are a real help to the people who wake up in the night with a strong feeling of anxiety that keeps them from falling back asleep. In order to avoid these symptoms it is recommended to have a spoon of powdered butterbur on an empty stomach three times a day, once every night before bed.

The butterbur tea is an efficient remedy for fever, breathing disabilities, arthritis, epilepsy and asthma.

Mixture: a spoon of grained butterbur roots are left to disolve in 1/4 litres over the night; in the morning the mixture is heated up and strained.

In fighting off stress and states of nervousness it is recommended to have a cup of tea every morning made from a half a spoon of linden flowers, half a spoon of butterbur and a bit of basil. The plants mentioned are scalded in a cup of boiling water after which they are left to cool off for fifteen minutes after which they're strained. It's recommended that the tea contain honey.

In the case of stomachaches - half a spoon of butterbur is left to boil in a cup of water for two minutes. Afterwards half a spoon of caraway and half of fennel are added into the mixture. Brewing time varies between 15-20 minutes; the tea should be drank hot and it can also be sweetened up and as a result, the stomachaches are expected to be gradually fade.

In order to reduce headaches it's recommended a daily mix of 75mg of butterbur with the food, two times a day. This special diet should be maintained for several months and should be stopped when the headaches don't occur for more than a month.

For treating the allergies that appear in the early spring, summer and autumn caused by inhaling pollen which causes a hypersensitivity reaction 8mg of butterbur taken 4 times a day no more than two weeks has proven to be effective.

Warning

It's well-known that butterbur contains an array of alkaloids which are toxic for the human body especially for the liver. Any consumption of extracts containing alkaloids is to be avoided. To avoid health risks, all the mixtures made of or containing butterbur will be taken only with the recommendation of a specialist. butterbur will not be administrated to pregnant women and children.

CARAWAY

It is said about caraway fruits that - by chewing them - one is able to disguise the alcohol in one's breath. The Romans would use it for flavoring and conserving meat. Nowadays, caraway is used in various types of medicine and the oil contained is used in cosmetics, at preparing soaps, lotions and perfumes.

Fig. 2.22: Caraway

Description

Caraway (*Carum Carvi*) is a biennial plant with a long history that started around 5000 years ago. Native to Egypt and east-Mediterranean countries, caraway is grown all over Europe, west Asia, Morocco, Turkey and America. It grows in a spontaneous way especially in mountainous regions and sunny dry areas. Due to its spicy flavour, it is an invaluable ingredient in Oriental, Indian, north-African and Mexican cuisines. It is also used in other countries of Europe. Its symbolical meaning is strongly represented in Germany, where young couples offer each other caraway as a symbol for fidelity. The Dutch use old recipes in which caraway fruits (also known as "seeds") are used in flavoring cheese. As a spice, caraway can be added in bread, soups, meat, salads and even cakes. It has a specific pungent taste to it; bitter and spicy at the same time. As medicine, only its seeds (*Fructus Carvi*) are used, and are appreciated for their property of stimulating food appetite and for alleviating stomach aches. Caraway is 30-50cm tall, has pinkish flowers and brown-yellowish seeds. In medi-cine, caraway has various uses and is easy to find in drug-stores. It is also used in veterinary medicine. Apart from that, caraway is a regular ingredient in perfume industry.

Proprieties

Caraway contains a considerable quantity of volatile oil (limonene, dehydrocarvon si dihydrocarveol), proteins, lipids, albuminoid substances, mineral substances, starch, tannins and so on.

Volatile oil is not only used in cosmetic industry in making perfumes, but also in therapeutic purposes, because it reacts efficiently in treating the gastro-intestinal tract. The main properties of the herb make it an effective stimulant of gastric secretion, it regulates stomach functions; it has anti-inflammatory properties for the intestines; it is a gastric and intestinal antiseptic and diuretic. Caraway plays an important part in stimulating food appetite and digestion. It also strengthens the body's immune system and alleviates cold symptoms.

Treatments and Mixtures

Caraway is recommended by therapists in treating bronchitis in eliminating intestinal worms at babies and pregnant women, because it increases the quantity of milk. At thee same time caraway eliminates intestinal inflammations, increases diuresis and eliminates stomach gases owing to the fact that it is a strong carminative (especially if it is associated with fennel or coriander.

Caraway Infusion

It is prepared from a spoonful of seeds in a cup with boiling water. It is then left to macerate for 15 minutes. The infusion is then administrated before every meal, three times a day to alleviate the loss of food appetite. As soon as inflammations of the skin occur, it is recommended to dab at the infected areas with caraway infusion.

Caraway Poultices

Warmed-up caraway seeds that are placed on a gauze can be used to eliminate intestinal worms in cases of children. The poultices are applied on the stomach area.

Caraway Powder

One gram of powder mixed with honey is another way of alleviating lack of food appetite and stimulating digestion. Against fermentation, colitis and diarrhoea, caraway powder is mixed with mint fruits and is administrated four times a day for four weeks.

Caraway Tincture

Owing to its energizing effects triggered by the volatile oil contained by the herb, the tincture mixture is used to ease brain circulation. Treatment with caraway tincture lasts one month by taking 4 spoonfuls of the mixture a day.

Note: The seeds can be harvested in August through the month of September.

Warning

Before starting treatment with products based on caraway it is recommended to see a specialist. It is known that it can trigger epilepsy states in children and overdoses taken by pregnant women can lead to miscarriages.

CASTOR OIL PLANT

Castor-oil plant is also known by its Latin name, *ricinus*, which means "mite", and is a persan plant from the Euphorbiaceae family. Other names the herb has are Christ's palm or the tree of the cross.

Description

The castor-oil plant is a herbaceous, annual herb of 1-3 metres in height, with a pivoting, ramified root, erect green or redish stems. The leaves are large. The flowers have a yellowish color. The fruit has the form of a capsule which holds 3 brownish or ash-colored, mottled seeds, rich in oil. The plant blooms from July to September.

Properties

The castor-oil plant seeds contain over 50% fat, 20% proteins, glucides, mineral salts, water, oleic acid, toxalbumine, enzymes and vitamin E. These give the plant laxative and purgative properties, leading to the agglutination of the red cells.

Treatments

Castor-oil plant is used most often as castor-oil. This exercises a benefitting action on the teguments, both at the epidermis' level and at the derm level.

Castor-oil is an efficient means of curing warts. The should be massaged for 10-15 minutes with the castor-oil. The treatment is followed 2 times per day, each day, until the warts start dissapearing.

For irritated mucous membrane and red eyes, 1-2 drops of castor-oil are applied on each eye.

In case of haemorrhoids, the annointing of the anus with castor-oil or the ingestion of 1-1/2 teaspoons of oil internally is recommended. The same oil is good for treating bruises, cuts, ulcerations or various erruptions of the skin.

A feather drenched in castor-oil is indicated to be used for annointing the affected areas. In cases of bronchitis and colds, the chest is massaged, using a mixture of 2 tablespoons of castor-oil and one of turpentine. The chest of the patient is rubbed with it, then enfolded in a wool scarf and then dressed in a cotton blouse.

Castor-oil has a stimulating effect of the growth of eyelashes and eyebrows. Also, it helps in some cases of alopecia and strengthens the roots. The hair roots are massaged with castor-oil. It is applied in the evening before going to sleep. The second day, the hair and the head's skin is washed well. The treatment is made 3 times per week until the wanted result is achieved. For reguilar usage, it is applied 2 times every month.

To soften the callosities and thick skin, the feet should be rubbed 3 times a week with castor-oil, dressed in cotton socks and left like that for the night.

Castor-oil is also recommended in treating moles and hepatic pigmentation. The affected areas are rubbed insistently with castor-oil in the evening and in the morning. The effects are visible after about a month.

For nails which are flaking off or which break off easily, the treatment with castor-oil is recommended. In the evening the oil is applied on the nails and rubbed well for an hour. The treatment should last two months.

Mixtures

Castor-oil is fabricated thus: the seeds are harvested at their complete maturity, manually or mechanically. They are dried, decorticated and cold pressed for obtaining the oil.

Warning

The therapeutic castor-oil is not toxic. The toxic effect is only manifested in cases of swallowing seeds which would lead to the coagulation of fibrine, the agglutination of eritrocites, lesions of the blood vessel walls, irritation of the gastro-intestinal mucous, hepatic and renal lesions.

CELANDINE

In North America, celandine dates back to the year 1672 when it was used for treating warts. But the plant has a longer history; it has been used as a medicinal herb starting from ancient times. Long ago it was used by nomads as a perfume for feet, while today its purgative properties are considerably appreciated.

Fig. 2.23: Celandine

Description

Celandine (*Chelidonium majus*) is a herbaceous, perennial herb, found on plains but also in mountainous areas at maximum altitudes of 800 to 1000 metres. It grows on soft, sometimes even sandy soils, in shaded places in forests, bushes or gardens, while developing itself in a ramified fashion and reaching heights of 30-100 cm. Its flowers are yellow and they blossom in the period between May and fall. Its leaves are serrated, similar to oak leaves. All parts of the plant contain latex, a milky, yellowish-orange colored substance that has a bitter taste, which gets darker in color when being in contact with air. The plant is of European origin, (it was discovered near the Mediterranean region). Despite that, however, it has spread out easily to other areas of the world.

Properties

Celandine contains alkaloids like chelidonine, homo-chelidonine, oxy-chelidonine, methoxy-chelidonine, sanguinarine, coptisine, protopine, alocryptopine, in a percentage of about 0.2 - 0.5% depending on the part of the plant and on the time of harvesting. It also contains smaller quantities of baberine and sparteine, vitamin C (especially the leaves), resins, essential oils and mineral salts. Chelidonine and homo-chelidonine act in a similar way as morphine, sedative and narcotic on the superior nervous centers. At the same time, they also have a slight stimulating action upon respiration. Chelidonine is also responsible for anti-spastic action that the herb triggers. Sanguinarine from celandine has a stimulating effect on the medullary centers, and it even presents anti-tumoral effects of a colchinic type while the cheleritrine has the property to reduce the arterial pressure and to stimulate intestinal peristalting and the contractions of the uterus.

Apart from the described properties, celandine extracts have a remarkable antibiotic effect on many pathogenic germs. Other actions: calming, anti-septic and anti-spastic.

Treatments and Mixtures

Celandine is used successfully in treating severe hepatic illnesses, biliary and renal diseases (it eases liver and bile pains). Having a depurative property (of purifying blood), but also a property of de-toxifying the liver, celandine is beneficial to metabolism. Externally, celandine is used to control skin diseases: treating skin tuberculosis, treating wounds, fistulas, psoriasis, warts or callosities. It is also efficient in cases of skin cancer and eczemas that are hard to treat. Celandine can be used as an adjuvant against baldness (alopecia), also having the property of fortifying the hair strands.

When preparing the mixtures that are presented here, the use of the plant's more fragile branches and stems are recommended. These are to be harvested in their full blossoming period (the months of April and May) because that is when the plant contains the highest amount of active elements. It can be dried artificially at temperatures of 35-40° Celsius or in the shade, stretched onto a thin layer and moved around once every three days.

Celandine Infusion

It is prepared by boiling a spoonful of grained herb in a cup of water. The infusion is recommended for treating hemorrhoids. In this purpose, two or three cups of tea are to be consumed every day in small drams.

Celandine Syrup

Is recommended in cases of hepatic afflictions. It is prepared by boiling a litre of water. After it starts bubbling slightly, five grams of dried celandine are added. The pot is covered with a lid and kept in a warm place over night, covered with pillows. The next day it is filtered and mixed with 200g of honey, until the honey dissolves completely. The resulting liquid is put into a bottle. This juice is administered ten times a day, a spoonful every hour. A wooden spoon is to be used. The syrup is well-known for the fact that it regenerates hepatic cells. The treatment should only be repeated after a pause of six months.

Celandine Tincture

It is a homoeopathic remedy recommended for treating icterus, biliary dyskinesias, biliary calculosis, bladder atony, spleen and intestinal diseases. For controlling hysteria, insomnia or restlessness, it can be mixed with tincture of valerian or St. Johns wort. Against warts, callosities, skin irritations, keratitis or skin cancer, a poultice will be applied on the affected area. In cases of uterine fibroids, the tincture poultice will be applied on the lower abdominal area.

Fresh Celandine Juice

To obtain celandine juice, the stems, leaves and flowers have to be washed, then the liquid is squeezed out of them. It is only used externally. It is a good caustic against warts.

The juice can be effective in cases of cataracts, cornea spots, or retinal bleedings. In this case, a moist celandine leaf is used from which the juice is squeezed out. The liquid is spread out toward the corner of the eye. The eyes are kept shut at this time. The same juice can be used for weak sight or overstressed eyes.

Warning erdoses are not recommended since they can trigger toxic reactions.

CELERY (*Apium graveolens*)

Celery is an alimentary herb as well as a special medicinal plant. Celery leaves are used for spicing up foods and drinks such as cocktails. The volatile oil extracted from this vegetable can be used for medicinal purposes as well as an ingredient for various perfumes.

Description

Usually, celery (*Apium graveolens*) is used in making salads, spicing up foods containing meat, etc. However, the roots, leaves and elery seeds are used for therapeutic purposes in treating and preventing diseases. In medicine, celery has been used as far back as Ancient Greece when it was highly valued for its properties as an aphrodisiac as well as its medicinal properties. Around the same time celery was also used as a decorative herb by the Romans, who used the leaves for their "Winner's Crown". In traditional medicine celery was used to eliminate intestinal parasites. Chinese medicine recommended celery to be used as a medicine to treat high blood pressure due to its stabilizing components. Apium graveolens initially grew on humid grounds of Europe and Asia. With the start of the 19th century, celery began to be grown in United States. Nowadays this vegetable is more commonly used in foods, due to the richness of its taste. It is also useful in stomach illnesses, rheumatism, obesity and diseases of the urinary bladder; celery keeps its therapeutic properties the best when it is consumed raw. Either used as a snack or as medicine, celery detoxifies the body, stimulates the nervous system and mineralizes the body.

Proprieties

One hundred grams of celery has an energetic value equal to 18 calories. It contains vitamins A, B_1, B_2, B_6, C, E, K, PP and minerals such as iron, calcium, phosphorus, magnesium and zinc. Vitamin C contained by celery strengthens the immunologic system and at the same time makes the body more resistant against new diseases. Calcium, potassium and magnesium act towards the same goal, straightening the body. Along with magnesium, iron is effective in alleviating the effects of anemia. Celery has the ideal quantities of iron and magnesium to stop oncological diseases from progressing. This plant has diuretic properties and dichloridic effects which are useful in renal afflictions (like renal colic and renal lithiasis) and heart disorders. In this purpose celery root is used. Due to its depurative properties, the consumption of celery is recommended for individuals who have a fast paced lifestyle and are unable to maintain a healthy diet. Because of these properties - diuretic and depurative - celery is the ideal ingredient for diets based on weight-loss. Diets based on celery have energizing and fortifying effects on the body due to the stimulation of the renal glands, reduction of the stress hormone and decreasing of the heart rate. But celery also has hypoglycemic properties, which means it can be used in treating sugary diabetes. Other properties: expectorant, emollient (effective against bronchitis), it adjusts hormonal dysfunctions (dysmenorrhea, infertility, disorders caused by menopause, various forms of acne, allergic dermatosis); cicatrizing (good for wounds, scratches, ulcerations.

Treatments and Mixtures

Celery is consumed as a diuretic and laxative by those who have urinary retentions or suffer from kidney illnesses;

it is also efficient in cases of asthenia, hoarseness, rheumatism, icterus, gout, arthritis, inflammations, dermatosis, diabetes, and obesity. Individuals with high cholesterol should add celery to their diets. Moreover, celery is effective for those who have lack of food appetite. Below are some mixtures based on celery.

Infusion of Celery Powder

To prepare the infusion, four spoonfuls of celery powder are put in one litre of boiling water. After that, the mixture is passed through a sieve and one cup of it a day is consumed to treat hoarseness, intestinal gases or for its laxative/diuretic properties. The infusion made from boiling two spoonfuls of grained celery stimulates the central nervous system. The infusion is taken daily in small amounts. If in one glass of cold water a spoonful of grained celery root is left to macerate, the resulting mixture taken before each meal treats anorexia. The infusion needs to be renewed each day.

Celery Decoct

Twenty-five grams of celery boiled in 1 litre of water are sufficient in preparing the mixture. The resulting decoct is taken in small quantities and is efficient against rheumatism, cough and hoarseness. A more concentrated decoct (containing between 30 and 40 grams of celery root in one litre of water) has a diuretic and depurative effect, treating slow digestions, obesity, gout, rheumatism.

Celery Juice

Celery juice is excellent in treating rheumatism, allergies, stomach disorders, eliminating toxins, stimulating digestion and food appetite, adjusting sexual functions (treats frigidity and impotence) and is known as an all-round aphrodisiac. The ideal dosage in which it should be consumed is 3 glasses a day.

Warning

For pregnant women the consumption of celery should be made in very small quantities. Celery can cause in very rare cases allergic reactions to some individuals (cases which occurred in Central Europe).

CHAMOMILE

Maticaria recutita or Chamomile - its popular name - is a herbaceous, annual and hibernating plant originating in south-eastern Europe, which nowadays has spread to all continents. The scientific name "*Matcaria*" derives from the latin word "*mater*" (mother) and suggests the many uses in mothers' diseases and generally in that of women. Because it is a common plant, it can be found anywhere, in uncultivated areas, on fields, on road edges and so on. The plant loves heat, light (which influences the essential oil contained), and moist soils. The chamomile stem, reaching growing up to 60 cm, is striated and ramified at its base, and each branch has flowers. The hemaphrodite flowers with their pleasant flavor, bloom from May until late August or early September. In this interval, the best harvesting period is noon. Noticeable is the fact that inflorescent flowers are harvested before becoming mature. For conservation the plants are put to dry in a thin layer in a dry and shady place, after which they are kept in paper bags. In ancient times, chamomile was used to control neuralgia and rheumatism (especially the articular one) and the ancient Egyptians used it to decrease fever. It is also mentioned in old books about medicinal plants that chamomile?s oil drives away fatigue from the limbs.

Properties

Chamomile flowers contain: essential oils (etheric oil: 0.38 - 0.81%), vitamins B_1 and C, mineral substances (phosphorus, potassium, silicon, iron, manganese, calcium, copper, lead, zinc, zirconium), glucides, lipids (in small quantities) and acids. The plant has calming, analgesic, disinfecting and antiseptic, antispasmotic and tonic actions. At the same time, chamomile has an antitoxic action through disactivating the bacterian and carminative toxins, favoring the elimination of intestinal gasses. Externally, chamomile has cicatrizant, emollient and anti-inflammatory effects. Because of its antiseptic (it destroys the microorganisms from the tegument) and decongestive properties, chamomile also has many aplications in cosmetics, being recommended for irritated, damaged or fat complexions.

Treatments and Mixtures

Chamomile can be used for an entire series of afflictions and diseases. No matter if we're talking about gingivitis, dental abscess (and dental pains generally), tonsillectomy, stomatitis, hyperacid gastritis, ulcer, enterocolitis, diarrhoea, hemorrhoids, flues, colds, sinusitis, bronchic asthma, rheumatism or insomnia, chamomile is a true adjuvant. Being a good sedative, it can be used against stress and anxiety. Chamomile also helps to drive away menstrual problems (as amenorrhea) and other pelvic diseases.

Chamomile Infusion

In preparing this infusion, a teaspoon of chamomile flowers is added to a litre of boiled water. The mixture is left a few minutes before being consumed. Inhaling the vapours emanated by the infusion helps in healing colds and sinusitis if the patient remains in a warm place. The tea can be administered to children, when they suffer from bad dispositions, cramps or colics - abdominal pains. Used externally, the infusion can be added to the bath water (four handfuls of flowers to a bathtub) or in the head washing water (one handful). The hair - especially the blond one - becomes silky and shiny. The complexion is also refreshed if it is cleaned with chamomile infusion. Also, conjunctivitis and eye inflammations heal faster with the help of this mixture. It can also be used for gargle (in cases of toothaches), cutaneous eruptions, or cleaning wounds.

Chamomile Oil

In a bottle filled with chamomile flowers, cold-pressed olive oil is poured. The bottle is then kept in the sun, well corked up, for a period of approximately two weeks. After this stage, the oil is conserved in the refrigerator.

Chamomile Ointment

It is obtained relatively easily, out of two handfuls of fresh chamomile flowers added to 200g of lard. The operation is done when the grease is already warmed. After it starts boiling and spume is formed at the surface, it is all covered and kept in a cool room. After 24 hours, the mixture is warmed again and filtered with the help of a cloth.

Chamomile Poultices

A tablespoon filled with chamomile is emptied in a litre of hot milk. After a few minutes, the mixture is filtered and used in poultices. Caution is required as the poultice has maximum effect with warmth. Another way of obtaining poultices: filling a small bag of textile material with dried chamomile flowers. The bag is then introduced into the oven on a tray and heated up for a short time. Then the bag is applied locally for eliminating corporal pains.

CHICORY

Although the medical usages of this herb are numerous, Chicory is known for the fact that it's considered an excellent coffee substitute. Moreover it contains insulin - a substance from the saccharoids group, very useful for transforming the non-alimentary substances into biodegradable ones.

Description

Chicory (*Chihorium intybus*) is an edible perennial herb native to North Africa, Europe and Asia. Today it can be found all over the world and especially on the lands with

Fig. 2.24: Chicory

a mild temperate climate. It gained its fame in Antiquity because of its therapeutic usages and the old Egyptians would use it to treat the liver and gallbladder problems. They consumed chicory in large quantities because they believed that the herb could purify the blood and eliminate the toxins from the liver. In France during Napoleonic times chicory was used as a coffee substitute. England and the United States soon followed this example. While the root of this herb is used as a coffee substitute, the other parts are used either in cooking (especially in salads), either as medicine. Compared to real coffee, chicory stimulates the nervous system by sustaining the mental capabilities and concentration. This herb is also recommended in fighting the sleepy states and asthenia. Owing to the substances that it contains (like chicorine and choline) the herb shows laxative-like characteristics. At the same time, chicory stimulates digestion and the pancreatic secretion, regulating the amount of glucose in the human body. Moreover, should one include in ones personal diet mixtures which contain chicory root, their body will adjust the level of cholesterol.

Proprieties

In the chemical composition of the herb substances can be found such as inulin, chicorine, choline, tanin, chicoric acid, aminated acids, starch, protids, minerals and vitamins (B, C, K, P). The root of the herb contains the highest concetration of the above-mentioned substances. Various studies show that inulin greatly reduces the risk of the intestinal cancer. The tanin works as an astringent, disinfectant, detoxicant tonic and has a light antibiotic effect to it. It further influences the gallbladder effects (by enlarging the gall and the fluid quantity). Under the influence of the compounds with bitter taste, the digestion is stimulated and also the drainage of the liver and spine. These compounds reduce hunger but stimulate the sensation of fullness. In this sense a short rise of hunger followed by a considerable diminution of hunger was noticed. Chicory helps the body to better absorb calcium and other minerals.

Owing to the detoxifying, cholagogue-like, anticatarralic and alkalizing effects, the mixtures containing chicory are effective in treating digestive problems, gastritis, hepatitis, gallbladder problems, statis, mild enterocolitis, intestinal worms, and hemorrhoids. Due to the active compounds from the herb, the glucose from the blood accumulates faster under the aspect of glycogen in the liver. This process leads to a decrease in the glycemia and cholesterol which reduces diabetes and artery sclerosis. Other afflictions treated by chicory are: acne, anemia, anorexia, heart problems, arthritis, asthenia, liver and gallbladder problems, hepatic congestions, splenic problems, depressions, dermatosis, the decrease in the biliary secretions, headaches, furunculosis, goutiness, hepatitis, hydropsy, jaundice, urinal infections, biliary insufficiency, lithiasis, tiredness, marsh fever, intestinal parasitosis, rheumatism.

Mixtures and Treatments

Chicory mixtures help detoxify the body and regulate metabolism and are recommended to those who have an inaccurate diet (hence a decreased metabolism) and also to those who are suffering from furunculosis, acne, intoxications.

When administrating the treatments based on chicory, in cases of people with a noticeable appetite, it is recommended that it should be done between eating hours. If the goal is to stimulate the appetite, the chicory mixture should be administrated just before dinner.

For reducing glycemia the consumption of two cups of chicory infusion a day or a cup of decoct before dinner is recommended. A cup of infusion of chicory before dinner stimulates digestion and is recommended during states of nervousness, asthenia, coughing. To prepare the infusion of chicory, two spoons of chicory are mixed in a litre of boiled water for 10-15 minutes. For the decoct tea it's necessary for a small amount of dry chicory root to be mixed in a litre of boiling water and then left to cool down for approximately 15 minutes. The chicory juice detoxifies the body. For this purpose it's recommended to have 2-3 spoons of it a day. To prepare chicory juice it?s necessary to boil 1 litre of chicory infusion which gets mixed with 1 kg. of sugar until the liquid becomes thick, like syrup. If needed, a type of jam from chicory root can be made to treat the lung problems.

Chicory leaves are efficiently used as bandages for cuts and bruises. Cataplasms can be made of Chicory infusion in cases of acne, furunculosis, cuts and bruises.

CIDER

"An apple a day keeps the doctor away, but having a glass of cider is a much more pleasant way of keeping healthy", were the words of a spokesperson for the National Association of cider production.

Description

Cider is an alcoholic drink obtained usually from apples. Harvesting is done manually from October until November. The level of phenol from cider depends a lot on the type of apples it was made from, on sun exposure, soil composition and also the storing conditions.

Proprieties

Owing to the high quantity of contained phenols, consuming cider daily can prevent cancer, heart diseases, strokes and can reduce a premature death caused by any illness.

Cider obtained from black currant has revitalizing effects and can protect the body from cancer. In order to obtain the desired effect, it is recommended to consume 100ml of cider before primary meals. Also, cider obtained from black currant has aphrodisiac effects and can protect the body against heart attacks and heart diseases. Moreover, it is efficient against headaches.

Mixtures

Apple cider is obtained from the fermentation fresh apple juice, preferably obtained from the autumn or winter apples, because they are rich in saccharine. Winter apples are kept for 4 to 6 weeks to become sweeter. After that time passes, the healthy apples are chosen and rinsed thoroughly. Then they are crushed and kept in large pots and are left to macerate for 6 to 12 hours and are then treaded with a wine press.

The mixture obtained from that is mashed in a large pot over which 20% water is poured; after 24 hours it gets mashed again and 40 litres of diluted juice is obtained. Fermentation of the juice takes places in big barrels thoroughly washed or in wicker bottles of 50 litres. Fermentation starts at 15 to 18 degrees C and lasts between

4 and 8 weeks. During that time fermentation takes place and foam is formed on the surface. When foam is formed, the cider clears up naturally. After carbon dioxide is emitted and the cider clears up, the content is moved to another barrel for the fermentation to continue. On top a lid is placed in such a way that lets out the carbon dioxide.

Depending on the fermentation period, cider has three different grades: raw cider with alcohol of 4 to 5.5 degrees; mild cider with alcohol of 1 to 3 degrees; and traditional cider of 5 to 6 degrees.

Warning

Cider is not recommended for children or adolescents.

CLOVER

Found in Europe, Central Asia, Northern Africa and Australia, the clover is a plant with numerous medicinal properties.

Description

There are two types of clover: white clover and the red clover.

White clover is a small, perennial, herbaceous plant, having its stem recumbent on the ground, from which its roots emerge. The leaves are trifoliated, sometimes spotted with white or a darker colored stain. Its flowers are white or slightly pink colored; as they bloom they turn darker toward a shade of brown.

The parts used from this plant are the flowers, leaves and the stem.

Properties

Clovers and especially the red ones have bioactive components: calcium, lecithin, chromium, magnesium, potassium, silicium, vitamins A, E, C, B_2, and B_3.

Fig. 2.25: Clover

Red clover is also considered one of the richest sources of isoflavon. Isoflavons are efficient in treating some forms of cancer and can even eliminate some cancerous cells. Studies have proved that clovers can protect against the development of breast cancer cells. Also, clover can reduce the risk of lymphatic, ovary and breast cancer.

The herb reduces breast inflammations (mastitis) and breast pains. It detoxifies the lymph, lungs, liver, kidneys, and blood. In cases of gout, it is useful for decreasing the concentration of uric acid.

Clover is a good expectorant; it soothes the spasms of the bronchi, convulsive cough and children's cough. It is also anti-asthmatic. It reduces the symptoms affections such as syphilis; it stimulates biliary secretion and relaxes the muscles.

The herb has other uses too: it decongests the salivary glands, decreases arthritis pains, and reduces ocular inflammations. It has a relaxing effect on the nervous system, adjusting the psycho-emotional balance and contributing to the development of communication abilities.

Also, in cases of a tuberculous nature, it reduces ganglionary inflammations, the effects concerning menopause and premenopause, hot flashes, depressive states and palpitations, being an excellent vaginal and urinal relaxant.

In external use, it is dermatomic, being used in treating acne, psoriasis, eczemas, insect stings, abscesses or ulcerations. Red clover is also used for detoxifying the blood.

Mixtures

The red clover infusion is obtained by adding a teaspoon of plants and one of mint to 200ml boiling water. It is recommended for ameliorating congestions and breast level pains, as well as colds or influenza.

CLUBMOSS

Clubmoss, commonly known as ground pine, is a plant used in treating and lessening various diseases of the body.

Description

Clubmoss is a procumbent, evergreen plant, which has a similar appearance to moss and can be found in beech and fir forests to an altitude of over 600 m. The plant's stems are procumbent, growing up to 1-2 metres in length with small, fine and thin roots. From the stalks, smaller stems of lengths of around 7-10 cm grow, they are small, ramified and have bushy leafs. These smaller stems generally end with 2 ears. The leaves are linear, small and persistent, having long, whitish hairs on top. The harvest is made in July and August, on sunny weather, after the dew has lifted.

Properties

The plant contains radium, triterpanes, alkaloids and mineral substances which give it diuretic, anti-alcoholic, anti-tobacco, anti-cirrhotic, and purgative properties.

Treatments

Fig. 2.26: Clubmoss

Clubmoss is recommended to those suffering from rheumatism and arthritis even in cases when the diseases present malformations of the articulations. Clubmoss tea is recommended in treating chronic constipation, and for hemorrhoids. This is also used for lessening diseases of the urinary system and the genital organs. Clubmoss tea prevents the formation of kidney stones and renal colics.

In hepatitis and tumors of the conjunctive tissue of the liver, clubmosss are indispensable. Hepatic cirrhosis or liver cancer can also be treated with the help of clubmoss tea. Because it contains radium, clubmosss are used for calming muscle cramps. For this purpose, a pillow can be stuffed with this plant.

The plant can also be used sometimes as a diuretic, and clubmoss spores are used for skin irritations. If 4 to 5 drops of tincture are added into the water meant for washing hair, the hair is strengthened, and is less friable.

Clubmoss tincture is also used in alcohol detoxification, or to discourage from smoking. For this the treatment can last between a week and 3 months. The tincture can also be used against the pains caused by muscle spasms and hypertension. Compresses are applied on the back and kept there for a few hours during the night.

Mixtures

Clubmoss tea is prepared from one teaspoon of clubmoss added to half a litre of boiled water. It is left like that for a short time. A cup per day is consumed slowly in the morning, on an empty stomach half an hour before breakfast.

Clubmoss decoct is obtained from the mixture of equal amounts of clubmoss, pansies, dandelion, birch, parsley, hip and bean pods. A quantity of 200 ml of the mixture is consumed 3 to 4 times per day, between meals, sweetened with honey.

The clubmoss pillow is made like so: a small pillow case is taken, filled with 2 handfuls of fresh clubmoss, and applied on wounds.

Hip baths are prepared the following way: in a bowl of 4 to 5 litres of hot water, 4 handfuls of clubmoss are added, it is left to macerate, then heated and added to bath water.

Warning

It is recommended that people suffering from diarrhoea use clubmoss tea cautiously so that it does not cause intestinal spasms.

CONEFLOWER

A natural substitute for antibiotics, coneflower is a truly miraculous plant for healing actions capable of treating many afflictions and diseases.

Fig. 2.27: Coneflower

Description

Originating in America, coneflower was used in the past for treating infections and fortifying the immune system. The native population used this plant for healing insect bites, snake bites as well as against abdominal pains. Today, a greater series of uses is assigned to it because its properties recommend it in cases of respiratory virosis (cold and flues), chronic fatigue, tooth aches, skin irritations and wounds as well as some gynecologic diseases. The plant was acclimated in Europe starting with the 16th century and the types of coneflower used most often are: *Echinaceea purpura, Echinaceea angustifolia* and *Echinacea pallida*.

Properties

The plant has the power of eliminating many types of toxins from the body. Moreover, based on researches, it has been proven that by consuming coneflower, the body is stimulated in producing more white cells, such as lymphocytes and interferon (the synthesizing substance in the cells which impedes the development of viruses and intercellular parasites) - substances which help prevent the development of malignant tumors. Also, coneflower improves the resistance of the body against venereal diseases and HIV. Skin lesions (such as furuncles, burns, wounds, psoriasis), gangrenes, acne, kidney diseases, the cardiovascular system are other areas in which coneflower proves to be efficient. An excellent blood purifier, coneflower improves the process of microcirculation and also has the quality of being an excellent cicatrizing medicine.

Treatments and Mixtures

The mixtures based on coneflower are recommended in treating all diseases which have in common weakened the immunity of the body. The most well-known and used mixtures are the coneflower tincture and the capsules from plant powder. Out of the two, based on scientific research, the tincture - along with the coneflower tea - is more efficient than the capsules. In cases of colds, influenza, sinusitis and intestinal infections, coneflower must be consumed carefully while seeking medical advice.

Coneflower Tincture

Recommended in cases of colds and influenza, it also heals viral and urinal infections. The dose is a teaspoon of tincture in every three hours for a period of two days. It is efficient in diets for the detoxification of the body. Taken four times a day, a teaspoon of tincture is dissolved in a glass half filled with water. Locally, on the areas affected by stings, tincture can be applied (dissolved according to its concentration - the indications of the product should be observed). In cases of chronic infections, half a teaspoon is prescribed three times per day for a period of three weeks.

Coneflower Ointment

The coneflower ointment is used especially because its antibacterial and cicatrizing effects. It is useful in treating wounds and skin affections - herpes, furuncle or stings. For rheumatism it is recommended to massage the wounded areas with coneflower ointment.

Coneflower Capsules

Usually used in a concentration of 300 mg of purple coneflower powder, the capsules are efficient in bronchopulmonary diseases, respiratory virosis, otitis and sinusitis, renal diseases and those of the genital-urinary system; diseases of the digestive system (gastritis, cholecystitis); functional disturbances of the cardiovascular and nervous system. In case of colds, one or two capsules in every two-three hours are recommended. The treatment lasts two days after which the dose is diminished to six capsules per day. In case of chronic infections, six capsules are administered (taken three times per day, two capsules every time) for three weeks with the possibility of lengthening the treatment after a week of pause.

Contraindications

Use caution for the symptoms which can be caused by the products based on coneflower. Some people have adverse reactions manifested by itches of the eyes and neck. Care must also be taken in case of interactions with other medicine and supplements. The doctor's recommendations should be heeded. Also, coneflower is not recommended for people who have suffered organ transplants.

CORIANDER

Coriander is an annual herb in the family *Apiacae*. Apart from being an aphrodisiac, condiment and medicament, coriander is used as a condiment in cuisine for preparing the finest foods, in the perfumery industry because of the volatile oil contained by its fruits but as a medicinal herb also. The coriander contains a powerful diuretic that red-uces the sanguine pressure and ameliorates a headache.

Description

Fig. 2.28: Coriander

Coriander (*Coriandrum sativum*) is a Mediterranean herb grown for its fruits that look like white-rose seeds and its leaves known as "cilantro". It came from the sunny and droughty areas of Asia. It was used a long time ago in India, Iran and China. The Indians used coriander not only in their culinary art, but also in the medicinal field. They used the herb to treat insomnia, the flu and constipation. The recognition of the herb's qualities encouraged its cultivation in Europe. Ancient Greeks and Romans used it to give flavor to their foods and wines. In the Middle Ages it was especially used to give flavour to wines, steaks and cakes. In the 17th century it was one of the ingredients used by the nuns from the Carmelite Order to prepare the Parisian Eau de Toilete. In the same period, coriander was used to prepare two well known drinks for that time: the Benedictine liqueur and Chartreuse. In the 18th century, people used coriander to avoid having an unpleasant breath (they chewed the seeds with sugar).

In our days, coriander is used mostly in the food industry as an aromatizer and condiment for meat products, fish and pickles. Dried yellow fruits have a nice smell and a sweet flavor. The bitterish taste is predominant to the sweet hot astringent taste. Coriander's leaves resemble the ones of parsley and they taste different from the fruits. It can grow up to 20 inches tall.

Coriander has many well know medicinal qualities. If the coriander seeds were used in Iran to treat insomnia and anxiety, the recently made experiments from many Middle Orient hospitals confirmed its anxiolytic and sedative effects. Then it was synthesized in the pharmaceutical industry a natural medicament used to treat panic attacks, the depressive-anxious syndrome and insomnia.

Fig. 2.29: Coriander Seed

Properties

Coriander fruits contain volatile oil, lipids, starch, pectins and mineral substances. In fact, coriander's flavor comes from the etheric oil contained in proportion of 1,5% - 2,0% . This oil contains linalool (60% - 80%), pinene, dipentene, etc. The fruits contain fatty acids like petroselinic acid, proteic substances, amino-acids, sitosterols, tocopherols, cumarins, caffeic acid and chlorogenic acid. The aromatic contained substance - coriandrol - is a very good adjuvant in the treatment of liver cancer. At the same time, coriander leaves represent a powerful source of vitamin A, C, thiamin, riboflavin, vitamin K, folic acid, calcium, iron, magnesium and potassium. In small quantities it contains also niacin, vitamin B_6, phosphor and zinc.

Furctus coriandri, in other words coriander fruits are used as a stimulant for the gastrointestinal secretion, sedative and carminative. They ameliorate the abdominal pains, reduce digestive spasms and distend. Coriander is also known as a bactericide, fungicide and anthelmintic. It has also a good influence over the neural system and stimulates memory.

Mixtures and Preparation

Modern phytotherapeutics recommends coriander fruits as adjuvant in: anorexia, dyspepsia, intestinal worms, hypogalactia, dysfunctions of the mammal glands and abdominal pains.

Coriander Infusion

Internally, coriander is used as an infusion, usually prepared from a half of spoon with fruits mixed in a cup, which is consumed during one day. For colic (distend caused by swallowed air or fermentative processes): infusion from a half of spoon of fruits for 3.5 oz of water - the concentration could vary with the baby's age. Adults can consume up to three cups of hot coriander seeds infusion. It's a powerful carminative (eliminates intestinal flatulencies) and spasmolytic agent. For those who suffer from diabetes, it should be taken into account that coriander seeds regulate the level of insulin and decrease the level of cholesterol. In order to obtain this result, one litre of coriander seeds infusion must be consumed each day. For digestive dyspepsia and as an appetite stimulant, the infusion will be prepared during the day from one spoon of mashed fruits boiled in 10oz of water. The infusion must be consumed during the day, two cups after each primary meal. The infusion is also efficient against intestinal worms. It must be taken on an empty stomach and it must be prepared from 0.44lb of fruits boiled in 34oz of water.

Coriander Powder

A simple treatment with coriander powder, recommended for pycho-emotional disorders, is the following: 0.004lb of powder tken four times a day, for a 49 days period with a pause of 10 ded to take four spoons of fresh coriander powder each day, for at least three months. The same treatment can be used for mammal cancer. The treatment must be sustained by a low fat diet. Any hydrogenated fats are completely forbidden.

Salad

It can be used to treat allergies. Coriander leaves contain natural antihistamines, vitamin C and bioflavonoids that decrease the llergic reactions such as hay fever. The cures must be 12 days log and they are especially recommended if the exposal to allergicfactors is intense. The high content of bioflavonoids from the leaes helps also in the cases of hemorrhoids, varices and other veins disorders.

Used externally, the juice made up from the fresh herb is good fr allergies and cutaneous eruptions. Dry coriander fruits can beused to obtain oil that will help against fatigue and lethargies. It can be used also for stomachal massage and abdominal massage in cases of bad digestion, colics, distend, diarrhoea. Because of its heating and analgesic effect, coriander is very useful for calming the rheumatic pains and states of flu or cold. It can be applied locally.

Caution

Caution at the volatile oil contained by coriander seeds, because it can trigger allergic reaction to some.

CORNFLOWER

Cornflower (*Centaurea cyanus*) is a herb that belongs to the *Compositae* family native in Europe. It is mostly used in cosmetics.

Description

Cornflower is a herbaceous plant with a lifespan of 1-2 years. The stem is ramified and covered with leaves which have a stretched out aspect, are deeply dented and displayed randomly. The stem is covered with fine puff, giving the whole plant a green-whitish silky look. The flowers are blue, sometimes white or pink and are grouped together. The herb grows on dry, rocky areas, edges of roads and near crop fields.

Only the blue flowers are used from a cornflower; the white-pinkish ones are removed. It is a good idea to remove them before the herb dries off. The harvesting is done in the months July-August, when the weather is dry and the dew has evaporated.

Fig. 2.30: Cornflower

Proprieties

Because it contains active substances like tannin and potassium salts, cornflower has astringent, weak diuretic, bitter-tonic anti-inflammatory and soothing proprieties.

Treatments

Along with being used as decorative flowers, cornflowers also have a benefic role in health.

Internally, cornflower is recommended in treating diarrhoea, renal and urinary afflictions, while being used in infusions. Cornflower is also recommended for alleviating rheumatism and anorexia.

Externally, cornflower has various applications. It has soothing and antiseptic effects and is used under the form of poultices in cases of conjunctivitis, irritations and inflammations of eye lids.

Due to its soothing effects, cornflower is used in treating facial muscles and wrinkles. It is also used in treating afflictions like eczemas and ulcerations.

In popular medicine, cornflower is used as infusion to threat the dark rings bellow the eyes. The active substances contained in cornflower deter the formation of the rings below the eyes, and at the same time smoothes the skin around the eyes. Locally, cornflower detoxifies the body.

Mixtures

Infusion of cornflowers is prepared from one and a half spoonfuls of cornflowers added to 300 ml boiling water. The pot is then left to cool down for 15-20 minutes. It is consumed lukewarm, half an hour before main meals. This is very useful for treating diarrhoea. The infusion obtained from mixing cornflowers with cowberry flowers is an efficient diuretic. Also, an infusion from one spoonful of cornflowers added to a cup of water can be easily prepared. Around 2 to 3 cups of this mixture are consumed daily, having the effect of eliminating intestinal parasites.

Poultices made of cornflower are made from on spoonful of cornflowers added to 200 ml water.

Cornflower facial mask is prepared from mixing 1 spoon of sour cream with 2 spoons of milk, a spoonful of honey, a vial of vitamin A and a yolk of an egg. The mask is then applied on the face where is left for 30 minutes. It has regenerative effects, making the face skin smooth and silky.

Face steam with cornflower relaxes the skin. Exposure to the steam lasts 10-15 minutes over a pot with hot tea made from cornflower, marigold and wild camomile. For more efficiency, a towel is placed on the back of the head and let its edges drop around the pot of tea to stop the steam from being wasted.

Warning

In case the sensation of discomfort appears, the treatment with cornflower should be ceased.

COWSLIP

Cowslip (*Primula officinalis*), is one of the most widely used medicinal herbs with beneficial effects over the human body.

Description

Cowslip is a small herb, about 10-30cm tall. It grows in glades and clearings, hayfields and also in mountainous regions. Underground it has a very small rhizome from which thick short roots start. The rhizome ends in a bud from which blossoms during spring season. From this bud a small velvety herbaceous stem grows and ends in oval-shaped leaves.

Fig. 2.31: Cowslip

Cowslip blossoms in May and its flowers of a golden-yellowish color spread a very pleasant scent. From this herb its rhizome, roots, flowers and sometimes leaves are used. The recommended time for harvesting is in spring when the herb is in bloom and continues until fruits start to form.

Proprieties

This herb can be used fresh as well as dry, and therapeutically only its flowers, stem and roots are used. Its flowers and leaves are rich in vitamin C and beta-carotene, potassium, calcium, sodium and salicylates which help strengthen the immune system through its antioxidant properties and by lowering the cholesterol level. Also, the herb contains saponoids which bring about expectorant and emetic effects.

The root and stem contain saccharum, amidine and tanoids. Cowslip is also a natural diuretic, soothing sedative.

Treatments

Owing to the substances contained, cowslip is used in treating lung disorders (virosis and bronchitis) and helps eliminate secretions.

The herb is used to eliminate insomnias in adults as well as children. For this a tea from this herb is prepared and for a more efficient effect over the body the herb is mixed with hop plant.

To treat gout and arthritis it is recommended to use cowslip. The treatment must be followed for a long period of time, depending how serious the illness is.

In cases of anxiety tea made from cowslip flowers and roots is prepared. This herb has beneficial effects on the heart especially if it is consumed as tea. It is recommended to be consumed by the individuals who suffer from heart diseases.

Against wounds a macerated mixture made from cowslip flowers is especially effective.

Cowslip tea is a sure way of strengthening the nervous system and heart; it can effectively alleviate headaches and also has a noticeable effect over the myocardium and the tendency towards apoplexy.

This herb is also used in cosmetics, by being an ingredient in many face creams due to its regenerating effects. Moreover it can be used externally in warm poultices applied on painful areas because of its calming nature.

Mixtures

Infusion of cowslip flowers is made from a spoonful of dried flowers over which a cup of boiling water is poured. It is then left to infuse for 10 minutes after which it is consumed and is effective against colds.

Decoct from cowslip roots is prepared by putting a spoonful of roots in a cup of water. The mixture is then left to boil and then set aside. After cooling it is consumed, bearing in mind that the mixture is strengthening for the heart.

Cowslip syrup is recommended in cases of breathing disorders and is obtained from crushed flowers mixed with honey and water.

Cowslip tea is used against insomnias and is obtained from 50g of cowslip herb, 25g of lavender flowers, 10g of St. John's wort herb, 15g of hop plant. A spoonful of the abovementioned quantities is mixed in a 0.25 litres of water and is let to sit for 3 minutes. The tea is consumed very warm in small gulps.

Boiled mixture of cowslip roots is a great cure for kidney problems. The tea is obtained from 50g cowslip, 50g common elder, 15g nettle leaves, 15g dandelion roots. A spoonful of these quantities is mixed in 0.25 litres of water. After that, the mixture is left to boil and to sit for 3 minutes. Two cups should be consumed throughout the day.

Cowslip wine is prepared from 2 litres of fresh flowers in a bottle of water, on top of which white wine is poured. The flowers must be covered. The bottle (covered with a cork) is then let to sit for 14 days in the sunlight. In treating heart diseases it is recommended that the whine be consumed each day 3 to 4 spoonfuls.

Warning

Cowslip is not recommended to those who are allergic to aspirins, because of its high quantity of salicylants which are the main basis for aspirin. It is also not recommended to be consumed by those who follow anticoagulant treatments or by pregnant women. It can be used, however by the women who breastfeed because cowslip tea stimulates lactation.

DANDELION

It is a large genus of following plants in the family *Asteraceae*. The powerful sun-like yellow color emites energy, reminding us that the dandelion is not just an ordinary garden herb, but it is one of nature's miraculous treatments.

Description

Dandelion or *Taraxacum officinale* is a well known herb that came from Greece. Old books about herbal medicine state that in order to have a shiny complexion, women used to use an infusion obtained by boiling the herb and its root. Nowadays, dandelion is consumed mostly in Japan, Italy, France, India and the USA. The whole herb has a curative effect. Raw or dry dandelion roots eaten with tea have a cleansing effect, stimulating digestion and the

Fig. 2.32: Dandelion

urinary system. They fluidize the blood and are considered to be an excellent remedy against thickened blood. A high appreciated salad with a distinctive bitter taste and containing more nutritive substances than spinach or tomatoes is prepared from its fresh leaves. With its 45 cal/ 100g, dandelion contains 2, 8% protids, 7, 5% glucids, vitamins (A, B_2, C, D and G) and minerals (potassium, sodium, calcium, phosphorus and iron). It is widely used either as a laxative or a natural diuretic or as an ingredient in the process of preparing the coffee (it can be added to regular coffee in order to enrich its taste or to prepare a drink similar to coffee or tea).

Properties

From a pharmaceutical point of view, the herb has many qualities: cholagogus, choleretic, alkalizing, laxative, diuretic, venotonic and astringent. The root contains a bitter compound - *taraxacina* - *pectins*, and sterols, vitamins B1, C and D, inulin, tannin and reshines. With a high amount of vegetal fibres, dandelion prevents the unwanted assimilations of glucose and facilitates the elimination of feaces. The contained potassium is responsible for the diuretic action. Dandelion also contains curative substances which are very important for treating metabolism disorders.

The substances contained by dandelion stimulates the stomach's activity as well as the liver's and bile's, causing a high diuresis and helping an organism to eliminate, trough urine, the toxic products of metabolism. Dandelion can be successfully used in cases of hypoacid gastritis, dyspepsia, biliary dischinesis and for preventing the formation of renal calculi. The diuretic effect also helps eliminate the renal calculi. Trough the diuresis it causes, dandelion eliminates toxins and indirectly helps treat eczema and other skin diseases.

Because of the contained vitamins A and C, dandelion is also known as an anti-oxidant and anti-cancer agent.

Mixtures and Treatments

Dandelion is recommended as an adjuvant in all the diseases that involve a glandular disequilibrium. Because of these qualities, the specialists are using it to successfully treat liver diseases. And its effect? It increases the biliary secretion, regulates the blood circulation and stimulates the appetite when in convalescence periods. Because of its diuretic action, it eliminates toxins efficiently. This way, it indirectly treats eczemas and other skin diseases, gout, rheumatism, atherosclerosis, varices, etc. It reduces the level of cholesterol. Dandelion is also efficient in treating the hepatic dermatosis, cleaning the blood from impurities and calming rheumatic pains. Here are some of its uses.

Internal Use

- Consumed as a drink or as salad, dandelion is a great remedy. A healthy salad can be prepared from a handful of dandelion leaves mixed with parsley and dill, oil and vinegar. It can be consumed two or three times a day, before primary meals.
- Decoct for lowering the cholesterol level: 15g of leaves and 15g of roots must be boiled in one litre of water for 30 minutes and it can be consumed a cup before each primary meal.
- Dandelion juice is obtained from hashed and pressed dandelions. If it's consumed immediately and in high quantities, the juice has a remarkable effect over the blood, by purifying it and enriching it with iron.
- In cases of liver disorders the following recipe can be applied: 25g of leaves and 25g of roots must be boiled in one litre of water for 30 minutes. It must be consumed before each meal, one cup only.
- Against anorexia and constipation, 20g of leaves and 20g of roots must be boiled in one litre of water and the product must be left for 24 hours, before consuming it, one cup before each meal.

- To ameliorate the acne and cellulite 25g of leaves and 25g of roots can be boiled for 5 minutes in one litre of water and left to infuse another 10 minutes.

External Use

- The decoct obtained from the hole herb is used to treat cataract. 10g of leaves, roots, flowers and stalks must be boiled in 3/4 litre of water for 20 minutes. The fresh mixture is then used to wash the area around the eye 4 or 5 times a day.
- For treating greasy hair, the following recipe can be applied fresh and hashed dandelion leaves must be applied on the dry hair and left there over night. The following morning, the hair must be washed with shampoo.
- For attenuating freckles it is recommended to use dandelion juice or a lotion prepared as follows: 15g of fresh flowers and leaves, boiled for 10 minutes in 1/2 litre of water.

ELDER

Elder is a plant with strong therapeutic effects which can be used to treat and prevent a great number of diseases. Many legends formed around elder, one of them stating that Judas hung himself from an elder tree.

Description

Elder is a tree 4 to 5 metres tall, with its stem and branches covered in a greenish-ashen bark, having a white herbage in its interior. The leaves have cogged margins and the flowers are white with a pleasant smell. The fruits are small, black and shiny, with 3 longish seeds inside. The plant can be found in mountainous areas, and in river valleys where the sun rays don't shine directly. The flowers are harvested when more than two thirds of them have blossomed, the fruits are only harvested on autumn when they are black. The parts used from this plant are its flowers, fruit and bark.

Properties

The flowers contain glycosides, tanins, mucilages, sapins, pectins, essential oil, vitamin C and mineral salts. In the fruits, alkaloids, carotene, tanins, organic acids and vitamins A, B and C can be found. The leaves contain vitamin C and the bark is rich in tanins, resines and valerenic acid. All these compounds give the plant diuretic, diaphoretic, sudorific, emolient, laxative, anti-inflammatory and antiseptic properties.

Treatments

Elder is a strong antiviral medicine, from stimulating the healing of degenerative diseases, to preventing cancerous diseases, to controlling benign tumors. For this a 30 day diet is recommended with tincture from elder fruit. This helps activate the immune system.

Elder also helps destroy intestinal worms. The flowers, fruits and the juice obtained from the fruits can calm neuralgia. Also, it is useful in case of rheumatism, diseases of the respiratory system or sciatica. The bark is recommended for nephritis and edemas. The tea of elder flowers helps detoxify the body, being recommended for treating cold, flues and bronchitis.

Elder can be used as a natural medicine in obesity because of its laxative properties and its properties of eliminating water from the tissues. It is also used in cases of renal attacks. It eliminates the toxins from the body through urine and also through perspiration, it increases the secretory activity of the sudorific glands and it intervenes directly though dropsy. Elder increases the secretion of the mammary glands for women who breastfeed.

Elder tea is used for furuncle, abcesses, eczemas, extrications, burns, swellings, and urticaria. As a compress it helps treat conjunctivitis, eyelid eczemas, having a role of reducing inflammations and of liquefying infections.

Mixtures

The infusion of elder flowers is prepared from a tablespoon of flowers added to 250 ml of boiling water. The bowl is kept covered for approximately 5 minutes. It is filtered, sweetened with honey and 3 cups per day are consumed after each main meal.

The elder flower decoct is obtained by boiling 50 g of flowers for a period of 3 minutes. The elder fruit juice is prepared with 20 g of fruit mixed with a tablespoon of honey and it is taken on an empty stomach in the morning as a laxative.

The decoct of elder bark is obtained like this: two handfuls of elder bark are boiled in one litre of water, until the water decreases to half of its initial quantity, it is then filtered and the whole quantity is divided into 3 parts. One is taken before each main meal.

Elder cordial is prepared from the following ingredients: 10-12 big elder flowers, 1 lemon, 1 small bag of lemon salt, 800 g sugar, a knife's tip of yeast, 10 litres of water. All ingredients are mixed in a jar. They are stirred every day two times in the jar, leaving them in the sun for 3-4 days. The mixture is then filtered and placed in bottles. It is served cold from the refrigerator.

Elder wine is obtained from ripe fruits, crushed, boiled in wine for 30 minutes. It is sweetened and consumed in proportion of 2-3 small glasses per day.

Fruit powder is prepared like this: the fruits are dried and crushed finely to be consumed in doses of 3-4 teaspoons per day on an empty stomach, for 3-4 weeks.

Warning

Elder brews are not recommended to be consumed in large doses of over 200 g of fruit. It can create symptoms of intoxication, vomit, throat irritations, stomachal burns, respiratory difficulties or convulsions.

FENNEL

Fennel is a herb native to the Mediterranean region which gained popularity ever since the Middle Ages when it was cultivated near monasteries. Also, fennel is one of the nine sacred herbs of the saxons which was capable to cure the nine instances of the illness.

Description

Fennel (*Foeniculum vulgare*) is an edible, perrenial herb which resembles dill. It was discovered in the Mediterranean region and south-east Asia (from east of Morroco and Portugal all the way to Pakistan). The biggest growers of fennel today are: the United States, France, India and Rusia. Fennel was brought to North America by the Spanish missionaires to be grown in their own medicinal gardens. The fact that this herb was used in the ancient times is shown by the traditions presented in mythology. In Greek myths this plant was associated with Dionysus (the god of feasts and wine). It is also said that intelligence came from the gods and reached the humans through a fennel stem. Fennel was considered to have magical characteristics. In the Middle Ages during the summer solstice this herb was placed by the door in order to fend off the evil spirits. What is more, the plant seeds were used to block the keyhole to keep the ghosts from entering the homes.

Fennel seeds are 4-8 cm long, thin and slightly curved with colors that vary from brown to light green. The bittersweet smell and the slightly minty taste make this herb similar to ansine. Many languages (like Hindoo, Indonesian, Hungarian) contain only one word for both fennel and ansine. Fennel fruits - seeds are an old type of seasoning found in the Mediterranean region. These are used to make pickles, scented bread, scented vinegar, meat, fish, sea fruits. The poor would use fennel to appease the hunger in the Lent period but also for spicing up meals.

Fig. 2.33: Fennel Seeds

Proprieties

It is believed from folklore that this herb has mysterious vitalistic characters. It was believed that snakes would digest fennel to shed their skin and to sharpen their vision. Likewise, it was believed that this herb has a rejuvenating effect on man and helps the eye sight. Moreover, fennel stimulates lactation and loss of weight. The consumption in excessive quantities of fennel is not indicated because it can lead to muscular convulsions and even hallucinations.

Fennel contains many minerals and vitamins: vitamin C, fibres, us substances from intestines. The herb is rich in potasium - an essential mineral which helps decrease the high blood pressure that can cause a heart attack.

Fennel seeds, leaves and roots are edible, but the fat extracted from the fennel seeds was proved to be toxic even in small quantities - leading to skin rashes, breathing problems and nausea.

Mixtures and Treatments

Cold and reduce the bouts of cough due to its expectorant nature (contains big quantity of alpha-pinen). The steam resulting from the boiling of the fennel leaves in water alleviates asthma and bronchitis.

Good remedy against intestinal worms by administering light infusions of fennel leaves and seeds. The fennel mixture is used to sharpen the eyesight and alleviate eye irritations. Fennel seeds and roots unclog the liver, spleen, billiary bladder and eliminate cramps. In order to prepare an infusion of fennel seed it is necessay to crush a spoonfull of fennel seeds in a cup of water or milk. The container in which the mixture is being prepared must not be made out of metal. After boiling the mixture, 10 minutes are necessary for it to cool. Two-three cups of this mixtures should be consumed daily.

The tea from fennel leaves and seeds is beneficial for removing intestinal worms and bacteria. The syrup made from fennel juice alleviates the violent bouts of cough. The volatile oil is antiseptic, sedative, carminative, expectorant and it is used in the making of soap and perfumes. The herb also has a very valued effect: if it is pulverized in coops and stables it keeps the flees away.

Warnings

It is recommended that pregnant women stay away from mixtures containing fennel. In large quantities fennel is an uterine stimulant. It does not cause any side effects if it is used in meals. In using the volatile oil any direct contact with the skin is to be avoided due to the fact that it can cause dermatitis for the individulas with sensitive skin.

GARLIC

Garlic (*Allium sativum*) is a plant native to Africa and Central Asia. It was discovered and used by the ancient

Fig. 2.34: Garlic

Egyptians, Babylonians, Jews, Greeks and Romans. Garlic earned a renowned place in the modern natural medicine. In the Middle Ages and Renaissance when the population was facing great plagues, garlic was used very often as a protective medicine. It gained its fame owing to some wrongdoers who fended off the plague by using antiseptic garlic vinegar. As a result, garlic was known as the best antidote against the plague under the name of "the vinegar of the four thieves". The diuretic qualities were discovered by Bartholius, who recommended it for treating ague, while Sydenham would recommend it as a dropsical treatment.

The active compounds of garlic are volatile oil, the mixture between sulfide and allyl oxide in an almost pure state, two very important mineral antibiotic components (sulfur, iodine, zinc, and manganese) and vitamins B and C.

The main therapeutic qualities of garlic describe it as being antiseptic, antibacterial, stimulating digestion, reducing high blood pressure, glandular regulator, diuretic and even cancer deterrent.

Internally, garlic is not used so much due to the strong smell that remains in the mouth. Yet it is still being used often for treating various afflictions: the consumption of 2-3 cloves of garlic a day has wonderful results in treating pharyngitis and intestinal infections. It also counteracts flu complications and helps treat gout and insures a general state of health.

Externally, garlic enemas are effective against intestinal worms. Other usages of garlic are:

- ground and mixed in grease or oil it is recommended as an ointment. This mixture is named "devil's mustard" and is used and is used at treating white tumors;
- the mixture obtained from a clove of garlic mixed with camphorated oil used in rubbing the back and chest with is effective against scabies;
- the disinfection of wounds can be successfully done by grinding a clove of garlic and mixing it until a solution is obtained (10% garlic juice and 1-2% alcohol) or by making dabs or garlic (30 g of ground garlic put to sit in 500 ml of vinegar for 10 days);
- the mixture obtained from a clove of garlic mixed with camphorated oil is successfully used in treating asthenia and rheumatism;
- for the individuals who are hypertensive it is recommended that they take a mixture prepared from garlic (2-3 cloves of garlic are grained and left to sit in 1 litre of alcohol for about 15 days). The resulting mixture is consumed by taking two spoonfulls everyday before eating;
- cases of bad acne get better by rubbing the inflamed spots with half of garlic clove;
- wounds [and] blackheads can be treated by applying poultices made of ground garlic. Results are visible after two weeks. Poultices of warm oven-cooked cloves of garlic can be further used to protect healthy skin.

Garlic juice is another useful treatment obtained from this herb. It has noticeable results in treating: hypertension, infectious diseases, lung problems, bronchitis, tuberculosis, asthma, intestinal parasites and can even deter cancer occurrence.

Indications

- several drops of garlic juice digested with a small quantity of sugar are efficient in stopping a bout of asthma;
- a wad of cotton soaked in garlic juice calms an ear ache;
- eliminating the intestinal worms, a mixture of 20 ml of garlic juice with 200 ml of warm milk drunk early in the mornings is very efficient as a treatment.

Caution! To eliminate the unpleasant smell of garlic it is advisable to chew 2-3 coffee beans, aniseed or caraway, an apple or a piece of parsley.

Another less known benefit that garlic has is its aphrodisiac effect. Research has shown that garlic is capable of improving the blood flow through the veins and also the sexual performance in men. Unfortunately, garlic consumed in normal quantities is unable to reach spectacular results, but the edible products containing garlic may aid you in this sense.

GENTIAN

Used for more than 2000 years as a sour, anti-toxic tonic, which stimulates liver functions, gentian is a medicinal herb. Its name comes from king Gentius of Illyaria, who mentioned it for the first time in a treaty.

Description

A vivacious herb (*Gentiana acaulis*), about 20-60 cm tall usually blue followed, with an erect, cylindrical stem without branches, gentian grows on cliffs. The herb's root is rhizome shaped and long, from which other roots derive. The leaves are big, oval and the flowers are light yellow colored and brown dotted. Only the herb?s roots and rhizomes are used. Harvesting the roots in spring is not recommended, since a weaker product in active substances is obtained. For use in medicinal purposes, these are dried right after being harvested.

Fig. 2.35: Gentian

Properties

As a medicine, the curative properties of the gentian roots are countless: gastric, tonic, simulative of the appetite, anti-febrile, anti-helmintic, and has choleretic-cholagogue actions. Because of its main components: gentio-pyrine, gentio-marine, amaragentine, tannin, gentianine, lipids, and mineral substances, gentian is recommended when treating dyskinetic biliary anorexia, for stimulating salivary secretion, for increasing gastric secretion and the bodys resistance.

Treatments

By stimulating the digestive glandular cells and having a bacteriostatic, anti-helmintic, choleretic and cholagogue effect, gentian stimulates the glandular cells of all digestive organs, quickening intestinal transit. The herb has an important role in stimulating the immune system, favoring the growth number of leucocytes and red blood cells.

For internal use, gentian, mixed with other depurative herb tinctures, favours the detoxification of the body. In treating diabetes, intestinal parasites, inflammatory or pancreas affections, the use of gentian tincture is recommended. For gastric and hepatic diseases, dilution in water of the gentian tincture is indicated.

Cholagen sponges with gentian violet are good antiseptics against gram-positive bacteria and some locally hypoestesiant protector and epithelising fungus. These are used in case of various wounds or ulcerations. The wound or the ulcerated zone is cleaned and the sponges are applied under gauze dressing. The dressings are changed once every 2-3 days.

In case of biliary fits, biliary dyskinesis, or for preventing biliary lithiasis, gentian tincture is administered in form of tincture, from which a teaspoon is taken, diluted in a quarter of a glass of water, 3-4 times a day - in the morning and a quarter of an hour before the main meals.

The gentian root has tonic hepatic effects, being thus used in liver diseases since it stimulates function and helps regenerate hepatic cells. The herb inhibits the development of viruses affecting the liver. In this case, gentian is used in the form of a powder, of which half a teaspoon is taken 3-4 times a day in treatments of 6-12 weeks.

Distension, dyspepsia and atonic constipation can be treated with treatments of 3-6 weeks by cold maceration of gentian, of which a quarter of a glass of water is taken 4 times a day, 15 minutes before meals.

Gentian tincture can treat indigestion or hyperacid gastritis with the power of eliminating hard sensations in the stomach or nausea before and after meals. A teaspoon of tincture is administered, diluted in a little water, 10-15 minutes before every meal.

The lack of appetite in the case of children can be treated through adding 10-15 drops of gentian to a teaspoon of honey. The mixture is administered a quarter of an hour before meals.

In treating hypothyroid and interfacing disorders, the gentian tincture is administered as an adjuvant, a teaspoon 4 times a day, in treatments of 3 months, with breaks of 15-30 days. It has strong stimulation effects of metabolism and it favors normal secretion of thyroidal hormones.

Mixtures

A decoct can be obtained from a teaspoon of the herb, cut into small pieces, to half a litre of cold water. It is boiled for 15 minutes and consumed before the most important meals.

The gentian macerate and tincture are obtained from 20 g of root to 100 g of 70 degrees alcohol for 8 days. fifteen drops are taken, in water, half an hour before meals, thus stimulating appetite.

Gentian syrup is prepared out of 10 g of root, soaked in 150 ml of boiling water, after which the liquid is filtered and squeezed out, 230 g of sugar is added, and then it is boiled and passed through a sieve.

The cataplasm of gentian root is prepared of root powder; it is put in a receptacle, in which progressively warm water is added while stirring continuously, until a paste is formed. It is then wrapped in gauze and applied in the affected area where it is kept for 1-3 hours.

Warning

It is not recommended being used for a period longer than three weeks when treating states of debility or acute weakness.

GINKGO BILOBA

This herb has grown on Earth for millions of years, also known as the "Tree of Life", the herb survived to our days from the times of dinosaurs. Its name is "*Ginkgo biloba*" and its strength is due to the chemical substances it contains.

Fig. 2.36: Ginkgo Biloba

Description

One of the most studied herbs, ginkgo biloba has some remarkable qualities in the benefit of health. This plant grows spontaneous in China and Japan and it is grown in many countries not only because it enriches the visual aspect of any land but also for its therapeutic uses. In ancient times, Japanese people used to grow this herb inside the gardens of temples and today they venerate the old ginkgo trees as gods. But the herb is older than that. The recently discovered fossilized leaves show that the gingko trees existed on Earth from the Permian period (approximately 250 million of years before).

South Carolina prides itself on having the biggest ginkgo tree plantation. Although they are kept at the dimension of little trees, a gingko tree can grow up to 30 metres tall with two-lobed leaves. The flowers determine the masculine or feminine type of the tree. The leaves change their color from light green in summer to yellow in fall.

Properties

The pharmaceutical action of the herb is given by the complexity of the chemical substances contained by the leaves. They contain flavonoids and terpenoids (ginkgolide,

A, B, C, bilobalide). The extract of the Ginkgo leaves contains flavonoids glycosides and terpenoids (ginkgolide, bilobalide) and has been used pharmaceutically. It has many alleged no-otropic properties, and is mainly used as a memory and concentration enhancer, and also as an anti-vertigo agent. Blood circulation is improved and brain cells are protected against afflictions. The brain is oxygenated better and due to the effect the herb has over the veins, the capillar permeability diminishes.

Treatments

Due to the fact that it has multiple effects on human health, *gingko biloba* can be used in cases of hearing and memory loss, in treating tuberculosis, gonorrhea, stomach pains, skin diseases, leucorrhea, angina pectoralis, dysenteries, high blood tension, vertigo and anxiety. It can be also used to treat impotence caused by the treatment with anti-depressives. Even more, it is known that the consumption of gingko biloba can diminish depressive states.

It helps in cases of asthma and bronchitis because of the contained flavonoids and it also contains an inhibitor that reduces blood clots. It can be used to treat blood pressure problems.

The critical illnesses such as benign tumor, cancer, diabetes, cardiac ischemia, hormonal disorders can be treated with the help of this herb. It is highly efficient even in the treatment of Alzheimer because it increases the secretion of dopamine and noradrenalin and also the tonus of the smooth muscles that cover the brain blood vessels.

Mixtures

There are a variety of products based on gingko biloba, such as: tea tablets, tincture, unguents, etc. Gingko biloba extract has a positive effect in cases of depressive and anxious states; it increases memory processes and endurance against tiredness. It can also be used for unguents against cellulitis because it activates the microcirculation. When it is used in the composition of shampoos, gingko biloba stimulates blood circulation at the scalp level.

Tea and unguents made from gingko biloba can treat varicose ulcer. The effects are predominant if the consumption of gingko tea is associated with an alimentary regime that can help the detoxification of the body.

Warning

The consumption of gingko biloba can cause vertigo, headaches and allergic reactions. It isn't recommended to use gingko biloba mixtures if you are having an anticoagulant treatment.

GINSENG

With a high variety of pharmaceutical actions, proving its powers not only in curative treatments but also in nutrition, ginseng truly represents an elixir of life due to its stimulant, tonic and energizing effects. It slows the ageing process offering the body a fresh sense of optimism.

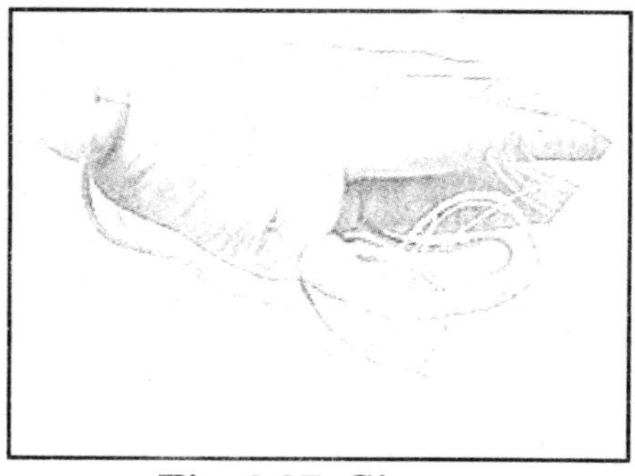

Fig. 2.37: Ginseng

Description

Ginseng (*Panax ginseng*) - native of Eastern Asia, Siberia and North America is a perennial species known and appreciated for its pharmaceutical properties for almost 5000 years. The Korean and Chinese ginseng is a tonic for the whole body. It was very precious in ancient times and its price was the same with the price of gold. Beginning with the 9th century, the herb was introduced in Europe by an Arab physician and after nine centuries it became one of the most popular natural remedies. It was used initially for its tonic effect over the immune system and for its power to heal virosis and fever states, but its area of use increased gradually and in our days it is used to treat fatigue, afflictions of the nervous system and lack of concentration. Protected by law, ginseng is intensively cultivated in China, Japan, Korea and Russia. Etymologically, its name comes from the word "gin" that means "human" and the word "seng" that means "the essence".

Properties

Ginseng contains 12 types of bio-active chemical substances also known as ginsenoids. It also contains panaxan (Panax Ginseng), which diminishes the level of glicemia and increases the effect of insulin. Ginseng has tonic (especially over the nervous system), anti-oxidant, anti-inflammatory, anti-depressive, hypotensive, hypoglycemic, hypocholes-terolemic and aphrodisiac effects. It increases the concentration and aids memory processes. It has a positive effect over blood circulation and it improves the function of lungs. Even more, it can revitalize weak bodies; reduce fatigue, and increase work and effort capacity as well as stimulating the secretion of adrenalin. Due to these properties, the consumption of ginseng is recommended to those who sustain serious physical efforts. It is recommended also during convalescence periods because it stimulates the healing process.

It is important to be aware that owing to its nutritive qualities, ginseng can be used by all people, irrespective of age. Because it stimulates the endocrine glands, ginseng increases mineral and vitamin absorption. Beca-use it is an adaptogen herb it contributes to the capacity of the body to adapt itself to the natural negative environment states such as cold, stress and malnutrition.

The quantity of active compounds is significantly larger if the root of the herb is older. The general belief is that the herb reaches its maturity after 6 years of life.

Treatments

According to Chinese tradition, ginseng treats hypertension as well as hypotension, anemia, asthenia, arthritis, digestive disorders, insomnia, and fatigue and increases body resistance during stress periods. The general belief is that ginseng prevents the ageing of tissues and treats impotence. Ginseng is included in the treatment of depressive and debilitative states, memory disorders and diabetes.

Because it is also a stimulant for the immune system, this herb is recommended in the treatment of low resistance to periods of cold. It is efficient in treating physical and intellectual fatigue that is generated by stress. It helps older and younger people as well.

It is recommended in the treatment of seasickness, airsickness and senility.

Mixtures

Used as capsules, powder, tea or nutritive supplements, ginseng can be easily found in any drug-store. The pharmaceutical products must be administrated by heeding the doctor's recommendations. It is important to know that the most efficient mixtures are obtained from the 5-year old herb roots. The soluble tablets are more efficient that the alcoholic extracts. The normal dose for an adult is about 0.03 oz and for a child the dose diminishes to half.

Caution

Small doses can increase the blood tension and big doses can diminish it. To avoid any side-effects you must see a doctor. Because ginseng can interact with other drugs causing side-effects, a doctor recommendation is needed.

HORSERADISH

Due to its medicinal characteristics and to the contribution it brings to the taste of meals, horseradish is one of the most used plants. It has thick pulpy yellowy roots, spicy taste and antibiotic, anti-inflammatory and aphrodisiacal properties.

Description

Horseradish (*Armoracia rusticana*) is a strong seasoning successfully used in phytotherapy. Because of its spicy flavor the horseradish root is used in conserving the canned food for the winter but is also used throughout the year in preparing various meal recipes. It originated in south-eastern Europe and western Asia and it is resistant to the low temperatures as well as to droughts. This herb grows in the shaded places as well as the warm ones but it does not grow on sandy soils, however argillaceous alkaline soils rich in humus are ideal for horseradish. It can grow up to 2m; it has large edible leaves and a branched stem.

Fig. 2.38: Horseradish

Proprieties

As a medicine horseradish root has many curative properties: strong antibiotic, expectorant, bronchodilatator, antibacterial, coronary vasodilatator, it increases the blood pressure, it heats up the body, stimulates the body's immune system, anti-inflammatory, anti-parasitic, anti-anemic, antiscorbutic, diuretic. It can stimulate the appetite. It has a cardiotonic effect and is recommended to the people that suffer from high blood pressure. Also it is known that horseradish has aphrodisiacal properties.

Treatments

Bronchitis, sinusitis, paradontosis, rheumatism, anemia, flu, stomatitis, and even facial paralysis can be treated by using horseradish. As for sinusitis and rhinitis it is enough for a cataplasm to be placed on the forehead along with two spoons of grained horseradish so that the nose gets immediately decongested. This treatment is repeated 4 to 5 days in a row and it gets interrupted once burns occur.

Against bronchitis, flu and lung congestions, horseradish flour is applied like a cataplasm on the chest area for a half an hour up to an hour. This treatment is repeated once every two or three days.

Pains caused by rheumatism disappear if a cataplasm of horseradish is used. If a burning sensation appears the treatment is to be stopped.

Gargling tincture of horseradish dosed in 3-4 spoons in a glass half filled with water alleviates stomatitis.

Against paradontosis, the person suffering from it would need to chew grained horseradish. It can be mixed with carrots to reduce the spicy taste. This herb is great for gums because of its strong stimulating effects.

Horseradish syrup is recommended in cases of asthma, bronchitis, breathing disorders.

Mixtures

The mixtures that can be obtained from horseradish are: tincture, horseradish vinegar, horseradish flour or horseradish cataplasm.

The tincture of horseradish is prepared by graining horseradish and filling it in a recipient in proportion of 80%. The recipient is then filled to the brim with white alimentary alcohol of 80 degrees and is left to mix for 8 days, after which the whole mixture is strained.

The horseradish syrup is obtained in the following way: grained horseradish root is mixed with 4 spoons of honey and are left to mix for several minutes. The mixture is strained and pressed with gauze. The raw syrup is obtained. The remains from the gauze are set to boil in a small quantity of water. After boiling, the mixture gets strained and then left to cool off, after which it gets mixed with the raw syrup. It is consumed by taking 3 spoons of the mixture a day.

To prepare the horseradish flour the horseradish root is cut into tiny squares which are left near a heating stove to dry up. After that they get grained. The whitish powder can be stored, however with the passing of the time it loses some of its characteristics.

Another very useful mixture for cases of facial paresis or seborrhea is horseradish vinegar, which is obtained by filling a bottle with grained horseradish over which apple vinegar is poured until it gets filled to the top. The mixture from the bottle is to be consumed in small quantities to treat the abovementioned illnesses.

Warnings

The consumption of horseradish is not advisable to the individuals suffering from gastric ulcer, goitrous problems or renal illnesses. Also the consumption of horseradish is forbidden to children younger than 4 years old.

HORSETAIL

Known from the oldest of times because of its hemostatic effect, horsetail was considered "irreplaceably priceless", especially in cases of bleedings and bladder problems. This herb cleanses toxins from inside the human body.

Description

Horsetail is a tall perennial herbaceous plant which grows in humid climates on plains, on the shores of mountain rivers or on railroads.

Fig. 2.39: Horsetail

In the spring from the herb's rhizome little stems burst out which rot after the plant blossoms and are replaced by sturdier summer stems up to 20-25 cm tall. These stems have small brown scaly leaves. The sturdier horsetail stems are harvested in the mouths between July and September on a sunny day after the dew has evaporated. It dries in the shade and it's kept in paper bags.

Proprieties

Horsetail contains 5-7% silicic acid, nicotine, palustrine, palustridine, phytosterol, beta-sitosterol, malic acid, vitamin C, volatile oil, potassium salts etc.

The active compo-nents from horsetail have antimicrobial, antiseptic, anti-inflammatory effects; they preserve eyesight and stimulate blood flow.

Treatments

The best herbs fit for digestion (under the forms of tea or tinctures) are the ones which can be found in forests or in argillaceous regions. The ones found in humid areas are good for being used in small quantities for treating various external illnesses (where the herb is being used without its root).

For treating digestive problems, gastric hyperacidity and ulcer 2-3 cups of tea are consumed daily which also do good for treating bladder and renal afflictions.

Horsetail helps retain water in pericardium, or in renal disorders after the occurrence of such illnesses as scarlatina and other infectious diseases which cause issues in eliminating water.

In cases of bronchitis and pneumonia it's recommended to consume three spoons a day containing the herb mashed to a powdered form because it has antiseptic and antibacterial properties.

Horsetail tincture is effective against sweaty feet. They are gently massaged using tincture. Also, it is recommended to consume a cup of horsetail every morning on an empty stomach. During the treatment it's necessary to follow a diet made of fresh juice which lasts 2 months; mixed with 2 litres of warm chamomile infusion it is used for enemas; three times a day 50ml of juice made of green barley juice or birch sap is consumed.

Dandruff is eliminated if hair is washed daily with infusion of horsetail and massaged with quality olive oil.

Also horsetail tea is recommended for gargling in treating amygdalitis, inflammations of the mouth, ulcerous stomatitis, gum bleedings, fistula and polypus.

Just like Richard Willfort, an Austrian botanist, stated - the prolonged consumption of horsetail tea prevents the malign tumor.

Arthritis, arthrosis, renal colics, gout, hemorrhoids, rheumatism could be alleviated by using horsetail in small amounts.

Horsetail tea is also recommended in dealing with headaches, weak states, tiredness, and stress. Its indicated in cases of blood pressure, in cardiovascular illnesses (asthma) and in cases of skin diseases: dermatosis, scars, gangrenes, nail inflammations.

Mixtures

Tea is prepared as follows: in a cup with boiling water one spoonful of horsetail, it is left to cool down for one minute and then it gets strained.

Horsetail tincture is obtained from 100g horsetail which is placed in a bottle on top of which refined alcohol is poured until it completely covers the herbs inside. Then it is left to sit in the sun or other heat source for 14 days.

Macerated horsetail is obtained from a couple of spoons of powder placed in a litre of water, left to macerate for a few hours and then strained; it is then consumed in a day. It's beneficial for the stomach because it has antitoxic effects and helps cleanse the kidneys.

Two handfuls of horsetail are placed in a sieve which is placed on a recipient with boiling water. When the plants have macerated they are placed in a clean gauze which is applied on the wound for about 4-5 hours.

The fresh herb is thoroughly washed, mashed until an unguent is obtained and applied on the painful spots (in case of hemohoids).

Baths are made in a following way: a pot gets filled with 5-6 litres of cold water over which two handfuls of horsetail are strewn and the mixture is let to settle till the next day. The pot is placed on the stove and it's left to boil, after which the mixture is passed through a sieve and used as bathing water. The bath lasts 20 minutes.

JASMINE

The most widely known chara-cteristic of this herb regards its distinctive smell. In order to extract 2.2 lb essence of jasmine it's necessary to use 2200 lb of fresh jasmine flowers. Nevertheless, its considerable effects conducive to a both healthy physical state and a state of mind are enough reasons to convince us that it's worth the effort.

Fig. 2.40: Jasmine

Description

Jasmine (*Jasminum officinale*) is a flowery shrub containing white or yellow flowers, native to Mediterranean countries (although there are a considerable number of people that say it comes from India). The shrub has a ramified crown, angular green long twigs, obtuse flowers and it is cultivated as a decorative plant (*Jasminum fretticans*), or for its industrial and medicinal uses. The flowers can be small or large, white with a nice perfume that increases in strength in the evening. Jasmine grows quickly. It can grow in the shade, but it grows better in sunny and breezy areas.

Widely known for its big consumption of jasmine tea, the Chinese civilization drinks green tea during the spring and summer times as well as in autumn and especially in winter, jasmine tea. This drinking tea habit appeared in the north and north-east region of China.

From jasmine flowers it is extracted the well-known and highly expensive oil. The high cost is explained by the fact that in order to extract 2.2lb of jasmine essence 2200lb of fresh flowers are needed. Nevertheless, its effects over an organism make that process worthwhile. The herb has the power to eliminate the stress and depression, and it can help regain self-confidence. The jasmine flowers are used in biotherapy and perfume industry.

Properties

The fresh jasmine flowers contain a high amount of etheric oil. Beside this oil, the flowers also contain benzilic acetate, linalcohol, benzilic alcohol, indole and jasmon. All these substances confer jasmine aphrodisiac properties. Among other properties of the jasmine flowers are: the improvement of digestion, adjuvant in the toxins elimination and the loose of weight. They also help the acceleration of metabolism, they improve the blood circulation and it is commonly known their aphrodisiac effect.

Mixtures and Treatments

How can the flowers be used? In the simplest way possible making tea out of them! Other ways: macerated in oil or alcoholic extract. The tea can be use to treat headaches, coughing and the macerate for rheumatism.

In aroma-therapy, the jasmine oil is recommended for any kind of physical pain. It is also good advisable to have it around in case of birth. Even more, it is a powerful antiseptic, sedative and tonic recommended for breathing difficulties, coughing and nervous debility. It also calms any skin affliction and it can be used in small amounts for calming pains.

Jasmine Tea

The jasmine tea is known by the majority of nutritionists as being an adjuvant in losing weight. The jasmine tea does not have any energizing properties like the green tea, but it has sedative properties and it can regulate blood circulation and arterial tension. The taste of one jasmine tea cup is sweet and combined with green tea will offer powerful tonic and energetic results.

Surely, it isn't one of the most powerful aphrodisiacs, but the jasmine tea helps an organism relax and regain its strength in the stress or physically and psychic overworking periods.

Jasmine Oil

The adepts of the aromatherapy use this jasmine oil in combination with drops of ylang ylang oil. This mixture helps regaining the healthy state of mind and body.

Warning

It isn't recommended to consume jasmine tea in big quantities, especially in cases of pregnancy. It is also not recommended to consume jasmine tea on an empty stomach, to prevent causing high acidity. After 5 pm it is best if the consumption of jasmine tea is ceased to prevent insomnia.

LADY'S MANTLE

This herb is known as a very efficient cure for women. Out of all the medicinal herbs, lady's mantle is the number one choice of specialists in phytotherapy when prescribing medication in cases of menstruation.

Fig. 2.41: Lady's mantle

Description

Lady's mantle (*Alchemilla vulgaris*) is a herbaceous perennial herb which grows at high altitudes, especially in mountainous regions. It also grows in forests, pasture and hayfields from April till the month of August. It is not a very tall herb. Its leaves are long, in a semicircular form, with denticulated edges; and its flowers are yellowish-light green, of small size without petals. For medicinal purposes the plant is harvested in June through July. Lady's mantle has been recommended by specialists in phytotherapy for centuries, owing to the beneficial effects that it has over women's bodies. It helps treat leucorrhoea, anxiety, problems caused by menopause, and combined with milfoil it constitutes an effective cure against menstruation disorders.

Proprieties

Among the active substances in the chemical composition of the herb tannins, flavonoids and mineral salts are also included. Due to the quantity of hormones from the herb lady's mantle can adjust hormonal disturbances and is recommended in cases of amenorrhea (absence of menstruation) and si hypermenorrhea (menstruation disorders), menopause disorders, cervicitis, small and medium uterine fibroma. It is also efficient in cases of headaches, dizziness, stomach aches and nausea. Mixtures made from this herb have astringent, antidiuretic, anti-inflammatory and heart strengthening properties. Moreover, because of its ability to stimulate the healing of wounds, the herb is used effectively in treating injuries.

Treatments

Believed to be very useful in treating sterility at women, lady's mantle helps and eases the process of giving birth. Furthermore, it can cure infections of the pelvic organs, fever, burns, boils, and hernia. It is also used in treating spasms and muscle pains, muscle weakness or general weakness, anemia, and growing problems at children. Traditional medicine teaches us that lady's mantle can be used effectively in obesity cases, rheumatism, arthrosclerosis and hydropsy.

For external use, lady's mantle is employed in healing wounds, cuts, and bee stings and also in treating ulcerous afflictions of the shank or for gargling.

Mixtures

Lady's mantle is used under various forms, starting with infusions to tinctures or macerated mixtures which can be found in stores specialized in selling medicinal herbs. It can even be used in its natural state in cases of cuts or stings. Bellow we have listed some of the main mixtures and their effects.

Lady's Mantle Tea

It is made from a spoonful of grinded herb, boiled in a cup of water. The mixture is then consumed two or three times a day and is recommended for diabetics and for those who suffer from obesity. The same tea if left to infuse for 5 to 10 minutes can help conquer insomnias. Children with weak muscles or those who do not gain any weight despite the accurate alimentation are advised to take two cups of lady's mantle tea a day. In cases of amenorrhea the tea should be more concentrated and the time left to infuse should be longer (about 15 minutes). For treating mild menstruation disorders an infusion of 4-5 minutes is recommended. Externally, for gargling, the infusion is made from three spoonfuls of lady's mantle macerated in a cup of water.

Tonic Wine

If your goal is to stimulate the food appetite, then the tonic wine made from lady's mantle is all that you need. Wine infusion is prepared following the same routine: a spoonful of lady's mantle fruits are added in a cup of hot wine. It is then consumed before meals.

Macerated Mixture of Lady's Mantle

After the herb is placed in water and left to macerate between 8 and 12 hours, the resulting mixture is then sieved and digested during meals.

Poultices

Poultices containing lady's mantle oil are used in cases of stomach aches and applied two or three times a day for 20 to 30 minutes. If applied on the heart area, they can alleviate heart problems.

For bathwater, 7 oz of dry lady's mantle are left to macerate all night in cold water. The next day the water gets warmed up and mixed with the bathwater. It is recommended that the bath should last no more than 30 minutes.

LEMON

The Romans used this fruit for improving the taste of their culinary preparations. Today lemon is well known not only as an aliment but also for its therapeutic properties. In aromatherapy, essential lemon oil is used in treating hepatic affections.

Description

The fruit of the tree named *Citrus limon* originates in India. The Arabs were those who have brought it later on to the area of the Mediterranean Sea. Starting with the 4th century, the Romans started using this fruit for improving the taste of their foods. Today lemon is well known not only as an aliment but also for its therapeutic properties. In aromatherapy, essential lemon oil is used in treating hepatic affections. Because of its chemical composition - especially because of its rich containment of vitamin C - lemon is also used successfully for preparing products with cosmetic purpose.

Properties

Lemon juice - with 30% fruit - contains citric acid, calcium and potassium citrates, glucides (glucose, fructose, sugar), mineral salts and oligoelements (iron, calcium, silicium, phosphorus, manganese, copper), vitamins (B_1, B_2,

B_3, C, PP, A, carotene). All these compounds help the body in its growing process. Citric acid, for example, stimulates the absorption of calcium through the intestines (mineralization action), neutralizes the effect of uric acid and reduces the gastric acidity. While vitamin C is richly contained by lemon, it has an anti-oxidizing role, vitamin PP offers vascular protection. Also, vitamin C has an important role in the synthesis of collagen in the tissues, cartilages and bones, also being anti-inflammatory. Furthermore, through the contribution of vitamin C, the burning of fat is also accelerated. A direct action of this is manifested through the fluidization of the blood - a process which does not limit the coagulation of blood in case of injuries. Therefore, the blood circulates easier though the blood vessels, becoming more fluid. We will now present the rest of the benefiting effects produced by lemon consumption: strong antioxidant, bactericide, febrifuge, tonic for the sympathetic nervous system, cardiac tonic, anti-gastric acid, diuretic, anti-rheumatic, anti-gout, anti-arthritic, sedative, anti-sclerotic, vein tonic, anti-scorbutic, depurative, remineralizing, anti-anemia, stimulates gastro-hepatic and pancreatic secretions, haemostatic, carminative, and vermifuge.

Treatments and Mixtures

Because of vitamin C in lemon, one can treat with great ease hepatic or respiratory diseases, varix or even obesity.

Lemon Juice

With its bactericide and antiseptic action, lemon juice activates the white cells and strengthens the body's immunity. Pulmonary, intestinal or renal infections, infectious maladies, febrile states, rheumatism, gout, hyperacidity, stomachal ulcerus, arteriosclerosis, varix and capillary fragility, sanguine hyper-sliminess, hypertension, pulmonary and bone tuberculosis, demineralization, growing deficiencies, convalescence, anemia, hepatic and pancreatic insufficiency, hepatic congestions, bleeding, intestinal parasites, asthma, bronchitis, influenza, colds and sinusitis are thus aimed at. The lemon juice diet usually starts with the daily consumption of the liquid obtained from 10 lemons and continues with the progressive decreasing of the number of lemons through the period of four to five weeks. Lemon juice drops can be placed in nostrils (repeatedly) for controlling colds and sinusitis. Lemon juice is also helpful against dandruff if the scalps skin is massaged with it. This way, blood circulation is intensified and the hair becomes shiny and healthy.

Used externally in cosmetic purposes, from lemon juice a numerous series of natural remedies can be prepared for various problems. For example in case of greasy complexions, a mixture of one teaspoon of lemon juice, one of grape juice and one of honey is recommended. The paste is applied on the face and then removed after fifteen minutes. For fragile nails, the following simple treatment can be used for a few minutes, several times per day, the fingers should be kept in lemon juice. Another remedy, for cuperosis, is based on mixing a white of an egg (mixed until it becomes spume) with lemon juice. The result is locally spread on the affected areas and this process is repeated up to 4 times a day.

Lemon-based Diuretic

In a bowl of hot water, lemon pieces are added. A tablespoon of marjoram is then added. After maceration (the mixture is kept macerating for a period of one night), it is filtered and consumed on an empty stomach. The diet can last for two or three weeks, depending on necessity. For the best results, it is advisable to consult a physician.

Lemon Rind Oil

In aromatherapy, this oil has multiple uses: from circulatory diseases (anemia, frost-bite, and varicosity) to digestive affections (diabetes, biliar lithiasis, and gastroenteritis), diseases of the respiratory system (asthma and bronchitis), liver diseases, headaches and so on.

LINDEN TREE

From earliest times, lime was a well-known tree for its therapeutic virtues. The Teutonic civilizations considered it a sacred tree, while the Celts saw in it a symbol of altruism. It is considered that this tree influences people to tell the truth, which is why in Medieval times, lovers swore eternal love in the shade of a lime tree.

Description

The lime is a tall tree, reaching 20-40 m, with big heart shaped leafs. The flowers have a yellowish-white color and a strong perfume. The tree is resistant to cold temperatures and wind, being found in mountainous regions. Lime is one of the most longevous trees, able to reach the age of 1000 years and to produce up to 100 kg of flowers.

Properties

Lime flowers have in their composition sugar, gallic and catechol acids, and also essential oil, which give the plant neurosedative and antispastic properties, reducing inflammations of the respiratory system.

Treatments

Because of the active substances it contains and the properties it has, lime is used as a sedative in cases of insomnia. It is successfully utilized against states of anxiety and irritability.

Having a sudorific, anti-thermic, emollient and expectorant action, lime is used as a tea for treating colds and influenza.

The tea stimulates abundant perspiration, decreasing body temperature. Lime flowers have a calming effect and help eliminate bronchic secretions. Associated with chamomile and mint, lime flowers ease digestion and tonify the gastric mucous.

Having a calming and decongestive action, the lime flowers, under the form of baths, are used for calming down fussy children and people suffering from convulsive cough. The lime flower pillow is recommended to those suffering of insomnia and nervous hyper excitability.

Lime flower tea mixed with sodium bicarbonate is used as throat wash for inflammations of the tonsils. In cosmetics, combined with cornflower flowers, helps reduce dark rings under the eyes. It is also used for calming irritated complexions.

Mixtures

Lime flower tea is prepared from a teaspoon of flowers added to 250 ml of boiling water. The pot is kept covered for 5-10 minutes, the tea is then filtered and consumed in a dose of 1-2 cups per day, sweetened with honey or sugar.

The infusion for gargle is prepared from adding 25 g of flowers to 250 ml of boiling water to which 5 g of sodium bicarbonate is added.

The sedative infusion is prepared from 20 g of flowers to a litre of hot water. One cup is consumed after the evening meal and one before bed.

Lime tea baths are prepared from 500 g of plant to 3 litres of water. The bath lasts about 15-20 minutes, at a temperature of maximum 37 degrees Celsius.

Lime flower macerate is obtained from 3 tablespoons of flowers macerated in a bowl with 250 ml of cold water, for a period of 8-10 hours, after which it is placed on the fire until it boils slightly. It is then filtered and left to cool down after which it is mixed with bee honey. One tablespoon, before bed, is administered from the honey mixed with lime tea.

The compress of lime flower infusion mixed with corn flowers is kept on the eyelids for 10-15 minutes before bed to reduce the dark rings under the eyes.

Lime flower mask with properties of nourishing and reviving pale complexions is made from 4 spoonfuls of lime infusion, a spoonful of milk powder and one of wheat bran. They are mixed until a paste is obtained which is kept on the face for 10-15 minutes. It is then washed off with lime infusion.

Warning

It is recommended to not have more than 3 cups of tea per day and to not use infusions which are too concentrated. If the doses are too big, the lime flower tea can have exciting effects on the nervous system, causing insomnia.

POT MARIGOLD

Pot marigold is native to southern and central Europe. Its name (*Calendula officinalis*) comes from the Latin word "Kalendae", which was the first day in the Roman calendar. They were named like that because of the fact that they bloom all year round. This herb is also known as the "flower of the rains", due to the fact that if the flower does not open in the morning it is a clear sign that it will rain with storm out that day.

For the people who lived in Antiquity, marigold flowers when given to a person, they symbolized everlasting love. Even then it was renowned for its effective treatment against stomach-aches, intestinal problems, and liver failures but also for speeding up wound healing.

Description

Marigold is a herb with a high stem supporting many ramifications, and with yellow flowers. It blossoms from May till September. The flowers which must be fully developed - are picked without their stems. The harvesting lasts for

3-4 days after the dew has evaporated. They are placed in thin layers and are left to dry in shaded places.

Proprieties

The active compounds found in marigold have the quality of stimulating blood circulation and speeding up the healing periods. Marigold flowers contain a bitter compound, volatile oil. They have healing, anti-inflammatory, anti-bacterial and soothing effects. They are a considerable source of flavonoids, carotenoids, vitamin C, proteins and resins, among others. The contained bio-flavonoids reduce the fragility of the capillary blood vessels.

Treatments

Marigold infusion and tincture are used to treat hyperacid gastritis, duodenal ulcer, infected icterus, cancerous ulcerations, inflammations and liver failures.

Marigold tincture is effective at stabilizing the menstrual cycle and marigold tea, if drunk a week before the appearance of the menstrual cycle, it can alleviate the pains, especially in cases of anemic persons.

Fig. 2.42: Pot Marigold

Leucorrhea, acne, burns, chilblains, infected wounds, skin cancer, breast cancer, tegumentary disorders, mycosis and ulcerous breast wounds are all treated with marigold lotions or with bath water containing marigold.

In cases of ulcerous pains or renal pains, it's recommended to hold on the belly a "pillow" containing marigold flowers. It is also used effectively in complexion disorders, by placing the "pillow" of marigold flowers directly on the face.

At the same time, in treating dry sensible skin, it is recommended that the marigold oil be used which speeds up the healing, has energizing and soothing effects and can also strengthen the vascular fragility of blood circulation. The oil is also recommended in skin inflammations and also in treating bruises and eczemas.

Against skin cancer as well as birth marks or dark spots marigold juice is recommended.

In cases of dizziness and headaches marigold decoct is recommended. It can be used in cases of bladder disorders, rachitis, cough, stomach aches.

Mixtures

The infusion is obtained from 2 spoonfuls of dry flowers over which 300ml of boiling water is poured. The pot is covered and left for 15-20 minutes after which it passes through a sieve. The tea is drunk warm three times a day, half an hour before primary meals. A more concentrated infusion is made from four spoonfuls of marigold flowers added in 200ml of boiling water from which four spoons are taken each day.

The infusion made from 10g of flowers added to 100g water can be used in vaginal baths to help destroy the protozoan Trichomonas vaginalis.

The marigold tincture is obtained by macerating 20g of flowers, freshly picked and put in 100ml of alcohol heated to 70 degrees for 8 days. The vessel is then left around a heating source or sunlight. To adjust the menstrual cycle it is necessary to dissolve 30 drops of tincture in a small quantity of water and then consume 3 spoons of the mixture a day.

A spoonful of tincture, obtained from macerating four spoons of marigold flowers in 100ml alcohol of 90 degrees for a period of 10 days, is mixed in 100ml distilled water. From this a mixture is obtained that can be used to treat pale or greasy complexions.

Marigold lotion is used for treating burns and chilblains and is prepared from 20g fresh marigold flowers which are cooked in 100g of lard. The lard must be preheated. It is then stirred for 10 minutes and the pan is left aside until the next day when it gets heated again and its content is passed through a fine sieve and into a jar. Excellent results are also obtained from mixing marigold lotion with comfrey roots, and the resulting ointment is used in treating wounds, chilblains, burns and varicose ulcer.

Bath water made from marigold flowers is prepared as follows: 30g of fresh marigold flowers are left to sit in cold water for 24 hours. After that they are boiled for 10 minutes and the water in which they were boiled is used in the bathtub. The baths should not last more than 15 minutes and should be taken twice a day for 12 days.

The "pillow" made from marigold flowers contains freshly picked flowers which were left in the shade for 24 hours to dry, after which they were placed in a little knapsack. It is then applied on sores on the face.

Marigold juice is obtained from the leaves, stems and flowers of the herb which are washed and then compressed and ready to add to other mixtures.

Marigold decoct, which is used for treating dizziness and headaches, is made from 10g of marigold flowers placed in 200ml of boiling water. It is consumed by taking 1 to 3 spoons of it three times a day. It is an excellent diuretic treatment.

MARIJUANA

Being most certainly one of the most controversial plants, marijuana has properties, which can be applied in medical purposes, but at the same time it is a plant that is appreciated because of its narcotic, sedative and euphoric properties as well.

Description

Believed to have originated in the area of the Himalayan mountains, cannabis has spread throughout all of India, China, Northern Africa, after which it reached Europe and North America, where it was extensively grown during the second world war. Marijuana (pronounced "*marihuana*") is the Spanish name of the dried leaves and flowering of the neck weed (*Cannabis sativa*). The latter - the scientific name - was assigned to the plant in the year A.D. 100 by the Greek physician, Dioscorides. However, the first references to the medicinal utilization of the plant. Ts'ao pharmacopoeia (a Chinese work, containing the description and indications for controlling the most important pharmaceutical substances and formulas and the presentation of mixtures, conservation and administering methods of medicines). For more than 4000 years, cannabis was used in medicinal purposes. Written evidence was discovered that in ancient India, the influences of the herb upon olism or of the dependence on other drugs, cannabis

Fig. 2.43: Marijuana

has proved to be useful. Despite this fact, cannabis remains a controversial plant because of its use, on a mass scale, as a stupefacient. In the 70's the smoking of marijuana by students and those belonging to the "hippie" movement symbolized the rebellion against authorities.

Properties

Cannabis contains a number of elements generically named, cannbinoids. The main substance present in cannabis is named tetrhydrocannabinol, a chemical compound, responsible for the euphoric effects. Also, tetrahydrocannabinol, as shown in recent studies, inhibits the development of streptococcus and streptolococcus bacteria. The various quantity of tetrahydrocannabinol and cannabinoids it contains, determines the textile or intoxicating character of the plant. The variations are caused by the difference between soils, temperature or light.

The main properties of marijuana studied in medicine are: analgesic and sedative (a reason why it was used during surgeries), anti-inflammatory, anti-convulsive and laxative. At the same time, marijuana produces a growth of appetite and reduces dizziness. Some investigations show the fact that the plant also presents anti-microbial and anti-bacterial actions. The medicinal properties are amplified in the case of species grown in more elevated areas and warm climates.

Treatments

Because of its properties and effects, marijuana was used in treating a number of diseases, like: insomnia, anxiety, panic attacks, depressions, neuralgias, rheumatism, gastrointestinal dysfunctions, ulcer, cholera, cancer, epilepsy, bronchitis, asthma (because of the property of bronchodilator), and gonorrhoea. It reduces intraocular pressure and because of this fact, it is recommended in treating glaucoma. The anti-spastic and anti-convulsive properties are indicated in cases of epilepsy, multiple sclerosis and spasms. In the case of cancer, cannabis (and especially the oil in cannabis) leads to the loss of states of dizziness and vomit which are specific to chemotherapy. For patients suffering of AIDS and hepatitis, marijuana helps with regaining their weight through increasing appetite and reducing states of nausea and vomit.

Warning

Because of the adverse effects and the causing of dependence, marijuana consumption is forbidden.

MINT

Known from antiquity, mint is a herb with curative properties. It is also used in the specific Arabian cuisine as a spice.

Description

Perennial herb, that spreads itself quickly, mint (*Mentha piperita, Mentha spicata*) has small violet or purple-white flowers that bloom all over its growing period. Depending on the type, the herb can grow up to 60 or 90cm tall. A particularity of this herb is represented by the "orange mint" that spreads a subtle orange perfume.

Fig. 2.44: Mint

Mint can be cultivated in any area with a temperate-continental climate. It can multiply by dividing its roots and can be planted anytime during its growing period. It tolerates sandy soil but needs to be planted in a sunny place. It needs high quantities of water, especially if the soil is argillaceous.

Properties

Because of its active compounds contained, mint has sedative, disinfectant and cicatrizing properties. It can be successfully used in gastro-intestinal disorders; it helps the liver and calms indigestion. It contains menthol, menthone, menthofuran, a-pinene, limonene, cardinene, acetic aldehide, isovaleriana, vitamin C and antibiotic substances.

Treatments

Because of its menthol, mint has a very good action over the digestive system, causing a small anesthesia of the gastric mucous membrane. It also stimulates digestion.

Mint can treat diarrhoea, gastric fever or toxic infections. It stimulates the biliary secretion and helps the digestion of fats.

It is recommended in cases of *asthma*, bronchitis and the flu because of its anti-spasmodic and sedative properties. Sinusitis can be treated with mint also, because menthol is a vasodilatator of the nasal mucous membrane. It can be used as an inhalation in small amounts as well as for chest massages.

Mental fatigue, stress, depressive states and headaches can be ameliorated if mint oil is applied over the temples and backhead. Mint oil is a powerful stimulant and tonic. Mint is recommended for the treatment of rheumatism, for disinfection of the oral pocket and in cases of ear inflammation. Due to the fact that it has an antibacterial action it can cure acne and blackheads.

Mixtures

- Mint can be used to make tea, mouth rinse or mint oil.
- To make tea, you must boil one mint spoon of leaves in 200ml of water. The tea must be drunk cold, three times a day.

- Mouth rinse is made out of 5g of mint oil dissolved in 95g of concentrate alcohol. This drink is refreshing, antiseptic and it can remove the unwanted smell or taste. Mint oil mixed with hot water is used to treat the flu, laryngitis and hoarseness. The product obtained from 5g of mint oil and 95g of alcohol can be used to treat rheumatic pains and itches.
- Rheumatism can be treated also with mint baths, obtained by boiling 200g of leaves in 3 litres of water and mixing the result with water at 37 degrees Celsius.
- Mint is also used as spice in the Arab cuisine. For example, a Lebanese recipe - lebneh (mint yoghurt) - is prepared by adding 2 or 3 green hashed mint leaves, 2 pieces of garlic and lemon juice in a cup of yoghurt. Mint leaves can be used also in summer drinks. Boiled vegetables will look better if they are decorated with mint leaves.

Caution

There are a few cautions regarding the use of mint oil: it is not recommended to use mint oil during pregnancy and lactation or to apply it on babies' skin. For external use, the mint oil must be diluted, no more then 30 drops of oil should be used in a skin cream.

MUSTARD

One of the oldest spices, dating back 3000 years ago, mustard has been used, since ancient times, as a medicine and an aliment. The name, "mustard", derives from the Latin word "mustum" which means "must".

Description

Mustard appears under three different forms: white mustard, black mustard and brown mustard.

White mustard has its leaves covered with small, rough puff. The flowers are arranged in clusters, and the fruits have elongated, podded shapes, covered with small rough puff. In these pods, round shaped, white-yellowish coloured seeds are formed. Each pod has approximately six seeds.

Fig. 2.45: Mustard

Black mustard, unlike the white one, has red-brownish, almost black seeds of a spherical shape. Its pods are black and crowned and can contain up to 12 seeds. These are round and rigid, varying in colour, from dark coffee-coloured to black. Black mustard has a strong pungent taste.

Brown mustard, by appearance, is similar to the black one; however, its leaves are broad and rounded at the base, getting thinner towards the tip, while the pods are 3-5 cm long. Its colour varies from light to dark brown. It is much spicier than the white mustard but less spicy than the black one.

Because of the presence of mucilages, mustard has laxative effects. The white seeded mustard has milder effects, being a source of vegetal oil and an excellent source of proteins, calcium, magnesium, and potassium. Combining it with warm water has the consequence of increasing arterial pressure and stimulating blood circulation. At the same time, mustard has anti-inflammatory properties.

Treatments

Mustard is a herb with various usages. Mustard baths are recommended for treating headaches, colds and cough. The consumption of one spoonful of mustard seeds 2 or 3 times a day could have laxative effects. Also, the mustard seeds, whether white or black, are used for treating respiratory problems.

The lack of food appetite can be alleviated through consuming black mustard seeds dissolved into a glass of milk, administered 15 minutes before a meal. Asthma can be treated by applying, during a period of 20 minutes, black mustard flour poultice on the chest area. Against headaches, or pains caused by long exposure to cold or to air drafts, it is recommended that a small bag of 200g of black mustard seeds be added into the bath water, kept inside for 10 minutes and then removed. The effects of rheumatic pains and neuralgias are also decreased through the use of general baths.

Intoxications can be treated by drinking, on an empty stomach, a glass of water, which was mixed with a spoonful of black mustard flour administered on an empty stomach. The mixture will induce a state of vomit, therefore permitting the elimination of toxic materials from the stomach.

Bronchitis, asthma and pneumonia are treated by applying a black mustard flour poultice on the chest area. It is maintained as long as the burning sensation is not strong, it is then removed and the area is to be covered with a warm material.

Mixtures

Mustard flour is obtained through grinding or crushing the mustard seeds. The dust is kept in dark coloured containers and in cool places. It is recommended that the mustard flour be used in the first 2-3 weeks after its preparation, after this period its curative capabilities are reduced considerably. Internally, the mustard flour is administered in milk or wine, and externally, at the preparation of poultices.

The poultice is prepared from 100g of mustard flour, mixed with warm water, of a temperature of 25-30° C. until a soft paste is formed. The paste is then put between two cloths and applied on the troublesome area. It is kept for about a quarter of an hour, then removed with the possibility of applying it on another area. For children, or for those who cannot tolerate the irritating property of mustard, the poultice is prepared with 50g mustard flour and 100g flax flour.

General or local bath water, used for treating rheumatism, colds, neuralgias or articulation inflammations, are obtained from 25-30g of mustard flour placed in a small bag, on which 2-3 litres of warm water, of about 25-30° C. is poured. In case of a general bath, a greater amount, 250g, of mustard seeds is added, and the bag is to be stirred in the water. The local bath, as the general one should not last more than 20-30 minutes.

Mustard is used in the alimentary industry, as a paste, as seeds, powder or flour. In the form of paste, mustard is used in the spicing of meat, of fish or of eggs. Mustard seeds are used for spicing pickles, sea fruits or meat. Mustard flour is used for spicing steaks.

Warning

Administering black mustard to children under the age of 6 is not indicated, since severe intoxications could occur. Also, administering mustard, black or white, for prolonged periods of time becomes irritating and toxic, especially in the case of individuals suffering from dyspepsia, with a sensitive stomach or colon and individuals who suffer from irritations of the urinary tract.

PARSLEY

A bright-green umbelliferous herb parsley behaves as an anticacerous herb (it protects the liver, the intestines against cancer), antirheumatic, stimulant of digestion, of kidneys, eliminating toxins and kidney stones. Moreover, parsley seeds stimulate fertility and helps against dependency upon alcohol and against brain tumors.

Description

Derived from two Greek words: "petros" which means "stone" and "selinon" which means "celery". Parsley (*Carum petroselinum*) seems to be native to the East Mediterranean part from Southern Europe, even though in the Middle Ages parsley was one of the most known spices, used even in Northern Europe. Earlier during the Middle Ages around 3rd century B.C. parsley was used in various foods and in antiquity people would use parsley leaves to keep a fresh breath. In oriental foods, parsley was a very appreciated ingredient. Presently the United States along with Canada and Europe are the main growers of parsley. The two types

Fig. 2.46: Parsley

grown are: petroselinum tuberosum (for the root) and petroselinum crispum (for the leaves). Due to their flavor, parsley leaves can stimulate food appetite (which is a reason why they are used in soups, salads, and meat foods), while the root is used as a vegetable. From a medicinal point of view, parsley behaves as an anticacerous herb (it helps protect the liver and intestines form cancer), antirheumatic, stimulant of digestion, of kidneys, eliminating toxins and kidney stones. It is important to bear in mind that parsley seeds have an outstanding aphrodisiac effect by stimulating the sexual glands. Moreover, they stimulate fertility and helps against dependency upon alcohol and against brain tumours.

Proprieties

Between 25-30 mg of parsley a day are enough to provide the daily dosage of vitamin C. It is important to mention that parsley contains more vitamin C than lemon, orange or any other fruit. It has abundant quantities of other vitamins and minerals such as: provitamine A, vitamine B, vitamine E, vitamine K, beta-carotene, magnesium, phosphorus, iron, manganese, sodium, potassium, sulfur and calcium. It acts like an antioxidant (eliminates toxins and maintains the elasticity of the blood vessels), it is a general stimulant, diuretic, antiseptic, antiinfectious, antirachitic and more. Apart from these, parsley is a great neutralizer of the negative effects brought about by smoking and dependence upon alcohol. Among other effects that it has: it straightens the body and immune system, has a beneficial effect over the liver, spleen, digestive and endocrine organs.

Mixtures and Treatments

From cosmetic solutions for face cleaning or removing of freckles up to treatments of various illnesses, parsley proves to be a wonderful herb. Whether it is asthma, anemia, obesity, rheumatic illnesses, toothaches, indigestions, intestinal parasites, menstrual disorders or even tumors, parsley leaves are an invaluable adjuvant. It is also beneficial for the stomach, kidneys, bladder, blood flow etc.

Parsley Infusion

Over two spoonfuls of grained parsley are put in 2 cups of hot water. After about an hour, the mixture is passed through a sieve and is consumed three times a day before meals. The same procedure is to be applied for the infusion made out of parsley seeds. The time for macerating is of about 8 hours, after which the mixture is passed through a sieve. Owing to the quantity of vitamin A (for beauty) and vitamin E (for elasticity) that it contains, parsley has multiple cosmetic effects. Infusion of parsley is used as a face tonic.

Parsley Powder

With the help of an electrical grinder, parsley seeds are ground. The resulting mixture is placed in a recipient hermetically closed which would then be kept in the fridge. It is enough to consume half a spoon of parsley 2 to 3 times a day in order to fully enjoy its effects.

Parsley Poultices

The powder obtained from parsley or from the crushed parsley leaves is used to make poultices from which are then applied on areas affected by mosquito bites or itchiness. Caution: in order to obtained the desired effect it is necessary that the poultice to be used for half an hour.

Warning

The products containing parsley are not advisable to pregnant women or those who breastfeed. However they can consume parsley in foods.

NETTLE

It can be said about nettle that it is one of the wonder-plants that nature has gifted us with. It is renowned because of its astringent, expectorant, tonic, anti-inflammatory, diuretic properties and as an important source of beta-carotene, vitamin A, C and E, iron, calcium, phosphates and minerals. All these qualities recommend it as being a powerful remedy against hepatic, arthritic or rheu-matic affections, and as an adjuvant in treating allergies, anemia and kidney diseases.

Fig. 2.47: Nettle

Description

In historical terms, it seems that nettle (*Urtica dioica*) has been used since pre-historic times. In Denmark, a tissue of this plant was found in a tomb from the Bronze Age. There is evidence of the fact that in the Neolithic era, the nettle's stem has been used to make strings. It is also a known fact that Caesar's Roman troops have brought nettle from England. Because of the uncommon properties of nettle fibres, it has also been used in textile industry; for example the uniforms of the German army during the First World War were made out of nettle.

Properties

Nettle contains a great number of amino acids, glucidic substances, amines, sterols, cetones, ketones as methyl heptenone, acetophenone, volatile oil, fat substances, sitosterols, formic and acetic acid, panthotenic acid, folic acid, chlorophyl 0.3-0.8, protoporphyrine and coproporphynine. It also contains vitamins C, B_2 and K, beta-carotene, Ca,

Mg, Fe and Si salts, phosphates etc. Because of these compounds, the plant has anti-anaemic, anti-diabetic, hemostatic and diuretic properties.

Mixtures and Treatments

Perhaps the most well-known property of nettle is that it stings. It is said that if this was not so, the plant would not have lasted through time. As a matter of fact, the Swiss priest, Kunzle, shows that nettle would have been destroyed by insects and animals by now, had it not defended itself by stinging. However, popular medicine has proved the usefulness of this property: fresh nettle leaves placed on the skin, and especially on the kidney area (a practice named urticaria) induces a stinging and burning sensation, with the effect of easing more profound rheumatic pains. In the present we can enjoy all benefits of this wonder-plant through the various brews and recipes. Here are some of them.

Nettle Tea

It cures diseases and inflammation of the urinary system, and also urinary retentions. It has a slightly laxative effect, being recommended in depurative remedies. For hepatic, biliary affections as well as for affections of the spleen, the treatment with nettle tea will last for a number of weeks. Nettle tea can also be of great help to those who suffer from diabetes, because it leads to the decrease of blood sugar and implicitly, of the glycaemia level. It is useful in eliminating virosis, and bacterial infections. Preparation: the tea can be prepared through soaking the fresh or dried leaves in boiled water. This method allows the retention of active substances.

Infusion

Washing the scalp with nettle (leaves or roots) infusion helps regenerate, grow and thicken the hair. Preparation: to prepare the infusion, 60g of finely crushed nettles are mixed with two and a half cups of water. The mixture is boiled, and then covered for 10 minutes. It can be consumed either hot or cold.

Nettle Tincture

It eliminates dandruff and leaves the hair silky. Moreover, this strengthens and revitalizes the hair. Preparation: for ten days, six-seven fresh leaves or two spoons of dried plant are kept macerating in half a litre of alcohol. The mixture is then used to rub the hair root.

Nettle Juice

For hypertension half a glass is drunk right before the most important meals. It has the effect of regulating arterial pressure and straightening blood vessels. In case of renal insufficiency, one glass of nettle juice per day should be consumed in the morning after waking up. The diet lasts for 20-30 days. In case of anemia and demineralization - one-two glasses of nettle juice are consumed daily for a period of two weeks. Preparation: nettle leaves and stem are gathered and put into the fruit juicer. The paste is then filtered and the resulting juice is kept cold in the refrigerator in dark colored bottles.

Root Powder

Against frail dry hair 60 day treatments are done, during which half a teaspoon of root powder is administered three times a day on an empty stomach. Preparation: the dried nettle roots are finely crushed using an electric coffee grinder.

Nettle helps strengthen the immune system, annihilating the predisposition towards colds. Anemia, states of fatigue, exhaustion and other effects of stress can be fought if we add nettle, rich in iron and mineral, to our daily nourishment or periodic remedies.

SESAME

One of the first spices used by people, sesame originate in India and the Far East. This plant is used in the most varied ways: in China it is used to fabricate ink and sesame flowers contain aromatic substances used in the perfume industry.

Fig. 2.48: Sesame

Description

Sesame (*Sesamum indicum*) is a herbaceous, annual and tropical plant which reaches heights of 1-2 metres. In the earth it has a tap root, only slightly developed, from which an erect stem emerges, tall, ramified and covered with puff. The leaves have varied shapes, they are either oval or lanceolate and fluffy on both sides. The flowers are either violet or white, and at their end, one can find pods of 3 cm containing many seeds. These are small and have a length of 3.5 mm. Their colour varies from yellowish-white to red, brown or black. The dried seeds have a nut-like taste which is intensified when pan-fried. When decorticated, they have a beige or milky white colour. If not decorticated, the black sesame seeds are less used and have a more concentrated fragrance than the white ones.

Properties

Sesame seeds contain fat substances, antioxidants, sesamol, proteinic substances, arginine and cellulose, mineral substances and calcium. This way, the sesame seeds have a very high nutritive and energetic value.

Treatments

The herb has remarkable therapeutic properties. Sesame seeds have a high energetic value and stimulate virility. The seeds can therefore be used in alimentation, strewed on pretzels or bread. From white sesame seeds, through cold pressing, an oil can be obtained which has a high therapeutic value and aphrodisiac effects, being used in massages.

Sesame is recommended in treating insomnia or as a protean infusion in various nutrition affections. Being rich in arginine, sesame seeds deters the development of tumors, help detoxify the liver and kidneys and improving the immune system. They also help increase fertility.

The plant has antirheumatic and anticancerous properties. Having antifungic and bactericide effects, the oil is used in treating gingival affections: gum bolls and gingivitis. In preventing paradontosis 2-3 drops of sesame oil are applied in the evening on the gums, after washing the teeth. The gums are massaged gently and the treatment is repeated every evening, for a period of minimum 3 months.

Sesame oil has laxative effects. The refined sesame oil is used in cosmetics for making soap. The sesame leaves, rich in mucilaginous substances, are used in combinations with other plants for treating dysentery and cholera.

Mixtures

Sesame oil is obtained through cold pressing which causes the preserving of aromatic compounds. The oil must be heated carefully so as not to lose this advantage. This type of oil is indicated for preparing salads. The sesame oil can also be obtained from seeds which are pan-fried before being cold pressed. The pressing is done at 60-80° Celsius. These are refined in order to remove the free fat acids. Margarine is obtained from this refined sesame oil.

Sesame milk is prepared from a cup of sesame, a quarter of a cup of honey and three cups of milk. The ingredients are mixed in the blender and the mixture is consumed cold.

Sesame flour results from the seeds. It is rich in amino acids and contains 3 times as much calcium as the same amount of milk. Sesame seeds are used in East Asia as a spice especially in Japanese and Korean foods. Halvah is also obtained from sesame seeds. They can also be used successfully in salads, poultry, pork or beef, cooked vegetables, cheese aromatizing, egg salads, sauces based on butter or bread aromatizing.

PUMPKIN

Because of its delicious and perfumed taste, the pumpkin is a favourite for many people. It is a vegetable with many uses: used as a basis for food, an ingredient for sweets and medicine, pumpkin is well known because of Halloween, when it is carved in the shape of a face and lit with candles to banish evil spirits.

Description

Pumpkin (*Cucurbita pepo*) being an annual, herbaceous plant, cultivated for its fruit, flowers and seeds, pumpkin has a flexible and climbing stem. Its leaves are big, heart shaped, with well marked nerves. Its flowers are yellow and pulpy. The fruit can be oval or spherical, of a green or intense orange colour. The fruits pulp is of a yellowish-orange colour, dense with a sweet taste.

Fig. 2.49: Pumpkin

Properties

Having a yellowish-orange colour, pumpkin is rich in anti-oxidants and beta-carotene. Beta-carotene is a vitamin that can be converted by the body into vitamin A. This helps the body in its process of regeneration, slowing down the aging process. Pumpkin pulp contains vitamins, especially pro-vitamin A, vitamins E and C, salts and minerals, carbon hydrates, and proteids. The seeds contain oil, proteids, resines and enzymes with antihelmintic properties. The pumpkins core contains lecithin, tyrosine, peporesine, phosphorus and vitamins B and A.

Treatments

Pumpkin seeds contain the strongest therapeutic effects. These help in eliminating intestinal parasites, cleaning blood vessels, adjusting cholesterol level and stimulating kidney activity.

In treating cancer, leukemia, sclerosis, or various diseases which are hard to cure, pumpkin seeds have an energizing role.

Pumpkin oil extracted from the seeds is recommended for reducing excess cholesterol. Pumpkin offers protection against heart diseases by containing antioxidants.

The vegetable has a laxative action, being useful in case of dyspepsia and constipation. Fried pumpkin is healthy for those who suffer from heart diseases.

Pumpkin juice is indicated for ulcer and high acidity. It has to be drunk three times a day, half an hour before meals. It is also useful in cases of insomnia, having sedative properties.

Pumpkin is also indicated in cases of hormonal disorders or adolescent behaviour, menopause disorder, intestinal parasites or sexual hyper-excitability. In external use, pumpkin is recommended for treating burns, inflammations and abscesses. It softens the skin and diminishes the inflammatory processes of mucous.

In case of insect stinging, cataplasms of crushed pulps can be used. These cataplasms are changed daily until healing is complete.

A number of hydrating and anti-wrinkle creams contain pumpkins. Pumpkin can be eaten either fried or under the form of a pie, raw and shaven in tomato, pickle or cauliflower salads or in soups. Before preparing them for food, pumpkins have to be cut and cleared of seeds. If fried, before inserting them into the hot oven, they can be anointed with olive oil, salt and pepper. They can be filled with cheese paste or rice and mushrooms.

Under the form of seed decoct, it is used for eliminating intestinal parasites. One kg. of pumpkin seeds is divided into 10 portions (100g for 10 days). Each portion along with the hulls are added into a mincing machine. The seeds are minced 5-6 times with the machine. They are mixed with 300-400 ml of savory tea. They are kept to macerate for 24 hours, and then filtered through gauze. The obtained liquid is divided into 3 equal portions, for 1 day (morning, noon and evening, ½ h before meals). The treatment lasts 10 days followed by 10 days of pause. If needed, the treatment is then repeated.

As a juice, it is used in treating cancer and vascular diseases.

For constipations and colitis, pumpkin is boiled. This way, 500 g of boiled core is grinded, added to the remaining boiled water and the mixture is homogenized. This brew is consumed in one day, in two portions.

Warning

Many of the pumpkin cake recipes are rich in cholesterol because they need an increased amount of eggs. This is why it is better for a substitute to be found which contains less cholesterol or to use fewer eggs.

RATTLE

Known from ancient times, rattle has gained a distinct place among other medicinal herbs because of its therapeutic powers and its various usages.

Description

A plant whose seeds rattle in the capsule — applied to two scrophulaceous plants, yellow rattle (*Rhinanthus crista-galli*) and red rattle (*Pedicularis palustris*) rattle is a herbaceous perennial plant with a straight woody stalk, with 4 longitudinal edges, that can reach up to 100cm tall. The leaves have an oval shape and because of the contained secretive glands they appear to have white dots if they are examined trough transparency. The flowers are yellow and they are grouped in inflorescences.

They have five petals black dotted. It blooms from June to September, the period being also recommended for picking it up in the morning, after the mist has vanished.

Fig. 2.50: Rattle

Properties

Rattle contains a brown-red substance called hypericine which can be easily spotted when the tincture is prepared. Apart from this substance rattle also contains pseudo-hypericine, volatile oil and tannin. Because of these substances, rattle has an antiseptic, astringent and cicatrizing action. The flavonoides are responsible for the vasodilatator and hypotensive action.

A group of scientists from the Benjamin Franklin University in Berlin brought evidence that rattle can replace the drugs recommended for depressive states.

Treatments

The lazy bile, chronic entero-colitis, hyperacid gastritis, gastric ulcer, hepatitis, chronic hepatitis and cholecystitis can be successfully treated with rattle infusion. At the same time, persons who retain water in tissues should consume one spoon of rattle tea after each meal.

The rattle tincture is used to treat arterial hypertension, neurovegetative dystonia, menopause, irascible states and psychomotor nervousness. A few drops can be consumed after each primary meal. The exact dose is established depending on age and illness.

The gingivitis and tooth abscesses can be treated with rattle gargles. During the day several gargles can be made and in the evening it is suggested to have another one.

The trigeminal neuralgia can be treated with rattle oil that must be applied on the damaged areas.

The speaking disorders, restless sleep, hysterical crises and somnambulism can be treated with rattle, as well as depressive states and urinary incontinence.

The rattle oil shouldn't be absent from any house, its curative powers being preserved for 2 years. It can be used to treat open wounds, hemathomes, inflammations of the ganglions, backaches, lumbago and rheumatic and sciatic pains.

A homemade cure for burns is represented by rattle flowers kept in linseed oil. The oil can also be used for sunburns.

Babies with colics relax if their belly is massaged with rattle oil.

In cosmetics the bloomed herb is used especially for its tonic action on dried and old skin tissues.

Mixtures

The infusion is prepared by adding one spoon of mashed herb in a cup of boiled water (200ml) that must be covered for 15-20 minutes and then filtered.

The tincture is prepared out of 40g of rattle, 30g of balm, 15g of odolean and 15g of lavender. All of these herbs must be macerated for 5-7 days in 700 ml of 60° alcohol and then filtered. The tincture must be kept in dark-colored glasses in cool places.

The oil macerate is prepared from 20g of mashed rattle with 20ml of 70% alcohol. After 12 hours, 200ml of sunflower must be added. It then must be steam-heated for 3 hours and left to macerate for 2 or 3 days. After it is filtered it must be kept in dark-coloured glasses.

The dabs are made with infusion prepared form 30g of herb boiled in 1 litre of water. The vessel must be covered for 20 minutes after which the infusion must be filtered and applied on dabs.

The gargles must be made with an infusion from two spoons of dried herb boiled in one cup of water.

Caution

It is recommended to avoid the exposal to sun of any rattle mixture, because photo-sensible reactions might occur. The consumption of rattle can induce headaches and stomachaches. Nevertheless, the secondary effects of the rattle consumption aren't as powerful as the side effects of the drugs recommended for treating depressive states.

ROSEMARY

After lavender, rosemary is probably one of the most often utilized and loved plant in aromatherapy. Its uses have extended in time from uses with culinary purposes to medicine and later to perfume industry, because of its aromatizing properties.

Description

Rosemary *(Rosmarinus officinalis)* to small fragrant pungent mediterranean labiate shrub, is known from ancient times as having many uses as a medicinal, ritual and seasoning herb. In those times it used to be consumed for relieving abdominal pain, gout, icterus, insomnia, cephalagia, for the calming of nerves etc. In Ancient Greece, people burned rosemary branches on the altars of the gods, considering it a sacred herb. However, the Greeks were not the only ones; the plant was also sacred for the Romans (those who gave it its name) and Egyptians (the evidence to that was finding traces of rosemary in the pharaohs' tombs.) The custom of burning rosemary branches has become a practice in hospitals in France - where it has been maintained until the 20th century - and used for cleaning the air. Also because of its antiseptic effect, the plant was appreciated and used for conserving meat, even in extremely hot weather - it was known that rosemary prevents and delays the alteration of meat foods.

The name "Rosemary" originates from the Latin words "ros", meaning "dew" and "marinus" meaning "sea". Originating in areas of Mediterranean coastlines, but also Uruguay, the plant has become a shrub which has spread very fast in the entire Europe, North America and Mexico.

Being a perennial, woody plant, it belongs to the Laminaceae family. This Mediterranean shrub with a pleasant flavor, ramified and displaying small, needle shaped evergreen leafs, with flowers of various colors (from white, pink, red, to purple and blue), has a medium height of 20-50 cm and can reach 150 cm in conditions of optimal heat and humidity.

Properties

Among the main properties of rosemary we can enumerate: analgesic, antiseptic, antidepressant, anti-inflammatory, expectorant, antiviral, aphrodisiac, disinfectant. Its active elements have choleric, antiseptic, diuretic and tonic aspects at a nervous level, stimulating bile secretion and eliminating it in the intestines, destroying microorganisms, increasing the quantity of eliminated urine, improving the blood flow and refreshing and energizing the mind. Apart from this, scientific researches indicate that rosemary is an ideal memory stimulant for both adults and students. Rosemary contains a series of secondary elements such as carnosol and carnosic acid, with a reflecting action in case of free radicals. Rosemary also has calming effects by working against fatigue, sadness, anxiety, calming muscle soreness, digestive pains and also, indigestion caused by stress.

In aromatherapy it is appreciated for bringing youth, protection, love, optimism, vitality health and a restful sleep.

Treatments and Mixtures

Rosemary can be consumed under the forms of tea, tincture, capsules or ethereal oils. Rosemary consumption improves digestion, fights against obesity, liver diseases, gastritis, cholesterolemia, bronchic asthma, edemas, and adjusts fast heart beats caused especially by irritability, coffee or tobacco excess. Because of its antiseptic and tonic properties, rosemary is extremely beneficial in cases of fainting, influenza, hangovers, asthma, bronchitis, cramps, constipation, cystitis, headaches, polypus, colds, cough, sinusitis or muscular pains. The plant also has a good influence on the blood circulation and blood pressure.

As a natural fortifier, rosemary is extremely efficient during convalescence because it increases energy and optimism, also being recommended in cases of asthenia. For long term periods it fortifies and revitalizes the body.

Rosemary Tincture

Indicated in cases of indigestion, diabetes, vomit, stomachal atony, colics, liver congestion, icterus, chronic and painful inflammations of the biliary bladder, high cholesterol, insomnia, dizziness, headaches, irritability, depressive states, convalescence, weak memory, asthenia, palpitations, asthma, and convulsive cough. Two teaspoons of tincture, diluted in a cup of water, are administered before main meals. Rosemary tincture is also used for sprains, swelling (articular or ankle swelling), rheumatism and torticolis. For this, a teaspoon of tincture is diluted in 100 ml of water and administered three to four times a day.

Essential Oil

The essential rosemary oil is a main ingredient in the industry of cosmetic products because of its analgesic, aromatizing, anti-inflammatory, peripheral blood circulation stimulating, antimicrobial and hair fall preventing action. Adding a few drops in a votive light or in the bath water, the essential rosemary oil is adequate for states of anxiety, headaches, debility, and weakness. It acts through unblocking the interior energies and in aromatherapy it is believed to help improve relationships with others.

Capsules

They are recommended in biliary dyskinesia, renal and rheumatic diseases, physical and intellectual overwork. Taken as a phytotherapic supplement (a capsule taken three times a day before the main meals) is efficient in abdominal diseases, anemia, rheumatism, coughs and minor cardiac disturbances.

Warning

Consumption during pregnancy or in cases of epilepsy or hypersensitivity should be avoided.

SEA BUCKTHORN

Abundant in vitamin C far more than brier or citrics are, sea buckthorn is used in the food industry, sylviculture, and pharmacy, and its positive effects can be seen in effectively treating illnesses, especially liver problems.

Description

Sea buckthorn (*Hippophae rhamnoides*) is a tall shrub measuring about 1.5-3.5 metres tall and is covered in thorns. It grows in clusters on river shores, in swampy areas and even on gravel.

Sea buckthorn is harvested in the period between August-September. It is recommended that sea buckthorn fruits be harvested before the first frost settles in so as to avoid the sudden diminish of the vitamin C that it contains.

Proprieties

Fig. 2.51: Sea buckthron

Sea buckthorn is an energizer, anti-anemic, abundant in vitamins, anti-inflammatory herb, and it also decreases appetite (in cases of treatments against obesity). At the same time it speeds up the recovery process after an illness, it's a good coronary protector and it can also slow down the aging process.

Due to the presence of a large amount of vitamins that it contains (C, A, B_1, B_2, B_6, B_9, E, K, P, F, as well as phosphoric microelements, calcium, magnesium, potassium, iron, and sodium), sea buckthorn is used effectively in treating liver failures, improving the detoxification of the hepatic cell. It contributes to the synthetization of proteins and through the considerable amount of carotene that it contains, it is also effective at preventing cancer. Furthermore it gives a relaxing sensation with slightly narcotic effects.

Treatment

Gamatism, neuro-endocrinological afflictions can be treated by using sea buckthorn oil. It can also be used against alcohol dependency, anemia, asthenia and stress.

Intreating ophtalmological afflictions, hypertension and gingivitis, sea buckthorn is an excellent treatment mixed with other medicinal herbs.

Extraordinary results were obtained from processing sea buckthorn in pharmaceutical laboratories. The products obtained were used in treating depressions, Parkinson diseases, tumors, adenomas and leukemia.

Thermal and chemical burns, chilblains and infectious eczemas are treated with the aid of products containing sea buckthorn or sea buckthorn oil.

Positive effects were obtained from treating psoriasis with sea buckthorn (under the form of tea or tincture).

Macerated sea buckthorn is used in cases of common cold or flu.

Mixtures

From sea buckthorn tea can be prepared containing a sort of oil obtained from fruits, syrup, macerated sea buckthorn, tincture, juice, nectar, jam, jelly, sweets, jelly fruit, liquors and various alcoholic drinks.

Tea is recommended in cases of diarrhoea, rheumatism, skin diseases, and nettle rash. It is obtained by putting two spoons of mashed fruits into 500ml boiled water. After leaving the pot covered for about 30 minutes its content is passed through a sieve.

Fruit oil is prepared from 150g of fresh fruits, over which 150ml of sunflower oil. The pot is kept at room temperature for 3 weeks stirred from time to time. After that, the seeds get crushed and placed in oil once again. After two days of being kept in a luminous warm place, the oil on the surface which should be clear is moved into another bowl. Thirty drops are administrated three times a day over a period of minimum three weeks.

By mixing half a litre of juice with half a litre of honey, fruit syrup is obtained. After homogenization the syrup is kept in the fridge. The treatment is long lasting and consists of taking from four to six spoons of syrup a day.

Macerated sea buckthorn is prepared by crushing 500g of sea buckthorn seeds over which 500g of honey is poured. This mixture is digested by taking a spoonful each day to keep the body resistant to cold and flu.

From sea buckthorn a decoct can be obtained by using two handfuls of sea buckthorn twigs which are left to sit in half a litre of water from morning till evening after which they are passed through a sieve. The macerated mixture is left aside and the twigs are crushed and boiled for 20 minutes after which it is passed through a sieve and left to cool down. It gets mixed with the other two mixtures and it is consumed in a day.

Sea buckthorn tincture is made from seven spoons of sea buckthorn powder which are put in a bottle. Over the powder 250ml of alimental alcohol heated to 70 or 80 degrees is poured. It is left to macerate for 15 days, stirred every once in awhile and is then passed through a sieve.

Sea buckthorn can also produce a disinfectant which is applied on the affected spots. A handful of sea buckthorn twigs finely cut are boiled in half a litre of vinegar for 10 minutes. It is then left to cool down and after that it gets strained. The remaining twigs are burnt and the resulting ash is mixed with the mixture based on vinegar obtained before; thus a sort of unguent is formed. This mixture is recommended in cases of scabs.

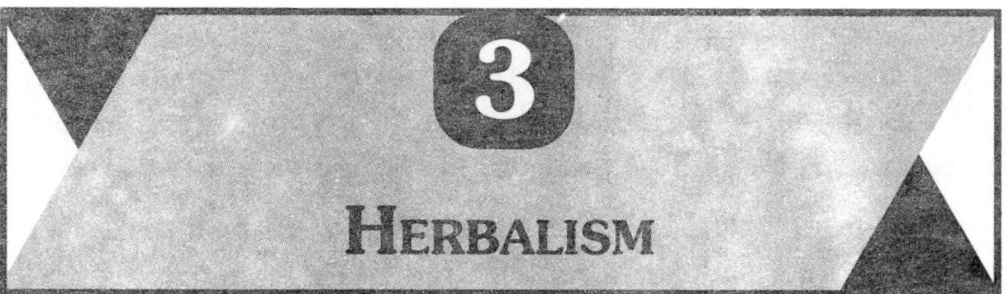

3 HERBALISM

Herbalism is a traditional medicinal or folk medicine practice based on the use of plants and plant extracts. Herbalism is also known as botanical medicine, medical herbalism, herbal medicine, herbology, and phytotherapy. Sometimes the scope of herbal medicine is extended to include fungi and bee products, as well as minerals, shells and certain animal parts.

Many plants synthesize substances that are useful to the maintenance of health in humans and other animals. These include aromatic substances, most of which are phenols or their oxygen-substituted derivatives such as tannins. Many are secondary metabolites, of which at least 12,000 have been isolated - a number estimated to be less than 10% of the total. In many cases, these substances (particularly the alkaloids) serve as plant defense mechanisms against predation by microorganisms, insects, and herbivores. Many of the herbs and spices used by humans to season food yield useful medicinal compounds.

Anthropology of Herbalism

People on all continents have used hundreds to thousands of indigenous plants for treatment of ailments since prehistoric times. The first generally accepted use of plants as healing agents was depicted in the cave paintings discovered in the Lascaux caves in France, which have been radiocarbon - dated to between 13,000-25,000 BC. Medicinal herbs were found in the personal effects of an "ice man", whose body was frozen in the Swiss Alps for more than 5300 years, which appear to have been used to treat the parasites found in his intestines. Anthropology or anthropologists theorize that animals evolved a tendency to seek out bitter plant parts in response to illness.

Indigenous healers often claim to have learned by observing that sick animals change their food preferences to nibble at bitter herbs they would normally reject Field biologists have provided corroborating evidence based on observation of diverse species, such as chimpanzees, chickens, sheep and butterflies. Lowland gorillas take 90% of their diet from the fruits of Aframomum melegueta, a relative of the ginger plant, that is a potent antimicrobial and apparently keeps shigellosis and similar infections at bay.

Researchers from Ohio Wesleyan University found that some birds select nesting material rich in antimicrobial agents which protect their young from harmful bacteria.

Sick animals tend to forage plants rich in secondary metabolites, such as tannins and alkaloids. Since these phytochemicals often have antiviral, antibacterial, antifungal and antihelminthic properties, a plausible case can be made for self-medication by animals in the wild.

Some animals have digestive systems especially adapted to cope with certain plant toxins. For example, the koala can live on the leaves and shoots of the eucalyptus, a plant that is dangerous to most animals A plant that is harmless to a particular animal may not be safe for humans to ingest. A reasonable conjecture is that these discoveries were traditionally collected by the medicine people of indigenous tribes, who then passed on safety information and cautions.

The use of herbs and spices in cuisine developed in part as a response to the threat of food-born pathogens. Studies show that in tropical climates where pathogens are the most abundant, recipes are the most highly spiced. Further, the spices with the most potent antimicrobial activity tend to be selected. In all cultures vegetables are spiced less than meat, presumably because they are more resistant to spoilage.

Herbs in History

In the written record, the study of herbs dates back over 5000 years to the Sumerians, who described well-established medicinal uses for such plants as laurel, caraway, and thyme. Ancient Egyptian medicine of 1000 B.C. are known to have used garlic, opium, castor oil, coriander, mint, indigo, and other herbs for medicine and the *Old Testament* also mentions herb use and cultivation, including mandrake, vetch, caraway, wheat, barley, and rye.

Indian Ayurveda medicine has been using herbs such as turmeric and curcumin possibly as early as 1900 B.C Many other herbs and minerals used in Ayurveda were later described by ancient Indian herbalists such as Charaka and Sushruta during the 1st millenium BC. The *Sushruta Samhita* attributed to Sushruta in the 6th century BC describes 700 medicinal plants, 64 preparations from mineral sources, and 57 preparations based on animal sources.

The first Chinese herbal book, the *Shennong Bencao Jing*, compiled during the Han Dynasty but dating back to a much earlier date, possibly 2700 B.C., lists 365 medicinal plants and their uses - including *ma-Huang*, the shrub that introduced the drug ephedrine to modern medicine. Succeeding generations augmented on the Shennong Bencao Jing, as in the *Yaoxing Lun* (Treatise on the Nature of Medicinal Herbs), a 7th century Tang Dynasty treatise on herbal medicine.

The ancient Greeks and Romans made medicinal use of plants. Greek and Roman medicinal practices, as preserved in the writings of Hippocrates and - especially - Galen, provided the patterns for later western medicine. Hippocrates advocated the use of a few simple herbal drugs - along with fresh air, rest, and proper diet. Galen, on the other hand, recommended large doses of drug mixtures - including plant, animal, and mineral ingredients. The Greek physician compiled the first European treatise on the properties and uses of medicinal plants, *De Materia Medica*. In the first century AD, Dioscorides wrote a compendium of more than 500 plants that remained an authoritative reference into the 17th century. Similarly important for herbalists and botanists of later centuries was the Greek book that founded the science of botany, *Theophrastus' Historia Plantarum*, written in the fourth century B.C.

Middle Ages

The uses of plants for medicine and other purposes changed little in early medieval Europe. Many Greek and Roman writings on medicine, as on other subjects, were preserved by hand copying of manuscripts in monasteries. The monasteries thus tended to become local centers of medical knowledge, and their herb gardens provided the raw materials for simple treatment of common disorders. At the same time, folk medicine in the home and village continues uninterrupted, supporting numerous wandering and settled herbalists. Among these were the "wise-women", who prescribed herbal remedies often along with spells and enchantments. It was not until the late Middle Ages that women who were knowledgeable in herb lore became the targets of the witch hysteria. One of the most famous women in the herbal tradition was *Hildegard of Bingen*. A twelfth century Benedictine nun, she wrote a medical text called *Causes and Cures*.

Medical schools known as Bimaristan began to appear from the 9th century in the medieval Islamic world, which was generally more advanced than medieval Europe at the time. The Arabs venerated Greco-Roman culture and learning, and translated tens of thousands of texts into Arabic for further study As a trading culture, the Arab travellers had access to plant material from distant places such as China and India. Herbals, medical texts and translations of the classics of antiquity filtered in from east and west. Muslim botanists and Muslim physicians significantly expanded on the earlier knowledge of materia medica. For example, al-Dinawari described more than 637 plant drugs in the 9th century, and Ibn al-Baitar described more than 1,400 different plants, foods and drugs, over 300 of which were his own original discoveries, in the 13th century. The experimental scientific method was introduced into the field of materia medica in the 13th century by the Andalusian-Arab botanist Abu al-Abbas al-Nabati, the teacher of Ibn al-Baitar. Al-Nabati introduced empirical techniques in the testing, description and identification of numerous materia medica, and he separated unverified reports from those supported by actual tests and observations. This allowed the study of materia medica to evolve into the science of pharmacology.

Avicenna's *The Canon of Medicine* (1025) is considered the first pharmacopoeia, and lists 800 tested drugs, plants and minerals. *Book Two* is devoted to a discussion of the healing properties of herbs, including nutmeg, senna, sandalwood, rhubarb, myrrh, cinammon, and rosewater. Baghdad was an important center for Arab herbalism, as was Al-Andalus between 800 and 1400. Abulcasis (936-1013) of

Cordoba authored *The Book of Simples*, an important source for later European herbals, while Ibn al-Baitar (1197-1248) of Malaga authored the *Corpus of Simples*, the most complete Arab herbal which introduced 200 new healing herbs, including tamarind, aconite, and *Nux vomica*. Other pharmacopoeia books include that written by Abu-Rayhan Biruni in the 11th century and Ibn Zuhr (Avenzoar) in the 12th century (and printed in 1491). The origins of clinical pharmacology also date back to the Middle Ages in Avicenna's *The Canon of Medicine*, Peter of Spain's *Commentary on Isaac*, and John of St Amand's *Commentary on the Antedotary of Nicholas*. In particular, the *Canon of medicine* introduced clinical trials, randomized controlled trials and efficacy tests.

Alongside the university system, folk medicine continued to thrive. The continuing importance of herbs for the centuries following the Middle Ages is indicated by the hundreds of herbals published after the invention of printing in the fifteenth century. Theophrastus' *Historia Plantarum* was one of the first books to be printed, but Dioscorides' *De Materia Medica*, Avicenna's *Canon of Medicine* and Avenzoar's Pharmacopoeia were not far behind.

Modern Era

The fifteenth, sixteenth, and seventeenth centuries were the great age of herbals, many of them available for the first time in English and other languages rather than Latin or Greek. The first herbal to be published in English was the anonymous *Grete Herball* of 1526. The two best-known herbals in English were *The Herball* or *General History of Plants* (1597) by John Gerard and *The English Physician Enlarged* (1653) by Nicholas Culpeper. Gerard's text was basically a pirated translation of a book by the Belgian herbalist Dodoens and his illustrations came from a German botanical work. The original edition contained many errors due to faulty matching of the two parts. Culpeper's blend of traditional medicine with astrology, magic, and folklore was ridiculed by the physicians of his day yet his book - like Gerard's and other herbals - enjoyed phenomenal popularity. The *Age of Exploration* and the *Columbian Exchange* introduced new medicinal plants to Europe. The *Badianus Manuscript* was an illustrated Aztec herbal translated into Latin in the 16th century.

The second millennium, however, also saw the beginning of a slow erosion of the pre-eminent position held by plants as sources of therapeutic effects. This began with the introduction of the physician, the introduction of active chemical drugs (like arsenic, copper sulfate, iron, mercury, and sulfur), followed by the rapid development of chemistry and the other physical sciences, led increasingly to the dominance of chemotherapy - chemical medicine - as the orthodox system of the twentieth century.

ROLE OF HERBAL MEDICINE IN MODERN HUMAN SOCIETY

The use of herbs to treat disease is almost universal among non-industrialized societies A number of traditions came to dominate the practice of herbal medicine at the end of the twentieth century:

- The herbal medicine system, based on Greek and Roman sources.
- The *Siddha and Ayurvedic medicine systems* from various *South Asian Countries.*
- Chinese Herbal Medicine (Chinese Herbology).
- Traditional African medicine
- Unani Tibb medicine
- Shamanic herbalism
- Native American medicine

Many of the pharmaceuticals currently available to physicians have a long history of use as herbal remedies, including opium, aspirin, digitalis, and quinine. The World Health Organization (WHO) estimates that 80 percent of the world's population presently uses herbal medicine for some aspect of primary health care. Pharmaceuticals are prohibitively expensive for most of the world's population, half of which lives on less than $2 U.S. per day. In comparison, herbal medicines can be grown from seed or gathered from nature for little or no cost. Herbal medicine is a major component in all traditional medicine systems, and a common element in Siddha, Ayurvedic, homoeopathic, naturopathic, traditional Chinese medicine, and Native American medicine.

The use of, and search for, drugs and dietary supplements derived from plants have accelerated in recent years. Pharmacologists, microbiologists, botanists, and natural-products chemists are combing the Earth for phytochemicals and leads that could be developed for treatment of various diseases. In fact, according to the World Health Organisation, approximately 25% of modern drugs used in the United States have been derived from plants.

Three quarters of plants that provide active ingredients for prescription drugs came to the attention of researchers because of their use in traditional medicine

- Among the 120 active compounds currently isolated from the higher plants and widely used in modern medicine today, 80 per cent show a positive correlation between their modern therapeutic use and the traditional use of the plants from which they are derived.
- More than two-thirds of the world's plant species - at least 35,000 of which are estimated to have medicinal value - come from the developing countries.

- At least 7,000 medical compounds in the modern pharmacopoeia are derived from plants.

Biological Background

All plants produce chemical compounds as part of their normal metabolic activities. These include primary metabolites, such as sugars and fats, found in all plants, and secondary metabolites found in a smaller range of plants, some useful ones found only in a particular genus or species. Pigments harvest light, protect the organism from radiation and display colors to attract pollinators. Many common weeds have medicinal properties.

The functions of secondary metabolites are varied. For example, some secondary metabolites are toxins used to deter predation, and others are pheromones used to attract insects for pollination. Phytoalexins protect against bacterial and fungal attacks. Allelochemicals inhibit rival plants that are competing for soil and light.

Plants upregulate and downregulate their biochemical paths in response to the local mix of herbivores, pollinators and microorganisms The chemical profile of a single plant may vary over time as it reacts to changing conditions. It is the secondary metabolites and pigments that can have therapeutic actions in humans and which can be refined to produce drugs.

Plants synthesize a bewildering variety of phytochemicals but most are derivatives of a few biochemical motifs.

- Alkaloids contain a ring with nitrogen. Many alkaloids have dramatic effects on the central nervous system. Caffeine is an alkaloid that provides a mild lift but the alkaloids in datura cause severe intoxication and even death.

- Phenolics contain phenol rings. The anthocyanins that give grapes their purple color, the isoflavones, the phytoestrogens from soy and the tannins that give tea its astringency are phenolics.

- Turpenoids are built up from terpene building blocks. Each terpene consists of two paired isoprenes. The names monoterpenes, sesquiterpenes, diterpenes and triterpenes are based on the number of isoprene units. The fragrance of rose and lavender is due to monoterpenes. The carotenoids produce the reds, yellows and oranges of pumpkin, corn and tomatoes.
- Glycosides consist of a glucose moiety attached to an aglycone. The aglycone is a molecule that is bioactive in its free form but inert until the glycoside bond is broken by water or enzymes. This mechanism allows the plant to defer the availability of the molecule to an appropriate time, similar to a safety lock on a gun. An example is the cyanoglycosides in cherry pits that release toxins only when bitten by a herbivore.

The word 'drug' itself comes from the Dutch word "druug" (via the French word Drogue), which means 'dried plant'. Some examples are inulin from the roots of dahlias, quinine from the cinchona, morphine and codeine from the poppy, and digoxin from the foxglove.

The active ingredient in willow bark, once prescribed by Hippocrates, is salicin, which is converted in the body into salicylic acid. The discovery of salicylic acid would eventually lead to the development of the acetylated form acetylsalicylic acid, also known as "aspirin", when it was isolated from a plant known as meadowsweet. The word aspirin comes from an abbreviation of meadowsweet's Latin genus Spiraea, with an additional "A" at the beginning to acknowledge acetylation, and "in" was added at the end for easier pronunciation. "Aspirin" was originally a brand name, and is still a protected trademark in some countries. This medication was patented by Bayer AG.

Herbal Philosophy

Most modern herbalists concede that pharmaceuticals are more effective in emergency situations where time is of the essence. An example would be where a patient had elevated blood pressure that posed imminent danger. However they claim that over the long term herbs can help the patient resist disease and in addition provide nutritional and immunological support that pharmaceuticals lack. They view their goal as prevention as well as cure.

Herbalists tend to use extracts from parts of plants, such as the roots or leaves but not isolate particular phytochemicals Pharmaceutical medicine prefers single ingredients on the grounds that dosage can be more easily quantified. Herbalists reject the notion of a single active ingredient. They argue that the different phytochemicals present in many herbs will interact to enhance the therapeutic effects of the herb and dilute toxicity. Furthermore, they argue that a single ingredient may contribute to multiple effects. Herbalists deny that herbal synergism can be duplicated with synthetic chemicals. They argue that phytochemical interactions and trace components may alter the drug response in ways that cannot currently be replicated with a combination of a few putative active ingredients. Pharmaceutical researchers recognize the concept of drug synergism but note that clinical trials may be used to investigate the efficacy of a particular herbal preparation, provided the formulation of that herb is consistent.

In specific cases the claims of synergy and multifunctionality have been supported by science. The open question is how widely both can be generalized. Herbalists would argue that cases of synergy can be widely generalized, on the basis of their interpretation of evolutionary history, not necessarily shared by the pharmaceutical community. Plants are subject to similar selection pressures as humans and therefore they must develop resistance to threats such as radiation, reactive oxygen species and microbial attack in order to survive Optimal chemical defenses have been selected for and have thus developed over millions of years. human diseases are multifactorial and may be treated by consuming the chemical defences that they believe to be present in herbs. Bacteria, inflammation, nutrition and ROS (reactive oxygen species) may all play a role in arterial disease. Herbalists claim a single herb may simultaneously address several of these factors. Likewise a factor such as ROS may underly more than one condition. In short herbalists view their field as the study of a web of relationships rather than a quest for single cause and a single cure for a single condition.

In selecting herbal treatments herbalists may use forms of information that are not applicable to pharmacists. Because herbs can moonlight as vegetables, teas or spices they have a huge consumer base and large-scale epidemiological studies become feasible. Ethnobotanical studies are another source of information. For example, when indigenous peoples from geographically dispersed areas use closely related herbs for the same purpose that is taken as supporting evidence for its efficacy. Herbalists contend that historical medical records and herbals are underutilized resources. They favour the use of convergent information in assessing the medical value of plants. An example would be when *in-vitro* activity is consistent with traditional use.

Popularity

A survey released in May 2004 by the National Center for Complementary and Alternative Medicine focused on who used complementary and alternative medicines (CAM), what was used, and why it was used. The survey was limited to adults, aged 18 years and over during 2002, living in the United States.

According to this survey, herbal therapy, or use of natural products other than vitamins and minerals, was the most commonly used CAM therapy (18.9%) when all use of prayer was excluded.

Herbal remedies are very common in Europe. In Germany, herbal medications are dispensed by apothecaries (e.g., Apotheke). Prescription drugs are sold alongside essential oils, herbal extracts, or herbal teas. Herbal remedies are seen by some as a treatment to be preferred to chemical medications which have been industrially produced.

In the United Kingdom, the training of medical herbalists is done by state funded universities. For example, Bachelor of Science degrees in herbal medicine are offered at Universities such as University of East London, Middlesex University, University of Central Lancashire, University of Westminster, University of Lincoln and Napier University in Edinburgh at the present.

Types of Herbal Medicine Systems

Use of medicinal plants can be as informal as, for example, culinary use or consumption of an herbal tea or supplement, although the sale of some herbs considered dangerous is often restricted to the public. Sometimes such herbs are provided to professional herbalists by specialist companies. Many herbalists, both professional and amateur, often grow or "wildcraft" their own herbs.

Some researchers trained in both western and traditional Chinese medicine have attempted to deconstruct ancient medical texts in the light of modern science. One idea is that the yin-yang balance, at least with regard to herbs, corresponds to the pro-oxidant and anti-oxidant balance. This interpretation is supported by several investigations of the ORAC ratings of various yin and yang herbs.

Eclectic medicine came out of the vitalist tradition, similar to physiomedicalism and bridged the European and Native American traditions. Cherokee medicine tends to divide herbs into foods, medicines and toxins and to use seven plants in the treatment of disease, which is defined with both spiritual and physiological aspects, according to Cherokee herbalist David Winston.

In India, Ayurvedic medicine has quite complex formulas with 30 or more ingredients, including a sizable number of ingredients that have undergone "alchemical processing", chosen to balance "vata", "pitta" or "kapha."

In Tami Nadu, Tamils have their own medicinal system now popularly called the Siddha medicinal system. The Siddha system is entirely in the Tamil language. It contains roughly 300,000 versus covering diverse aspects of medicine such as anatomy, sex ("kokokam" is the sexual treatise of par excellence), herbal, mineral and metallic compositions to cure many diseases that are relevant even today. Ayurveda is in Sanskrit, but Sanskrit was not generally used as a mother tongue and hence its medines are mostly taken from Siddha and other local traditions.

In addition there are more modern theories of herbal combination like William LeSassier's triune formula which combined Pythagorean imagery with Chinese medicine ideas and resulted in nine herb formulas which supplemented, drained or neutrally nourished the main organ systems affected and three associated systems. His system has been taught to thousand ceship programs during his lifetime, the William LeSassier Archive and the David Winston Center for Herbal Studies.

Gawo, a herb used in traditional treatments, has been tested in rats by researchers from Nigeria's University of Jos and the National Institute for Pharmaceutical Research and Development. According to research in the *African Journal of Biotechnology*, Gawo passed tests for toxicity and reduced induced fevers, diarrhoea and inflammation.

Routes of Administration

The exact composition of a herbal product is influenced by the method of extraction. A tisane will be rich in polar components because water is a polar solvent. Oil on the other hand is a non-polar solvent and it will absorb non-polar compounds. Alcohol lies somewhere in between. There are many forms in which herbs can be administered, these include:

Tinctures

Alcoholic extracts of herbs such as echinacea extract. Usally obtained by combining 100% pure ethanol (or a mixture of 100% ethanol with water) with the herb. A completed tincture has a ethanol percentage of at least 40-60% (sometimes up to 90%).

Herbal Wine and Elixirs

These are alcoholic extract of herbs; usually with an ethanol percentage of 12-38% Herbal wine is a maceration of herbs in wine, while an elixir is a maceration of herbs in spirits (e.g., vodka, grappa, etc.)

Tisanes

Hot water extracts of herb, such as chamomile.

Decoctions

Long-term boiled extract of usually roots or bark.

Macerates

Cold infusion of plants with high mucilage-content as sage, thyme, etc. Plants are chopped and added to cold water. They are then left to stand for 7 to 12 hours (depending on herb used). For most macerates 10 hours is used.

Vinegars

Prepared at the same way as tinctures.

Topicals

Essential oils

Application of essential oil extracts, usually diluted in a carrier oil (many essential oils can burn the skin or are simply too high dose used straight – diluting in olive oil or another food grade oil can allow these to be used safely as a topical).

Salves, oils, balms, creams and lotions

Most topical applications are oil extractions of herbs. Taking a food grade oil and soaking herbs in it for anywhere from weeks to months allows certain phytochemicals to be extracted into the oil. This oil can then be made into salves, creams, lotions, or simply used as an oil for topical application. Any massage oils, antibacterial salves and wound healing compounds are made this way.

Poultices and compresses

One can also make a poultice or compress using whole herb (or the appropriate part of the plant) usually crushed or dried and re-hydrated with a small amount of water and then applied directly in a bandage, cloth or just as is.

Whole herb consumption

This can occur in either dried form (herbal powder, or fresh (juice, fresh leaves and other plant parts. Just as Hippocrates said "Let food be thy medicine", it has become clear that eating vegetables also easily fits within this category of getting health through consumables (besides medicinal herbs). All of the vitamins, minerals and antioxidants are phytochemicals that we are accessing through our diet. There are clearly some whole herbs consumed that are more powerful than others. Shiitake mushrooms boost the immune system and are also tasty so they are enjoyed in soups or other food preparations for the cold and flu season. Alfalfa is also considered a health food Garlic lowers cholesterol, improves blood flow, fights bacteria, viruses and yeast.

Syrups

Extracts of herbs made with syrup or honey. Sixty five parts of sugar are mixed with 35 parts of water and herb. The whole is then boiled and macerated for three weeks.

Extracts

Include liquid extracts, dry extracts and nebulisates. Liquid extracts are liquids with a lower ethanol percentage than tinctures. They can (and are usually) made by vacuum distilling tinctures. Dry extracts are extracts of plant material which are evaporated into a dry mass. They can then be further refined to a capsule or tablet. A nebulisate is a dry extract created by freeze-drying.

Inhalation as in aromatherapy can be used as a mood changing , to fight a sinus infection or cough, or to cleanse the skin on a deeper level.

Examples of Plants used as Medicine

Few herbal remedies have conclusively demonstrated any positive effect on humans, mainly because of inadequate testing. Many of the studies cited refer to animal model investigations or in-vitro assays and therefore cannot provide more than weak supportive evidence.

- *Aloe vera* has traditionally been used for the healing of burns and wounds. A systematic review (from 1999) status that the efficacy of aloe vera in promoting wound healing is unclear, while a later review (from 2007) concludes that the cumulative evidence supports the use of aloe vera for the healing of first to second degree burns.
- *Agaricus blazei* mushrooms may prevent some types of cancer.
- *Artichoke* may reduce production cholesterol levels according to in vitro studies and a small clinical study.
- Blackberry (*Rubus fruticosus*) leaf has drawn the attention of the cosmetology community because it interferes with the metalloproteinaxses that contribute to skin wrinkling.
- *Black raspberry* may have a role in preventing oral cancer.

- *Butterbur* (*Petasites*)
- Calendula (*Calendula officinalis)* has been used traditionally for abdominal cramps and constipation. In animal research an aqueous-ethanol extract of *Calendula officinalis* flower was shown to have both spasmolytic and spasmogenic effects, thus providing a scientific rationale for this traditional use. There is "limited evidence" that calendula cream or ointment is effective in treating radiation dermatitis.
- *Cranberry* may be effective in treating urinary tract infections in women with recurrent symptoms.
- *Echinacea* extracts may limit the length and severity of rhinovirus colds; however, the appropriate dosage levels, which might be higher than is available over-the-counter, require further research.
- *Elderberry* may speed the recovery from type A and B influenza However it is possibly risky in the case of avian influenza because the immunostimulatory effects may aggravate the cytokine cascade.
- *Feverfew* is sometimes used to treat migraine headaches. However, many reviews of these studies show no or unclear efficacy. However a more recent RTC showed favorable results, Feverfew is not recommended for pregnant women as it may be dangerous to the fetus.
- *Gawo*, a traditional herbal medicine in West Africa, has shown promise in animal tests Garlic may lower total cholesterol levels.
- *German Chamomile*
- *Ginger*
- *Green tea* components may inhibit growth of breast cancer cells and may heal scars faster. Purified extracts of the seeds of *Hibiscus sabdariffa* may have some antihypertensive, antifungal and antibacterial effect.

Toxicity tested low except for an isolated case of damage to the testes of a rat after prolonged and excessive consumption. Honey may reduce cholestero. May be useful in wound healing. Lemon grass can lower cholesterol.

- *Nigella sativa* (Black cumin) has demonstrated analgesic properties in mice. The mechanism for this effect, however, is unclear. *In vitro* studies support antibacterial, antifungal, anticancer, anti-inflammatory and immune modulating effects However few randomized double blind studies have been published.
- *Ocimum gratissimum* and tea tree oil can be used to treat acne.
- *Oregano* may be effective against multi-drug resistant bacteria.
- *Pawpaw* can be used as insecticide (killing lice, worms)
- *Peppermint* oil may have benefits for individuals with irritable bowel syndrome.
- *Phytolacca* or *Pokeweed* is used as a homeopathic remedy to treat many ailments. It can be applied topically or taken internally. Topical treatments have been used for acne and other ailments. It is used to treatment tonsilitis, swollen glands and weight loss.
- *Pomegranate (Rauvolfia serpentina)*, high risk of toxicity if improperly used, used extensively in India for sleeplessness, anxiety, and high blood pressure.
- Rose hips – Small scale studies indicate that hips from *Rosa canina* may provide benefits in the treatment of osteoarthritis. Rose hips show anti COX activity.
- *Salvia lavandulaefolia* may improve memory.
- *Saw Palmetto* can be used for BPH. Supported in some studies, failed to confirm in others.

- *Shiitake Soy* and other plants that contain phytoestrogens (plant molecules with estrogen activity) (black cohosh probably has serotonin activity) have some benefits for treatment of symptoms resulting from menopause.
- *St. John's wort*, has yielded positive results, proving more effective than a placebo for the treatment of mild to moderate depression in some clinical trials. A subsequent, large, controlled trial, however, found St. John's wort to be no better than a placebo in treating depressionHowever more recent trials have shown positive results or positive trands that failed significance. A 2004 meta-analysis concluded that the positive results can be explained by publication bias but later analyses have been more favorable. *The Cochrane Database* cautions that the data on St. John's wort for depression are conflicting and ambiguous.
- *Stinging nettle*. In some clinical studies effective for enign prostatic hyperplasia and the pain associated with osteoarthritis. *In-vitro* tests show anti-inflammatory action. In a rodent model, stinging nettle reduced LDL cholesterol and total cholesterol. In another rodent study it reduced platelet aggregation.
- *Valerian root* can be used to treat insomnia. Clinical studies show mixed results and researchers note that many trials are of poor quality.
- *Vanilla*.

Safety

Standardization of purity and dosage is not mandated in the United States, but even products made to the same specification may differ as a result of biochemical variations within a species of plant Plants have chemical defense mechanisms against predators that can have adverse or lethal effects on humans. Examples of highly toxic herbs include poison hemlock and nightshade. They are not marketed to the public as herbs, because the risks are well known, partly due to a long and colorful history in Europe, associated with "sorcery", "magic" and intrigue. Although not frequent, adverse reactions have been reported for herbs in widespread use On occasion serious untoward outcomes have been linked to herb consumption. A case of major potassium depletion has been attributed to chronic licorice ingestion Black cohosh has been implicated in a case of liver failure Few studies are available on the safety of herbs for pregnant women.

Herb drug interactions are a concern. In consultation with a physician, usage of herbal remedies should be clarified, as some herbal remedies have the potential to cause adverse drug interactions when used in combination with various prescription and over-the-counter pharmaceuticals.

Dangerously low blood pressure may result from the combination of an herbal remedy that lowers blood pressure together with prescription medicine that has the same effect. Some herbs may amplify the effects of anticoagulants. Certain herbs as well as common fruit interfere with cytochrome P450, an enzyme critical to drug metabolism.

Effectiveness

Running total of the number of research papers listed on *PubMed from 1990-2007* containing the word "phytotherapy." The gold standard for pharmaceutical testing is repeated, large-scale, randomized, double-blind tests. Some plant products or pharmaceutical drugs derived from them are incorporated into mainstream medicine. To recoup the considerable costs of testing to the regulatory standards, the substances are patented by pharmaceutical companies and sold at a substantial profit.

Many herbs have shown positive results *in-vitro*, animal model or small-scale clinical tests but many studies on herbal treatments have also found negative results. The quality of the trials on herbal remedies is highly variable and many trials of herbal treatments have been found to be of poor quality, with many trials lacking an intention to treat analysis or a comment on whether blinding was successful. The few randomized, double-blind tests that receive attention in mainstream medical publications are often questioned on methodological grounds or interpretation. Likewise, studies published in peer-reviewed medical journals such as *Journal of the American Medical Association* receive more consideration than those published in specialized herbal journals. This preference may be due to the possibility of location bias for such trials. One study found that non-impact factor alternative medicine journals published more studies with positive results than negative results and that trials finding positive results were of lower quality than trials finding negative results. High impact factor mainstream medical journals, on the other hand, published equal numbers of trials with positive and negative results. In high impact journals, trials finding positive results were also found to have lower quality scores than trials finding negative results Another study found studies of phyomedicine to have superior quality to matched studies of pharmaceuticals. However, this study used a matched pair design and excluded all herbal trials that were not controlled, did not use a placebo or did not use random or quasi random assignment.

Herbalists criticize mainstream studies on the grounds that they make insufficient use of historical usage. They maintain that tradition can guide the selection of factors such as optimal dose, species, time of harvesting and target population.

Dosage is in general an outstanding issue for herbal treatments: while most conventional medicines are heavily tested to determine the most effective and safest dosages (especially in relation to things like body weight, drug interactions, etc.), there are fewer varieties of dosages for various herbal treatments on the market. Furthermore, herbal medicines taken in whole form cannot generally guarantee a consistent dosage or drug quality, since certain samples may contain more or less of a given active ingredient.

Several methods of standardization may be applied to herbs. One is the ratio of raw materials to solvent. However different specimens of even the same plant species may vary in chemical content. Another method is standardization on a signal chemical.

Clinical Studies

In 2004 the U.S. National Center for Complementary and Alternative Medicine of the National Institutes of Health began funding clinical trials into the effectiveness of herbal medicine.

Name Confusion

The common names of herbs (folk taxonomy) may not reflect differences in scientific taxonomy, and the same (or a very similar) common name might group together different plant species with different effects. For example, in 1993 in Belgium, a formula created by medical doctors including some Traditional Chinese medicine (TCM) herbs for weight loss. One herb (*Stephania tetrandra*) was swapped for another (*Aristolochia fangchi*) whose name in Chinese was extremely similar but which contained higher levels of a renal toxin, aristolochic acid; this mistake resulted in 105 cases of kidney damage. Note that neither herb used in a TCM context would be used for weight loss or given for long periods of time.

In Chinese medicine these herbs are used for certain forms of acute arthritis and edema.

Standards and Quality Control

The issue of regulation is an area of continuing controversy in the EU and USA. At one end of the spectrum, some herbalists maintain that traditional remedies have a long history of use, and do not require the level of safety testing as xenobiotics or single ingredients in an artificially concentrated form. On the other hand, others are in favor of legally enforced quality standards, safety testing and prescription by a qualified practitioner. Some professional herbalist organizations have made statements calling for a category of regulation for herbal products. Yet others agree with the need for more quality testing but believe it can be managed through reputation without government intervention The legal status of herbal ingredients varies by country.

In the United States, most herbal remedies are regulated as dietary supplements by the Food and Drug Administration. Manufacturers of products falling into this category are not required to prove the safety or efficacy of their product, though the FDA may withdraw a product from sale should it prove harmful.

The National Nutritional Foods Association, the industry's largest trade association, has run a program since 2002, examining the products and factory conditions of member companies, giving them the right to display the GMP (Good Manufacturing Practices) seal of approval on their products.

In the UK, herbal remedies that are bought over the counter are regulated as supplements, as in the US. However, herbal remedies prescribed and dispensed by a qualified "Medical Herbalist", after a personal consultation, are regulated as medicines.

Some herbs, such as cannabis, however, are outright banned in most countries for various reasons. Since 2004, the sales of ephedra as an dietary supplement is prohibited in the United States by the FDA.

Danger of Extinction

On January 18, 2008, the Botanic Gardens Conservation International (representing botanic gardens in 120 countries) stated that "400 medicinal plants are at risk of extinction, from over-collection and deforestation, threatening the discovery of future cures for disease." These included Yew trees (the bark is used for cancer drugs, paclitaxel); Hoodia (from Namibia, source of weight loss drugs); half of Magnolias (used as Chinese medicine for 5,000 years to fight cancer, dementia and heart disease); and Autumn crocus (for gout). The group also found that 5 billion people benefit from traditional plant-based medicine for health care.

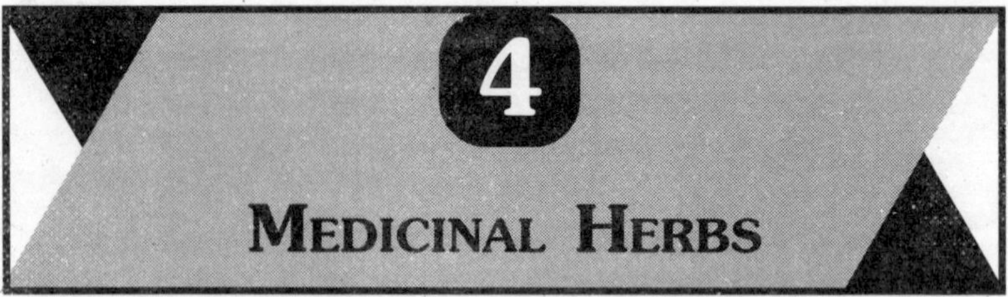

4 MEDICINAL HERBS

Medicinal Herbs continue as an alternative to main line pharmaceuticals

Modern medicine and more importantly the pharmaceutical industry have long desired to refute the claimed benefits of consuming medicinal herbs, however, there are those who believe that the healing power of herbs live on. May it be recognized that contradicting many research studies is the fact that many herbs are used in the manufacture of today's medicine, thereby cementing the notion that medicinal herbs can be useful in protecting and curing some illnesses.

In the early days of modern medicine, testing of a medicinal herb was based on patients use to record its effects. In a simplistic wayIf the result was positive as well as repeatable, the herb was prescribed for the particular illness for which id had been used. On the other hand, if the results were singular and its effect could not be repeated, its use was discontinued and put on a list of worthless theories.

In hindsight, many herbalists believe that requirements of the test may have been slanted. As with some conventional medicine, medicinal herbs do not have the same effect on every patient and they believe the test groupings may have been too small to accurately depict the benefit of the medicinal herb.

In most cases the taking of a medicinal herb usually shows no sign of ill effects, however, there are some natural herbs that can cause problems in humans. Therefore, as with modern medicine, any medicinal herb should be taken with caution and only in prescribed dosages given by a trained herbalist.

Herbs have Centuries of History on their Side

It is commonly believed that the Chinese were the first to use any medicinal herb for treating illnesses. In fact there are medical journals that date back around 5000 years listing various known herbal medications, it has also been discovered that ancient Greece and Egypt counted the medicinal herb as an important part of health care, thousands of yeards ago. Many of the herbs they used are still being used by naturalists around the world and many are also marketed for the specific ailments for which they have been used back then.

Unfortunately, the use of medicinal herbs has been a cause of concern for many medical professionals due to the lack of control over their use in over the counter products sold in many drug stores and health stores. Owing to the lack of control in the manufacturing process of these herbal medicines, the claim is that mixing certain herbs and other natural products may cause side effects of which the consumer is unaware.

An example of one of the medicinal herbs used today is red clover, which grows wild in many parts of the country. It is claimed to have healing tendencies for skin ailments such as eczema and psoriasis as well as chronic degenerative diseases and dry cough. Unfortunately, there is little information concerning the proper dosage and application of the clover to achieve the most benefits.

Irrespective of the innumerable documented successful treatments of cases of eczema, psoriasis etc. modern medicine still refuses to recognize that medicinal herbs do have healing qualities preferring to promote the products of large pharmaceutical companies instead.

Herbal medicine, also known under the names of phytotherapy and herbalism, is a well-defined branch of the ancient alternative medicinal system that involves the use of plants and plant extracts to cure diseases and alleviate symptoms. The great healing powers of many medicinal herbs and herbal supplements can never be contested for thousands of years plants have been successfully used to fight against a wide spectrum of diseases and disorders, and many of these ancient natural cures are still being used today, sometimes in combination with modern medical treatments.

According to recent archeological findings, herbal medicine dates back ever since man had first walked on this earth, more than 60,000 years ago. For ages, man has continued to perfect the ways of herbal medicine and has been permanently looking for new medicinal herbs with strong curative effects.

The ancient character of herbal medicine is also revealed in the Bible, which suggests the strong relation between man and nature, as well as man's timely preoccupation with herbalism:

> ". . . Along the bank of the river, on this side and that, will grow all kinds of trees used for food; their leaves will not wither, and their fruit will not fail. They will bear fruit every month, because their water flows from the sanctuary. Their fruit will be for food, and their leaves for medicine. . ." Ezekiel 47:12.

Another Scriptural view on herbal medicine can be found in *Ecclesiasticus*:

> ". . . Honor the healer for his services, for the Lord created him. His skill comes from the Most High, and he is rewarded by kings. The healer's knowledge gives him high standing and wins him the admiration of the great. The Lord has created medicines from the earth, and a sensible man will not disparage them. . ."

Anthropologists speculate that over the ages, early tribal communities had acquired a good level of knowledge on herbal supplements and medicinal herbs through simple processes of trial and error. This accumulated knowledge was passed from one generation to the other and has been gradually expanded and polished, carrying the print of many distinctive cultural influences: Western, based on Greek and Roman medicinal wisdom, the Ayurvedic from India and Oriental, particularly Chinese influences. Unfortunately, many secrets of the ancient herbal medicine had been lost, and nowadays herbalists are constantly aiming to recover reminiscences of our ancestors' medicinal wisdom. At present, herbalists, botanists, pharmacologists and microbiologists from many corners of the world have joined forces in an attempt to discover lost medicinal herbs and herbal supplements, as well as new specimens of plants which could be developed for treatment of various diseases in the near future.

In recent years, herbal supplements and medicinal herbs have been extensively used for treating diseases in non-industrialized societies of the world, but also in well developed urban societies. Many people have realized the great efficiency of herbal supplements and medicinal herbs and have decided to use them as substitutes for synthetic drugs or as enhancements for modern medication treatments.

Used wisely and with care, the right herbal supplements and medicinal herbs can successfully protect against diseases and help in curing already existent health problems. Nature has supplied us with so many natural ingredients with great curative effects, and it would be foolishness not to take full advantage of its offerings. We should make efforts to discover nature's mysteries and use its provided ingredients to create efficient, safe cures and remedies.

Of all the products for skin care out there have you ever wondered if there are effective medicinal herbs for skin conditions? Let's look at the ingredients in some of the herbal skin care products on the market and see what they are really good for.

Balm of Gilead

This is included in products designed to treat eczema and repair damage. It was not one of the traditional medicinal herbs for skin. Although it has a long history as fragrant cologne, there are no known benefits for the skin's health.

Gardenia

This is included in herbal skin care products designed to moisturize, although the oil is not known for its moisturizing abilities. Once again, it is prized for its sweet scent. Unfortunately, the scent is known to cause headaches, trigger asthma attacks and cause other adverse reactions. No benefits for this one either.

Citric Acid

This is not one of the traditional skin care medicinal herbs. Yet, it is found in numerous creams, some of which claim to be "extra gentle". It is a weak acid, but it is still an acid. It is known to damage the skin, as well as the hair. There are extracts from citrus fruits that are non-acidic and provide the antioxidant benefits that products containing citric acid claim to provide.

Manuka Honey

This is often listed alongside other medicinal herbs for skin conditions. It is not, of course, an herb, but bees gather their pollen from plants and to many of us,traditional remedies do not necessarily have to be herbaceous.

Honey has longed been valued for its benefits to the skin's health and the overall health of the body. Scientific evaluation has proven that all varieties of honey have some antibacterial and antioxidant activity. Manuka is simply the most active variety.

Benefits have been seen when it is used to heal blemishes, acne, eczema and psoriasis. It has been recommended recently for treating the antibiotic resistant staph infections and for treating diabetes related skin ulcers. Many herbal skin care products contain some type of honey. Manuka is the one to look for.

Jojoba and Coffeeberry

These two are traditional medicinal herbs to treat skin injuries, burns and other conditions. They are, in actuality, the same plant.

Herbal skin care products containing jojoba have been shown to moisturize, but are also beneficial for treating acne. A component of the plant balances the production of sebum, the skin's natural oils.

Jojoba herbal skin care products have numerous benefits. It helps to reduce wrinkles and stretch marks. It lightens and helps heal scars. It is useful in treating psoriasis and other problems. For moisturizing, it has a dual benefit, in that it forms a non-greasy layer that prevents water-loss through the skin. It is also quickly absorbed by the skin's cells, to soften and nourish them.

It is one of the natural extracts that is rich in vitamin E, a necessary nutrient and beneficial antioxidant. Antioxidants help repair and prevent damage from the sun and pollution.

There are many other beneficial medicinal herbs for skin problems. There's just no way to list all of them here, but you have a good start.

Why would anyone use artificial cosmetic products when there are medicinal herbs for skin which are far more effective and safe? The answer to that question is obvious. Not a lot of people know about medicinal herbs and their extraordinary effects on human skin. So, naturally, they fall for the glitz and glamour of artificial cosmetic stuff from big brands.

The best part about using medicinal herbs for skin is that they are completely safe. Artificial cosmetic items, however good they may be, are not completely safe for your skin. In fact, some of the chemicals used in skin care products today are not only unsafe for your skin, but also for your internal organs. By using them regularly, you can cause some serious damage to your health. Let me explain this a little further.

Your skin is capable of absorbing anything that is applied on it. So, whatever you apply, be it a moisturizer, anti-aging cream, or hydrating mask, some of it actually goes into your body. So, when you apply artificial cosmetic products with hazardous chemicals, they get ingested by your skin and get into your system. So, there is every chance of a serious health problem while using such things. This is why a lot of people, including skin care experts around the world, suggest using herbal skin care products.

Some of the most dangerous ingredients found in artificial cosmetic products include alcohols, phenol carbolic acid, toluene, artificial fragrance, mineral oils, and parabens. If you find any of these ingredients mentioned in your skin care cream, don't even think of buying it.

Herbal skin care products are gentle on your skin and they deliver the best results in the shortest possible time. When you use medicinal herbs for skin, there is absolutely no risk involved even if they get into your body as they are organic. Moreover, they are far more effective than artificial cosmetic products. However, choosing a good herbal skin care cream is not an easy task. There are quite a few products in the market that claim to have herbal ingredients, but only have traces of them. In order to get the best results, you need to go for products with the best herbal ingredients and you should not settle for anything less. So, let us take a look at the best organic ingredients that you should go for.

Some of the best herbal ingredients include wakame (extract from Japanese sea kelp), allantoin (comfrey and bearberry herbal extract), nutgrass plant, beeswax, functional keratin, and jojoba. Especially, functional keratin and wakame are considered miracle ingredients as far as skin care products are concerned. So, look out for these ingredients while buying a skin care product. As with any other thing in life, you need to spend a little time every day for skin therapy to get the results you want.

Now that you know everything you need to know about medicinal herbs for skin, don't settle for anything else. Treat your skin with the goodness of nature and experience the difference.

Medicinal herbs for skin can be the best way to take care of it. This is not just a claim made by herbal skin care companies, but skin care experts around the world also agree with this fact. With so many different skin care products available in the market, what makes herbal skin products so special and different?

There are two important reasons why you should use medicinal herbs for skin:

1. They are very, very effective. Contrary to what many people think, products from the big, famous brands are not necessarily the ones that give the best results. Herbal skin products have some of the most effective

organic ingredients that can produce miraculous results in a short period of time. So, they are considered the best.

2. Medicinal herbs for skin are very safe to use. They go easy on your skin and there are absolutely no risks associated with using them, no matter what your skin type is. No artificial cosmetic product can claim the same, since they are known to have tons of artificial chemicals, which are extremely harmful to your health.

Now that you know herbal skin care products are good, let us take a look at why artificial skin care products are bad. The most dangerous thing about using artificial cosmetic products is that you are taking a big risk. They contain a lot of chemicals, which are extremely harmful to your health. Most of the artificial cosmetic products contain chemicals like alcohol, phenol carbolic acid, toluene, artificial fragrance, triclosans, and parabens which are capable of causing health problems like severe allergic reactions, paralysis, depression, anemia, renal failure, and even cancer. This is why you should stay away from them by all means.

When you are looking for herbal skin care products, there is one thing you need to remember. Only the best organic ingredients give you the best results. So, you need to choose your products pretty carefully. According to skin care experts, some organic ingredients like manuka honey, awake, functional keratin, knotgrass root extract, comfrey and bearberry extracts, and natural oils like avocado oil, macadamia oil, and olive oil are very, very effective. So, make sure you look out for products with these ingredients to get the best results.

So, what are you still waiting for? You now know that herbal skin care products are the best and you know what kind of ingredients you should look out for to get the best results. Now, there is only one thing left in this equation. You need to go get these products and start using them.

5

VARIETIES OF PLANTS

Plants are living organisms belonging to the kingdom Plantae. They include familiar organisms such as trees, herbs, bushes, grasses, vines, ferns, mosses, and green algae. About 350,000 species of plants, defined as seed plants, bryophytes, ferns and fern allies, are estimated to exist currently. As of 2004, some 287,655 species had been identified, of which 258,650 are flowering and 18,000 bryophytes. Green plants, sometimes called metaphytes or viridiplantae, obtain most of their energy from sunlight via a process called photosynthesis.

Definition

Aristotle divided all living things between plants (which generally do not move), and animals (which often are mobile to catch their food). In Linnaeus' system, these became the Kingdoms Vegetabilia (later Metaphyta or Plantae) and Animalia (also called Metazoa). Since then, it has become clear that the Plantae as originally defined included several unrelated groups, and the fungi and several groups of algae were removed to new kingdoms. However, these are still often considered plants in many contexts, both technical and popular.

When the name Plantae or plants is applied to a specific taxon, it is usually referring to one of three concepts. From smallest to largest in inclusiveness, these three groupings are:

Land plants, also known as Embryophyta or Metaphyta. As the narrowest of plant categories, this is further delineated below:

– *Green plants* - also known as Viridiplantae, Viridiphyta or Chlorobionta - comprise the above Embryophytes, Charophyta (i.e., primitive stoneworts), and Chlorophyta (i.e., green algae such as sea lettuce). It is this clade which is mainly the subject of this chapter

– *Archaeplastida* - also known as *Plantae sensu lato*, Plastida or Primoplantae - comprises the green plants above, as well as Rhodophyta (red algae) and Glaucophyta (simple glaucophyte algae). As the broadest plant clade, this comprises most of the eukaryotes that eons ago acquired their chloroplasts directly by engulfing cyanobacteria.

Informally, other creatures that carry out photosynthesis are called plants as well, but they do not constitute a formal taxon and represent species that are not closely related to true plants. There are around 375,000 species of plants, and each year more are found and described by science.

Algae

Most algae are no longer classified within the Kingdom Plantae. The algae comprise several different groups of organisms that produce energy through photosynthesis, each of which arose independently from separate non-photosynthetic ancestors. Most conspicuous among the algae are the seaweeds, multicellular algae that may roughly resemble terrestrial plants, but are classified among the green, red, and brown algae. Each of these algal groups also includes various microscopic and single-celled organisms.

The two groups of green algae are the closest relatives of land plants (embryophytes). The first of these groups is the Charophyta (desmids and stoneworts), from which the embryophytes developed. The sister group to the combined embryophytes and charophytes is the other group of green algae, Chlorophyta, and this more inclusive group is collectively referred to as the green plants or Viridiplantae. The Kingdom Plantae is often taken to mean this monophyletic grouping. With a few exceptions among the green algae, all such forms have cell walls containing cellulose, have chloroplasts containing chlorophylls a and b, and store food in the form of starch. They undergo closed mitosis without centrioles, and typically have mitochondria with flat cristae.

The chloroplasts of green plants are surrounded by two membranes, suggesting they originated directly from endosymbiotic cyanobacteria. The same is true of two additional groups of algae: the Rhodophyta (red algae) and Glaucophyta. All three groups together are generally believed to have a common origin, and so are classified together in the taxon Archaeplastida. In contrast, most other algae (e.g. heterokonts, haptophytes, dinoflagellates, and euglenids) have chloroplasts with three or four surrounding membranes. They are not close relatives of the green plants, presumably acquiring chloroplasts separately from ingested or symbiotic green and red algae.

Fungi

Fungi were previously included in the plant kingdom, but are now seen to be more closely related to animals. Unlike embryophytes and algae which are generally photosynthetic, fungi are often saprotrophs: obtaining food by breaking down and absorbing surrounding materials. Most fungi are formed by microscopic structures called hyphae, which may or may not be divided into cells but contain eukaryotic nuclei. Fruiting bodies, of which mushrooms are most familiar, are the reproductive structures of fungi. They are not related to any of the photosynthetic groups, but are close relatives of animals. Therefore, the fungi are in a kingdom of their own.

Diversity

About 350,000 species of plants, defined as seed plants, bryophytes, ferns and fern allies, are estimated to exist currently. As of 2004, some 287,655 species had been identified, of which 258,650 are flowering plants, 16,000 bryophytes, 11,000 ferns and 8,000 green algae.

Embryophytes

Dicksonia antarctica, a species of tree fern. Most familiar are the multi-cellular land plants, called embryophytes. They include the vascular plants, plants with full systems of leaves, stems, and roots. They also include a few of their close relatives, often called bryophytes, of which mosses and liverworts are the most common.

All of these plants have eukaryotic cells with cell walls composed of cellulose, and most obtain their energy through photosynthesis, using light and carbon dioxide to synthesize food. About three hundred plant species do not photosynthesize but are parasites on other species of photosynthetic plants. Plants are distinguished from green algae, which represent a mode of photosynthetic life similar to the kind modern plants are believed to have evolved from, by having specialized reproductive organs protected by non-reproductive tissues.

Bryophytes first appeared during the early Palaeozoic. They can only survive where moisture is available for significant periods, although some species are desiccation tolerant. Most species of bryophyte remain small throughout their life-cycle. This involves an alternation between two generations: a haploid stage, called the gametophyte, and a diploid stage, called the sporophyte. The sporophyte is short-lived and remains dependent on its parent gametophyte.

Vascular plants first appeared during the Silurian period, and by the Devonian had diversified and spread into many different land environments. They have a number of adaptations that allowed them to overcome the limitations of the bryophytes. These include a cuticle resistant to desiccation, and vascular tissues which transport water throughout the organism. In most the sporophyte acts as a separate individual, while the gametophyte remains small.

The first primitive seed plants, Pteridosperms (seed ferns) and Cordaites, both groups now extinct, appeared in the late Devonian and diversified through the Carboniferous, with further evolution through the Permian and Triassic periods. In these the gametophyte stage is completely reduced, and the sporophyte begins life inside an enclosure called a seed, which develops while on the parent plant, and with fertilisation by means of pollen grains. Whereas other vascular plants, such as ferns, reproduce by means of spores and so need moisture to develop, some seed plants can survive and reproduce in extremely arid conditions.

Early seed plants are referred to as gymnosperms (naked seeds), as the seed embryo is not enclosed in a protective structure at pollination, with the pollen landing directly on the embryo. Four surviving groups remain widespread now, particularly the conifers, which are dominant trees in several biomes. The angiosperms, comprising the flowering plants, were the last major group of plants to appear, emerging from within the gymnosperms during the Jurassic and diversifying rapidly during the Cretaceous. These differ in that the seed embryo (angiosperm) is enclosed, so the pollen has to grow a tube to penetrate the protective seed coat; they are the predominant group of flora in most biomes today.

Fossils

Paleobotany and Evolutionary History of Plants

A petrified log in Petrified Forest National Park. Plant fossils include roots, wood, leaves, seeds, fruit, pollen, spores, phytoliths, and amber (the fossilized resin produced by some plants). Fossil land plants are recorded in terrestrial, lacustrine, fluvial and nearshore marine sediments. Pollen, spores and algae (dinoflagellates and acritarchs) are used for dating sedimentary rock sequences. The remains of fossil plants are not as common as fossil animals, although plant fossils are locally abundant in many regions worldwide.

The earliest fossils clearly assignable to Kingdom Plantae are fossil green algae from the Cambrian. These fossils resemble calcified multicellular members of the Dasycladales. Earlier Precambrian fossils are known which resemble single-cell green algae, but definitive identity with that group of algae is uncertain.

The oldest known fossils of embryophytes date from the Ordovician, though such fossils are fragmentary. By the Silurian, fossils of whole plants are preserved, including the lycophyte *Baragwanathia longifolia*. From the Devonian, detailed fossils of rhyniophytes have been found. Early fossils of these ancient plants show the individual cells within the plant tissue. The Devonian period also saw the evolution of what many believe to be the first modern tree, Archaeopteris. This fern-like tree combined a woody trunk with the fronds of a fern, but produced no seeds.

The Coal Measures are a major source of Palaeozoic plant fossils, with many groups of plants in existence at this time. The spoil heaps of coal mines are the best places to collect; coal itself is the remains of fossilised plants, though structural detail of the plant fossils is rarely visible in coal. In the Fossil Forest at Victoria Park in Glasgow, Scotland, the stumps of Lepidodendron trees are found in their original growth positions.

The fossilized remains of conifer and angiosperm roots, stems and branches may be locally abundant in lake and inshore sedimentary rocks from the Mesozoic and Caenozoic eras. Sequoia and its allies, magnolia, oak, and palms are often found.

Petrified wood is common in some parts of the world, and is most frequently found in arid or desert areas where it is more readily exposed by erosion. Petrified wood is often heavily silicified (the organic material replaced by silicon dioxide), and the impregnated tissue is often preserved in fine detail. Such specimens may be cut and polished using lapidary equipment. Fossil forests of petrified wood have been found in all continents.

Fossils of seed ferns such as Glossopteris are widely distributed throughout several continents of the southern hemisphere, a fact that gave support to Alfred Wegener's early ideas regarding Continental drift theory.

Life Processes

Most of the solid material in a plant is taken from the atmosphere. Through a process known as photosynthesis, plants use the energy in sunlight to convert carbon dioxide from the atmosphere, plus water, into simple sugars. These sugars are then used as building blocks and form the main structural component of the plant. Chlorophyll, a green-colored, magnesium-containing pigment is essential to this process; it is generally present in plant leaves, and often in other plant parts as well.

Plants rely on soil primarily for support and water (in quantitative terms), but also obtain compounds of nitrogen, phosphorus, and other crucial elemental nutrients. For the majority of plants to grow successfully they also require oxygen in the atmosphere and around their roots for respiration. However, some plants grow as submerged aquatics, using oxygen dissolved in the surrounding water, and a few specialized vascular plants, such as mangroves, can grow with their roots in anoxic conditions.

The leaf is the primary site of photosynthesis in plants.Factors affecting growthThe genotype of a plant affects its growth, for example selected varieties of wheat grow rapidly, maturing within 110 days, whereas others, in the same environmental conditions, grow more slowly and mature within 155 days. Growth is also determined by environmental factors, such as temperature, available water, available light, and available nutrients in the soil. Any change in the availability of these external conditions will be reflected in the plants growth.

Biotic factors (living organisms) also affect plant growth. Plants compete with other plants for space, water, light and nutrients. Plants can be so crowded that no single individual makes normal growth.

Many plants rely on birds and insects to effect pollination. Grazing animals may affect vegetation. Soil fertility is influenced by the activity of bacteria and fungi. Bacteria, fungi, viruses, nematodes and insects can parasitise plants.

Some plant roots require an association with fungi to maintain normal activity (mycorrhizal association). Simple plants like algae may have short life spans as individuals, but their populations are commonly seasonal. Other plants may be organized according to their seasonal growth pattern:

- *Annual:* live and reproduce within one growing season. Biennial: live for two growing seasons; usually reproduce in second year.
- *Perennial:* live for many growing seasons; continue to reproduce once mature. Among the vascular plants, perennials include both evergreens that keep their leaves the entire year, and deciduous plants which lose their leaves for some part of it. In temperate and boreal climates, they generally lose their leaves during the winter; many tropical plants lose their leaves during the dry season.

The growth rate of plants is extremely variable. Some mosses grow less than 0.001 mm/h, while most trees grow 0.025-0.250 mm/h. Some climbing species, such as kudzu, which do not need to produce thick supportive tissue, may grow up to 12.5 mm/h.

Plants protect themselves from frost and dehydration stress with antifreeze proteins, heat-shock proteins and sugars (sucrose is common). LEA (Late Embryogenesis Abundant) protein expression is induced by stresses and protects other proteins from aggregation as a result of desiccation and freezing.

Internal Distribution

Vascular plants differ from other plants in that they transport nutrients between different parts through specialized structures, called xylem and phloem. They also have roots for taking up water and minerals. The xylem moves water and minerals from the root to the rest of the plant, and the phloem provides the roots with sugars and other nutrient produced by the leaves.

The photosynthesis conducted by land plants and algae is the ultimate source of energy and organic material in nearly all ecosystems. Photosynthesis radically changed the composition of the early Earth's atmosphere, which as a result is now 21% oxygen. Animals and most other organisms are aerobic, relying on oxygen; those that do not are confined to relatively rare anaerobic environments. Plants are the primary producers in most terrestrial ecosystems and form the basis of the food web in those ecosystems. Many animals rely on plants for shelter as well as oxygen and food.

Land plants are key components of the water cycle and several other biogeochemical cycles. Some plants have coevolved with nitrogen fixing bacteria, making plants an important part of the nitrogen cycle. Plant roots play an essential role in soil development and prevention of soil erosion.

Distribution

Plants are distributed worldwide in varying numbers. While they inhabit a multitude of biomes and ecoregions, few can be found beyond the tundras at the northernmost regions of continental shelves. At the southern extremes, plants have adapted tenaciously to the prevailing conditions.

Plants are often the dominant physical and structural component of habitats where they occur. Many of the Earth's biomes are named for the type of vegetation because plants are the dominant organisms in those biomes, such as grasslands and forests.

Ecological Relationships

The Venus flytrap, a species of carnivorous plant. Numerous animals have coevolved with plants. Many animals pollinate flowers in exchange for food in the form of pollen or nectar. Many animals disperse seeds, often by eating fruit and passing the seeds in their feces. Myrmecophytes are plants that have coevolved with ants. The plant provides a home, and sometimes food, for the ants. In exchange, the ants defend the plant from herbivores and sometimes competing plants. Ant wastes provide organic fertilizer.

The majority of plant species have various kinds of fungi associated with their root systems in a kind of mutualistic symbiosis known as mycorrhiza. The fungi help the plants gain water and mineral nutrients from the soil, while the plant gives the fungi carbohydrates manufactured in photosynthesis. Some plants serve as homes for endophytic fungi that protect the plant from herbivores by producing toxins. The fungal endophyte, Neotyphodium coenophialum, in tall fescue (*Festuca arundinacea*) does tremendous economic damage to the cattle industry in the U.S.

Various forms of parasitism are also fairly common among plants, from the semi-parasitic mistletoe that merely takes some nutrients from its host, but still has photosynthetic leaves, to the fully parasitic broomrape and toothwort that acquire all their nutrients through connections to the roots of other plants, and so have no chlorophyll. Some plants, known as myco-heterotrophs, parasitize mycorrhizal fungi, and hence act as epiparasites on other plants.

Many plants are epiphytes, meaning they grow on other plants, usually trees, without parasitizing them. Epiphytes may indirectly harm their host plant by intercepting mineral nutrients and light that the host would otherwise receive. The weight of large numbers of epiphytes may break tree limbs. Many orchids, bromeliads, ferns and mosses often grow as epiphytes. Bromeliad epiphytes accumulate water in leaf axils to form phytotelmata, complex aquatic food webs.

A few plants are carnivorous, such as the Venus flytrap and sundew. They trap small animals and digest them to obtain mineral nutrients, especially nitrogen.

Importance

- *Potato plant.* Potatoes spread to the rest of the world after European contact with the Americas in the late 1400s and early 1500s and have since become an important field crop.
- *Timber* in storage for later processing at a sawmill.

A section of a Yew branch showing 27 annual growth rings, pale sapwood and dark heartwood, and pith (centre dark spot). The dark radial lines are small knots.The study of plant uses by people is termed economic botany or ethnobotany; some consider economic botany to focus on modern cultivated plants, while ethnobotany focuses on indigenous plants by native peoples. Human cultivation of plants is part of agriculture, which is the basis of human civilization. Plant agriculture is subdivided into agronomy, horticulture and forestry.

Food

Much of human nutrition depends on land plants directly or indirectly. Human nutrition depends to a large extent on cereals, especially maize (or corn), wheat and rice. Other staple crops include potato, cassava, and legumes. Human food also includes vegetables, spices, and certain fruits, nuts, herbs, and edible flowers. Beverages produced from plants include coffee, tea, wine, beer and alcohol. Sugar is obtained mainly from sugar cane and sugar beet. Cooking oils and margarine come from maize, soybean, rapeseed, safflower, sunflower, olive and others. Food additives include gum arabic, guar gum, locust bean gum, starch and pectin. Livestock animals including cows, pigs, sheep, and goats which are all herbivores, are feed primarily or entirely on cereal plants, particularly grasses.

Non-food Products

Wood is used for buildings, furniture, paper, cardboard, musical instruments and sports equipment. Cloth is often made from cotton, flax or synthetic fibers derived from cellulose, such as rayon and acetate. Renewable fuels from plants include firewood, peat and many other biofuels. Coal and petroleum are fossil fuels derived from plants. Medicines derived from plants include aspirin, taxol, morphine, quinine, reserpine, colchicine, digitalis and vincristine. There are hundreds of herbal supplements such as ginkgo, Echinacea, feverfew, and Saint John's wort. Pesticides derived from plants include nicotine, rotenone, strychnine and pyrethrins. Drugs obtained from plants include opium, cocaine and marijuana. Poisons from plants include ricin, hemlock and curare. Plants are the source of many natural products such as fibres, essential oils, dyes, pigments, waxes, tannins, latex, gums, resins, alkaloids, amber and cork. Products derived from plants include soaps, paints, shampoos, perfumes, cosmetics, turpentine, rubber, varnish, lubricants, linoleum, plastics, inks, chewing gum and hemp rope. Plants are also a primary source of basic chemicals for the industrial synthesis of a vast array of organic chemicals. These chemicals are used in a vast variety of studies and experiments.

Aesthetic Uses

Thousands of plant species are cultivated to beautify the human environment as well as to provide shade, modify temperatures, reduce windspeed, abate noise, provide privacy and prevent soil erosion. People use cut flowers, dried flowers and house plants indoors. Outdoors, they use lawn grasses, shade trees, ornamental trees, shrubs, vines, herbaceous perennials and bedding plants. Images of plants are often used in art, architecture, humour, language and photography and on textiles, money, stamps, flags and coats of arms. Living plant art forms include topiary, bonsai, ikebana and espalier. Ornamental plants have sometimes changed the course of history, as in tulipomania. Plants are the basis of a multi-billion dollar per year tourism industry which includes travel to arboretums, botanical gardens, historic gardens, national parks, tulip festivals, rainforests, forests with colorful autumn leaves and the National Cherry Blossom Festival. Venus flytrap, sensitive plant and resurrection plant are examples of plants sold as novelties.

Scientific and Cultural Uses

Tree rings are an important method of dating in archeology and serve as a record of past climates. Basic biological research has often been done with plants, such as the pea plants used to derive Gregor Mendel's laws of genetics. Space stations or space colonies may one day rely on plants for life support. Plants are used as national and state emblems, including state trees and state flowers. Ancient trees are revered and many are famous. Numerous world records are held by plants. Plants are often used as memorials, gifts and to mark special occasions such as births, deaths, weddings and holidays. Plants figure prominently in mythology, religion and literature. The field of ethnobotany studies plant use by indigenous cultures which helps to conserve endangered species as well as discover new medicinal plants. Gardening is the most popular leisure activity in the U.S. Working with plants or horticulture therapy is beneficial for rehabilitating people with disabilities. Certain plants contain psychotropic chemicals which are extracted and ingested, including tobacco, cannabis (marijuana), and opium.

Negative Effects

Weeds are plants that grow where people do not want them. People have spread plants beyond their native ranges and some of these introduced plants become invasive, damaging existing ecosystems by displacing native species. Invasive plants cause billions of dollars in crop losses annually by displacing crop plants, they increase the cost of production and the use of chemical means to control them affects the environment.

Plants may cause harm to people. Plants that produce windblown pollen invoke allergic reactions in people who suffer from hay fever. A wide variety of plants are poisonous. Several plants cause skin irritations when touched, such as poison ivy. Certain plants contain psychotropic chemicals, which are extracted and ingested or smoked, including tobacco, cannabis (marijuana), cocaine and opium, causing damage to health or even death. Both illegal and legal drugs derived from plants have negative effects on the economy, affecting worker productivity and law enforcement costs. Some plants cause allergic reactions in people and animals when ingested, while other plants cause food intolerances that negatively affect health.

6

MEDICINAL TREES

The coming of spring is announced by pileated woodpeckers, migrating geese, the movement of sap in trees, and many other exciting changes.

While many people notice the seasonal arrival of birds, the first awakening of the trees is usually only noticed by those who are cutting or tapping them and allowing their freshly flowing vital juice to flow outside of the protective outer bark. Tapping trees and making maple syrup is an activity that marks the change of seasons and allows syrup producers to be intimately aware of the awakening of the trees.

When we make maple syrup we get to spend quality time with the majestic beings we call trees. It is such quality time that has inspired this article. Most people know that lumber comes from trees,and apples, pears, and nuts (especially hickory, black walnut, and butternut in our area) come from trees. Along with lumber, food, and air, trees provide us with many significant medicines and this is what I would like to bring your attention to.

Areca (*Areca catechu*) - A palm tree of Malaysia, the areca yields a seed or nut once chewed by the natives to dye their mouths fashionably red. Although not relied on in human medicine, the alkaioid arecoline, the seed's extractive, has the ability to destroy and repel worms in animals.

Balsam poplar (*Populus balsamifera*) - Growing across the northern reaches of North America, balsam popular bears buds coated with a gooey, fragrant substance. In the drug industry, it's called "balm-of-Gilead," and as an expectorant, it becomes a constituent of cold medicine. It also keeps ointment from going rancid. Applied externally, it helps heal wounds.

Benjamin (*Styrax benzoin*) - Native to Java and other Southeast Asian countries, this large tree has grayish, fluffy bark. When wounded, it exudes a white, aromatic gum universally known as gum benzoin. It's a productive expectorant when used in medicine. As the compound called tincture of benzoin, it relieves bronchitis when employed in a steam inhaler.

Birch Beer - Even just scratching the twigs reveals a strong root beer aroma, and chewing on the twigs releases the flavor. The decoction is a good diuretic and counters rheumatic pains. Other Birches, both aromatic and not, have similar properties, though the aromatic quality is both distinct in taste and in medicinal action.

Birch (*Betula papyrifera, nigra, lenta*) - Native to northern and eastern North America, birch trees possess concentrations of salicylic acid, the predecessor of aspirin. Although birch products were never widely used, folk medicine called for chewing birch twigs to relieve headache and pain. Willows (Salix spp.) also contain the pain-reducing acid.

Black Birch - Birch bark decoction is one of my favorite herbal beverages. It was the main ingredient of the original root beer(along with Sassafrass and Sarsaparilla, a vine) and of the original.

Camphor (*Cinnamomum camphora*) - In both China and Japan, the evergreen camphor tree grows to great size. An extractive of its bark, camphor acts as a counterirritant when included in ointments for relieving muscle pain.

Cascara (*Rahmnus purshiana*) - In the Pacific Northwest and British Columbia, this small tree is called cascara buckthron. Since 1877, its bark has been dried, baled and shipped to dealers who grind it into a find powder for medicinal use as an effective laxative or purgative.

Cherry - Cherry bark is a specific remedy for coughs and lung congestion. I often wonder if Cherry flavored cough syrups were originally inspired by the real Cherry bark syrups. Although the bark tastes different than the fruit, it is quite pleasant. It is usually recommended to use thoroughly dried bark for medicine because of its cyanide content. The fruits are a great source of anti-oxidants. There are several species of Cherry, small and large.

Cinnamon - Cinnamon bark, ground or as "sticks", is found in many spice cabinets. It is a warming circulatory stimulant, beneficial for arthritic complaints, mucusy conditions, and other illnesses where increased circulation of blood and Chi is indicated. If you want to use Cinnamon medicinally, be sure to get good quality. Most spices are irradiated (exposed to radiation), so buying Organic spices or at least those that are labeled as non-irradiated. Also, bottles of Cinnamon that have been sitting in spice racks for many years may not be that medicinal.

Dogwood (*Cornus florida*) - A medicine made from the bark of this tree native to the eastern United States often has been substituted for quinine. During the Civil War, Confederate doctors used it to treat malaria cases. Although it grows in abundance, drug companies looked past it to the more powerful quinine that comes from the cinchona tree of South America and the tropics.

Hemlock - The infusion of Hemlock needles and twigs is another of my favorite beverages. It is good for the onset of colds and flu, and for lung congestion. I suspect that it has many uses that I am not yet aware of. The Native Americans used it for boils and the like. This was also on of their most commonly used scurvy cures, as it is high in vitamin C.

Kola (*Cola nitada, C. acuminata*) - Do you get a lift from a carbonated soda? The large kola trees of tropical West Africa, the West Indies, and South America are responsible. Their dried seeds, which contain much caffeine, provide the stimulant in some medicines. But they also provide an energizing ingredient in many soft drinks.

Nux vomica (*Strychnos nux-vomica*) - The deadly poison strychnine comes from the seeds of this Asian tree. In smaller amounts, or mixed with other drugs, strychnine can become a heart stimulant or tonic.

Oak - Another nourishing tonic is made with prepared acorns. I enjoy pancakes and muffins made with acorn flour. I also eat acorns by themselves or mixed with rice or other grains. The bark, leaves, and unprepared acorns all have a distinct astringent quality, making them useful for the treatment of inflammatory conditions. Astringent medicines are especially useful for mucusy discharges, bleeding, and other instances where the tissue needs to be toned or constricted. For sore throats the bark decoction can be gargled. It can be used as a wash or as a poultice for external conditions. And the decoction can be used internally for diarrhea and other damp, inflammatory conditions. Oaks can be hard to identify to species, especially since there is hybridization. The astringent quality can be detected by taste, as it has a distinct drying and constricting effect when chewed.

Pine - Also high in vitamin C and used like Hemlock. Turpentine is derived from Pine. White Pine (Pinus strobus) is the most common wild species in our area. There are many other species, which are used similarly.

Prickly Ash - This tree is a circulatory stimulant. Where that iscalled for in arthritis treatment, Prickly Ash bark could be helpful. It also helps cold fingers and toes and digestive problems.

Quassia (*Quassia amara*) - The wood of this tree from Mexico and Central and South America has been an item of commerce since the min-1700s. The wood's bitter extractive, which has been relied on to expel parasites and reduce fever, is water soluble. Thus in the 1800s it frequently was turned into popular "bitter cups." The substance also has uses as an insecticide.

Rauwolfia (*Rauwolfia serpentina*) - More like a shrub than a tree in most places where it grows in India, rauwolfia produces extracts in its roots that have for centuries been used to treat nervous disorders. The extract also provides an antidote for snake-bites and insect stings. In the 20th century it was discovered that powdered rauwolfia root as a clinical medicinal ingredient would treat hypertension and mental disorders. Many drugs that make up tranquilizers have their origin in rauwolfia root.

SASSAFRAS - This tasty root is one of the main ingredients of traditional root beer. The root is commonly used as a blood cleanser to remove toxins from the body in such cases as skin rashes and inflammatory conditions. Sassafras is used to make gumbo, both as a spice and as a thickener (the leaves are used for the latter). The leaves have three distinct shapes. One is three lobed, one is mitten-shaped, and one has no lobes.

Slippery Elm - The name "slippery" comes from the moistening properties of the bark. Chewing on the twigs, sucking on lozenges, or using the powdered bark allows the slippery quality of this plant to sooth sore throats and other inflammatory conditions. The bark gruel is used as a nourishing tonic. Other elms can also be useful.

Willow - Aspirin was originally synthesized from willow. The bark has similar properties as drugs such as Asprin- it is antiinflammatory, analgesic, and fever reducing. As mentioned already, the bark is used for flu and pain, including arthritis. It has a dry and cool energetic nature and is used for damp and hot conditions. Many Native Americans use willow branches to make sweat lodges, both because the wood is flexible and because the bark is associated with healing. Many other trees have similar properties as Willow (as they contain the natural Aspirin-like chemicals, known as salicylic acid), including Poplar, Birch, and Ash.

A Medically Important Plant

Traditional medicine systems are part of India's culture. Today the whole world has become increasingly interested in Indian ayurveda and other traditional health systems. The demand for medicinal plants is increasing in both developing and more-developed countries as a result of recognition of the non-narcotic nature, lack of side effects and easy availability of many herbal drugs. Most often the medicinal plants are collected from the wild. This uncontrolled harvesting has resulted in the extinction of many plants and created huge issues related to the potency and quality of medicinal products derived from those plants.

There are numerous data on the uses of medicinal plants. Gadgil and Vartak have reported the uses of such plants in India. The therapeutic potential of various herbal drugs ranges from the use of parts of plants to simple extracts to isolated active constituents. In the present paper we have attempted to briefly summarize the information available on the potency of *Trichosanthes tricuspidata* because of its immense medicinal potential.

Botany and Distribution

T. tricuspidata, also known as *T. palmata Roxb.*, *T. bracteata Lamb.*, *T. pubera Blume* or *Modeccca bracteata*, belongs to the family cucurbitaceae and is known by various vernacular names. In Hindi it is known as *Lal Indrayan*; in English, *Redball snakegourd*; in Malaya, *Kalayar*; in Marathi, *Kaundal*; in Telugu, *Avudua*; in Thai, *Khe-Ka-Daeng* and in Nepal, *Indreni*.

T. tricuspidata is a vine which is found at an elevation of 1200 to 2300 m. It ranges from the Eastern Himalayas in India and southern China through southern Japan, Malaysia, and tropical Australia. In India it is a large climber, often attaining a height of 9-10 metres. It has a robust stem that is woody below, and has 3-cleft tendrils. The leaves are variable, palmately 3-5 lobed with a cordate base, and the lobes are ovate to oblong with serrate or dentate margins. Male flowers are in axillary 5-10 flowered racemes with large bracts, while the female flowers are solitary. The corolla petals are wedge-shaped, fringed and white in colour. The fruits are globose, and when ripe are red with ten orange streaks.

Medicinal Uses

T. tricuspidata is considered to be medicinally important in several traditional systems. In ayurvedic medicines, the fruits are used in the treatment of asthma, earache and ozoena (intranasal crusting, atrophy and fetid odour). In the Unani system of medicine, the fruits are used as a carminative (an agent that relieves flatulence), a purgative, and an abortifacient, to lessen inflammation, cure migraines, and reduce heat of the brain, as a treatment for opthalmia (inflammation of the eye), leprosy (infectious disease caused by *Mycobacterium leprae*), epilepsy (episodic impairment or loss of consciousness, abnormal motor phenomenon) and rheumatism, (painful local inflammation of joints and muscles) as well as other uses. The seeds are emetic and a good purgative. In the Thai traditional system of medicine, the plant is used as an anti-fever remedy, a laxative, an anthelmintic as well as in migraine treatments The roots of the plant are used to treat lung diseases in cattle and for the treatment of diabetic carbuncles and headaches. Gaur has reported the use of this plant in curing bronchitis, and the application of seed paste for hoof and mouth disease in cattle.

The vaidyas, or practictioners of ayurveda, also use the fruits in treating stomatitis. The oil extracted from the roots is used as a pain killer. In Bastar District, Chhattisgarh, India, the plant is used for curing snakebite poisoning and the juice of the plant is applied externally for skin eruptions. In Nepal the roots are used to cure bleeding in chickens.

Chemical Constituents

Mohamed isolated a tetrahydroxy pentacyclic triterpene "trichotetrol" from the root extract of this vine. From the fruits of *T. tricuspidata*, 14 cucurbitane glycosides were isolated An extract of the fruits of this plant was found to be cytotoxic in KB cells, and two new cucurbitacins were reported: tricuspidatin and 2-O-glucocucurbitacin J. Kaneda and Uchikoba reported a protease from the sarcocarp of the fruits of this plant. The root contains methyl palmitate, palmitic acid, suberic acid, a-spinasterol, stigmast-7-en-3-beta-ol, a-spinasterol 3-O-beta-D-glucopyranoside, stigmast-7-en-3-beta-ol-3-O-beta-D-glucopyranoside, glyceryl 1-palmitate, glyceryl 1-stearate, bryonolic acid, cucurbitacin B, isocucurbitacin B, 3-epi-isocucurbitacin B, 23,24-dihydrocucurbitacin D, isocucurbitacin D and D-glucose. The roots of *T. tricuspidata* contain more than 6 times more cucurbitacin than the roots of T. kirilowii Maxim. Var. *japonicum* Kitam. Researchers isolated three new cycloartane glycosides, named cyclotricuspidosides A, B and C, from the leaf and stem parts.

Conclusion

A perusal of the literature shows that T. tricuspidata has been widely used for curing asthma, migraine, fever, diabetic carbuncles and other maladies. A number of pharmacologically important phytochemicals, such as cucurbitacins and trichotetrol, have been isolated from this plant. This report has provided an introduction to the panoply of reported therapeutic uses of T. tricuspidata. Clearly, further efforts are required in order to better understand the biological activities reported, and to isolate, purify, and chemically characterize the active principles of T. tricuspidata. Randomized trials should ultimately be conducted to rigorously evaluate the safety and efficacy of some of the most widely reported curative applications of this popular medicinal plant.

Effects of Radiation

In light of the various nuclear power plant accident, military and terrorism scenarios that have entered the world consciousness over the past two generations, there is tremendous practical value to understanding how to neutralize or reduce the damaging (and lethal) effects of radiation on the body. Despite substantial research over the past three decades, no chemical compounds have been found to be perfectly safe and effective for this purpose. Research on the use of plant extracts to protect against radiation exposure is not widely known, however the low toxicity and minimal side effects of many plant products are well known in both western science and traditional medicine. Examining the benefits of plant-based therapy with rigorous quantitative science is beginning to gain a toehold in the field of radioprotection. There are now a number of mechanism-based reports of substantial *in vitro* and *in vivo* activity from plant preparations. By presenting the following per-reviewed study, we hope to add to that body of evidence and to stimulate further research in this neglected arena.

Radiation protection is at a cross-road after radiation incidents event of planned and unplanned exposure (i.e., clinical oncology, radiation site cleanup, military scenarios, radiological terrorism, radiation accidents, etc.).

A substantial amount of research has been carried out in the field of chemical radioprotection during the last few decades; however, no safe and ideal synthetic radioprotectors are available to date. Recently, interest has generated in developing the potential drugs of plant origin for the amelioration of radiation effects. Plants and their products are well known to have an advantage over the synthetic compounds in terms of their potential low/no toxicity at the effective dose with minimum or no side effects. However, the use of medicinal plants suffers from lack of robust scientific evidence to support their use. Therefore, studies supporting or rejecting their role in the treatment of various health disorders is of great need.

Rosemary (*Rosmarinus officinalis*), belonging to the family Lamiaceae, is a common medicinal and aromatic plant grown in many parts of the world. It is indigenous to Southern Europe, particularly on the dry rocky hills of the Mediterranean region. Rosemary is used as a culinary herb, a beverage drink, as well as in cosmetics; in folk medicine it is used as a tonic and stimulant, analgesic, antirheumatic, carminative, diuretic, expectorant, anti-epileptic, anti-spasmodic in renal colic, dysmenorrhoea, for relief of respiratory disorders, effects on human fertility, and the stimulation of hair growth . Rosemary has been shown to be safe in toxicity studies in animal models when added as an antioxidant to food.

Since time immemorial, the plant has been used traditionally by people for curing various health disorders around the world. Caribs of Guatemala use rosemary to cure various human diseases. Rosemary has been described as a wonder-drug in literature and in various medieval drug monographs as well. Thus, wide acceptability and diverse pharmacological and anti-oxidative properties of the plant stimulated us to evaluate the radio modulatory effect of *Rosmarinus officinalis* in Swiss albino mice exposed to various doses of gamma radiation.

Male Swiss albino mice (*Mus musculus*), 6-8 weeks old, weighing 20-24 g., from an inbred colony were used for the present study. The animals were provided standard mice feed (procured from Hindustan Lever Ltd., India) and water ad libitum and were maintained under controlled conditions of temperature and light (Light: dark, 10 hrs: 14 hrs.). Four animals were housed in a polypropylene cage with locally procured paddy husk (*Oryza sativa*) as bedding throughout the experiment. Tetracycline-containing water (0.13 mg/ml) was provided once a fortnight and was given as a preventive measure against infections. Animal care and handling were performed according to the guidelines set by the World Health Organization (WHO), Geneva, Switzerland and the INSA (Indian National Science Academy), New Delhi, India. The Departmental.

Irradiation

The cobalt teletherapy unit (Co-60) at the Cancer Treatment Centre, Radiotherapy Department, SMS Medical College & Hospital, Jaipur, India, was used for irradiation. Unanaesthetized animals were restrained in well-ventilated Perspex boxes and exposed to various doses of gamma radiation (i.e., 3, 6 and 9 Gy) at a distance (SSD) of 80 cm from the source at a dose rate of 0.85 Gy/min.

Taxonomic Description of the Plant

Rosemary is an evergreen shrub growing to 1.5 m by 1.5 m at a medium rate. The leaves of rosemary are about 1 inch long, linear, revolute, dark green above and paler and glandular beneath, with camphoraceous aromatic odour. The scented hermaphrodite flowers are small and pale blue. Much of the active volatile principle resides in their calyces. There are various other varieties of the plant, but the green-leaved variety is the kind used medicinally.

Preparation of Plant Extract

The identification of the plant *Rosmarinus officinalis* (family: Lamiaceae) was done by a botanist, Dr Deepak Acharya, (Voucher Specimen No: DDC/2001/DEPTBT/ACHARYA2430) of the Department of Botany, Danielson College, Chhindwara, Madhya Pradesh (India). The non-infected leaves of the plant were collected, carefully cleaned, shade dried and powdered in a grinder. The plant material was prepared by extracting 200 gm of leaf powder with double distilled water by refluxing for 36 hrs (12 hrs. × 3) at 55 ± 5°C. Pellets of the extract were obtained by evaporation of its liquid contents in the incubator. An approximate yield of 22% extract (w/w) was obtained.

The required dose for treatment was prepared by dissolving the drug pellets in double distilled water and administered by oral gavage with a micropipette (100 µl/animal) at a dose of 1000 mg/kg body wt./animal (1000 mg of 22% of original plant weight). Henceforth, rosemary leaf extract will be called RE.

Experimental Design

Optimum dose Determination

A dose selection of *Rosmarinus officinalis* (RE) was done on the basis of a drug tolerance study. For this purpose, various doses of RE extract (100, 200, 400, 800, 1000, 1500 and 2000 mg/kg body wt.) were tested for their tolerance (once in a day for 5 consecutive days) in Swiss albino mice. One hour after the last administration of RE, mice were exposed to 8 Gy gamma irradiation. All these animals were then observed for 30 days for scoring signs of radiation sickness or mortality. Thus, the optimum tolerated dose of RE (1000 mg/ kg b. wt.) was determined and used for further detailed experimentation.

Modification of Radiation Response

A total of 48 animals used for the experiment were assorted into 4 groups. Mice of group 1 (sham irradiated) were orally administered double distilled water (DDW) at a dose of 1000 mg/kg body weight, volume equal to RE. Animals belonging to group 2 (RE alone) were given daily rosemary extract at a dose of 1000 mg/kg/animal for 5 consecutive days, one hour before irradiation. Animals of group 3 (radiation control) were exposed to various doses of gamma rays alone (i.e., 3, 6 and 9 Gy) one hour after DDW treatment on day 5. Group 4 (RE experimental) received RE (1000 mg/ kg body wt./animal) as in group 2. One hour after last administration of RE, mice were exposed to various doses of gamma rays, (i.e., 3, 6 and 9 Gy), respectively. These animals were observed daily for any sign of sickness, morbidity, behavioral toxicity and mortality. A minimum of 6 animals from each group were necropsied on days 1, 3, 5, 10, 20 and 30 post-treatment intervals to study hematological and biochemical parameters.

Biochemical Determinants

Biochemical alterations were studied in animals of all the groups at one hour post- exposure to gamma radiation. The level of glutathione (GSH) was determined in blood. The lipid peroxidation (LPx) level in the serum was measured by the assay of thiobarbituric acid reactive substances (TBARS).

Statistical Analysis

The result for all the groups at various necropsy intervals were expressed as mean ± standard error of the mean (S.E.M.) to evaluate whether the mean of the sample drawn from experimental (RE experimental) deviated significantly from respective control (Irradiation control). Student's 't' test was used. The significance level was set at different levels as $p<0.05$, $p<0.01$ and $p<0.001$.

Results

The radioprotective effect of rosemary leaf extract (RE) was studied in mice treated with 1000 mg/kg body wt. RE before exposure to 3, 6 and 9 Gy of gamma radiation. No noticeable signs of behavioral change, sickness or mortality were observed in Sham irradiated/RE-treated group. Animals exposed to 3 and 6 Gy gamma rays alone did not show mortality throughout the experimental period, but slight laziness was observed in some animals. Animals exposed to 9 Gy gamma rays exhibited epilation, ruffled hair, watering of eyes, weight loss and became lethargic. No animal could survive in the 9 Gy irradiated alone group beyond day 10. Animals pretreated with RE did not exhibit mortality or any symptoms of radiation sickness. General health, activeness, food and water intake were found to be normal in RE pretreated irradiated animals.

After whole body exposure to different doses of gamma radiation (i.e., 3, 6 and 9 Gy), lymphocyte percentages remained significantly lower than normal, and could not regain a normal value even by the last day of autopsy interval (day 30). No significant changes in monocytes, eosinophils and basophil counts were registered in any of the groups. However, monocytes followed a pattern similar to lymphocytes. Following irradiation, a significant increase above normal was observed in neutrophil counts. A normal value could not be restored in any of the irradiated groups till day 30 post-exposure.

Daily administration of 1000 mg/kg of RE for 5 consecutive days rendered recovery in the different types of leucocytes (i.e., lymphocytes, monocytes, eosinophils, basophils and neutrophils) in comparison to irradiated alone groups, and values close to normal were registered in a dose dependent manner (3> 6> 9 Gy) by post-treatment day 30.

Biochemical Determinants

There was no significant difference observed in the levels of glutathione (GSH) and lipid peroxidation (LPx) in the blood content of sham irradiated (group 1) or RE alone treated animals (group 2). In concomitant treatment of RE and radiation (group 4), GSH was found to be further lowered than the radiation treated group. A significant elevation in the values of blood GSH as compared to group 3 was estimated in RE experimental animals. An increase in LPx levels above normal was evident in serum of irradiated mice, while a significant decrease in such values was evident in the RE pretreated irradiated group.

Discussion

Radiation injuries are manifested as a result of enhanced production of free radicals due to oxidative stress. Exposure to radiation causes ionization of molecules in the cells, which sets off potentially damaging reactions via free radical production. Free radical mediated processes and oxidative stress have been implicated in the pathogenesis of the aging process and various diseases such as atherosclerosis, liver damage, arthritis, cancer, and neurodegenerative disorders . The prevailing view is that intake of antioxidant nutrients can reduce the risk of free radical-related health problems and may prove to be protective against ionizing irradiation.

The present study revealed that the number of lymphocytes declined in a dose dependent manner after exposure to 3, 6 and 9 Gy gamma irradiation. A rapid depression was observed at early intervals which may be attributed to direct destruction of such cells in peripheral blood of mice No significant changes in monocytes, eosinophils and basophils were observed after whole body exposure to different doses of gamma radiation. It may be attributed to the fact that mature granulocytes are radioresistant whereas lymphocytes are extremely sensitive to radiation Furthermore, neutrophil granules altered inversely as compared to lymphocytes. These cells exhibited an early rise while lymphocytes and monocytes declined soon after exposure thus showing an opposite behavior. This can be explained by an abortive rise phenomenon as described earlier by workers.

According to Hall, by the time the number of circulating cells in the blood reaches minimum value as the mature circulating cells begin to die off, the supply of new cells from the depleted precursor population becomes inadequate to replace these, thereby making radiation effects become apparent. Also, this abrupt increase may have appeared due to an abortive rise phenomenon or can be interpreted as stimulation effect. Hastening the maturation of granulocyte precursors in bone marrow and their release into general circulation can be attributed to a rise in neutrophil counts.

It is evident from the present study that administration of RE reduced radiation sickness and mortality, and provided protection to differential leucocytes counts (i.e., lymphocytes, monocytes, basophils, eosinophils and neutrophils) in the peripheral blood of mice from the damaging gamma radiation. It has been observed that rosmarinic acid (found in rosemary) is effective in relation to blood circulation and to improve hemodynamics in occlusive arterial diseases Rosemary has been found to contain certain antioxidative and free radical scavenging activity in its active compounds like caffeic acid, carnosolic acid, chlorogenic acid, rosmanol, rosmarinic acid, carnosol, different diterpenes, rosmari-diphenol, rosmariquinone and other natural antioxidants such as ursolic acid, alkaloid rosmaricine and glucocolic acid In a recent study, carnosic acid was found to render protection to UVA irradiated human skin fibroblasts.

The basic effect of radiation on cellular membranes is believed to induce lipid peroxidation (LPx) by the production of free radicals that have the potential to damage DNA and cause cell death. The level of radiation-induced LPx increased considerably in a dose dependent manner in the entire group 3 irradiated animals, whereas a decrease in the values was observed in RE-treated group 4. The inhibition observed in the LPx level in blood of RE administered animals may have been responsible for the observed radioprotection by plant extract. This view is supported by the investigation of an anti-lipoperoxidant activity of young sprouts of *Rosmarinus officinalis* that significantly reduced the formation of malondialdehyde in rat hepatocytes. Sotelo-Felix *et al.* proposed that carnosol could scavenge free radicals induced by carbon tetrachloride, consequently avoiding the propagation of lipid peroxides in the liver of mice.

Glutathione (GSH) is one of the antioxidant enzymes that act as the first line of defense against pro-oxidant stress, thus performing as a free radical scavenger. Oral administration of DDW or RE did not significantly influence the endogenous GSH level in blood. In the present study, GSH levels were found to be lower in the blood of irradiated alone animals than that observed in the RE pre-treated mice. The levels of GSH were found to be elevated in the blood of mice after RE administration.

One of the mechanisms of RE protection against radiation can be an elevation in the glutathione level that is mediated through the modulation of cellular antioxidant level. Rosmarinic acid has been experimentally found to have a significant antioxidant role through free radical scavenging activity Kilic et al. observed that lipid peroxidation starts as soon as the endogenous GSH gets exhausted, and the addition of GSH stops further peroxidation promptly. Increase in the GSH concentration, towards normal, could have resulted in reduced levels of LPx, thereby protecting against damage caused by radiation in the RE pre-treated irradiated group.

The mechanism of the radioprotective action of Rosmarinus officinalis leaf extract in this animal model may thus be its free radical scavenging activity and its ability to thus protect cellular molecules from oxidative damage. Furthermore, it inhibited lipid peroxidation and modulated GSH levels in blood of these Swiss albino mice. The activity of rosemary may also be attributed to stimulating or protecting hematopoiesis in bone marrow and a subsequent increase of hematological constituents in the peripheral blood. Since significant protection was obtained at a non-toxic low dose, RE may have an advantage over the known radioprotectors. Further investigations are in progress to study the exact mechanism of action and clinical applicability of R. officinalis in radioprotection.

7

Importance of Trees

A tree is a perennial woody plant. It is most often defined as a woody plant that has many secondary branches supported clear of the ground on a single main stem or trunk with clear apical dominance. A minimum height specification at maturity is cited by some authors, varying from 3 m to 6 m some authors set a minimum of 10 cm trunk diameter (30 cm girth) Woody plants that do not meet these definitions by having multiple stems and/or small size, are called shrubs. Compared with most other plants, trees are long-lived, some reaching several thousand years old and growing to up to 115 m (379 ft) high.

Trees are an important component of the natural landscape because of their prevention of erosion and the provision of a weather-sheltered ecosystem in and under their foliage. Trees also play an important role in producing oxygen and reducing carbon dioxide in the atmosphere, as well as moderating ground temperatures. They are also elements in landscaping and agriculture, both for their aesthetic appeal and their orchard crops (such as apples).

Wood from trees is a building material, as well as a primary energy source in many developing countries. Trees also play a role in many of the world's mythologies (see trees in mythology). As of 2005, there were approximately 400 billion trees on Earth, about 61 per person.

Classification

A tree is a plant form that occurs in many different orders and families of plants. Trees show a variety of growth forms, leaf type and shape, bark characteristics, and reproductive organs.

The tree form has evolved separately in unrelated classes of plants, in response to similar environmental challenges, making it a classic example of parallel evolution. With an estimate of 100,000 tree species, the number of tree species worldwide might total 25 percent of all living plant species The majority of tree species grow in tropical regions of the world and many of these areas have not been surveyed yet by botanists, making species diversity and ranges poorly understood.

The earliest trees were tree ferns, horsetails and lycophytes, which grew in forests in the Carboniferous Period; tree ferns still survive, but the only surviving horsetails and lycophytes are not of tree form. Later, in the Triassic Period, conifers, ginkgos, cycads and other gymnosperms appeared, and subsequently flowering plants in the Cretaceous Period. Most species of trees today are flowering plants (Angiosperms) and conifers. For the listing of examples of well-known trees and how they are classified, see List of tree genera.

A small group of trees growing together is called a grove or copse, and a landscape covered by a dense growth of trees is called a forest. Several biotopes are defined largely by the trees that inhabit them; examples are rainforest and taiga. A landscape of trees scattered or spaced across grassland (usually grazed or burned over periodically) is called a savanna. A forest of great age is called old growth forest or ancient woodland (in the UK). A young tree is called a sapling.

Morphology

Beech Leaves

Tree roots anchor the structure and provide water and nutrients. The ground has eroded away around the roots of this young pine tree.The parts of a tree are the roots, trunk(s), branches, twigs and leaves. Tree stems consist mainly of support and transport tissues (xylem and phloem). Wood consists of xylem cells, and bark is made of phloem and other tissues external to the vascular cambium. Trees may be grouped into exogenous and endogenous trees according to the way in which their stem diameter increases. Exogenous trees, which comprise the great majority of trees (all conifers, and almost all broadleaf trees), grow by the addition of new wood outwards, immediately under the bark. Endogenous trees, mainly in the monocotyledons (e.g., palms and dragon trees), but also cacti, grow by addition of new material inwards.

As an exogenous tree grows, it creates growth rings as new wood is laid down concentrically over the old wood. In species growing in areas with seasonal climate changes, wood growth produced at different times of the year may be visible as alternating light and dark, or soft and hard, rings of wood In temperate climates, and tropical climates with a single wet-dry season alternation, the growth rings are annual, each pair of light and dark rings being one year of growth; these are known as annual rings. In areas with two wet and dry seasons each year, there may be two pairs of light and dark rings each year; and in some (mainly semi-desert regions with irregular rainfall), there may be a new growth ring with each rainfall In tropical rainforest regions, with constant year-round climate, growth is continuous and the growth rings are not visible nor is there a change in the wood texture. In species with annual rings, these rings can be counted to determine the age of the tree, and used to date cores or even wood taken from trees in the past, a practice is known as the science of dendrochronology. Very few tropical trees can be accurately aged in this manner. Age determination is also impossible in endogenous trees.

The roots of a tree are generally embedded in earth, providing anchorage for the above-ground biomass and absorbing water and nutrients from the soil. It should be noted, however, that while ground nutrients are essential to a tree's growth the majority of its biomass comes from carbon dioxide absorbed from the atmosphere. Above ground, the trunk gives height to the leaf-bearing branches, aiding in competition with other plant species for sunlight. In many trees, the arrangement of the branches optimizes exposure of the leaves to sunlight.

Not all trees have all the plant organs or parts mentioned above. For example, most palm trees are not branched, the saguaro cactus of North America has no functional leaves, tree ferns do not produce bark, etc. Based on their general shape and size, all of these are nonetheless generally regarded as trees. A plant form that is similar to a tree, but generally having smaller, multiple trunks and/or branches that arise near the ground, is called a shrub. However, no precise differentiation between shrubs and trees is possible. Given their small size, bonsai plants would not technically be 'trees', but one should not confuse reference to the form of a species with the size or shape of individual specimens. A spruce seedling does not fit the definition of a tree, but all spruces are trees.

Record Breaking Trees

The world's champion trees can be rated on height, trunk diameter or girth, total size, and age.

Tallest Trees

The heights of the tallest trees in the world have been the subject of considerable dispute and much exaggeration. Modern verified measurement with laser rangefinders combined with tape drop measurements made by tree climbers, carried out by the U.S. Eastern Native Tree Society has shown that some older measuring methods and measurements are often unreliable, sometimes producing exaggerations of 5% to 15% above the real height. Historical claims of trees of 130 m (427 ft), and even 150 m (492 ft), are now largely disregarded as unreliable, and attributed to human error. (however, see "Tallest specimens" chapter in Eucalyptus regnans article). Historical records of fallen trees measured prostrate on the ground are considered to be far more reliable. The following are now accepted as the top five tallest reliably measured species in recent years:

Coast Redwood (Sequoia sempervirens): 115.55 m (379.1 ft), Redwood National Park, California, United States Australian Mountain-ash (Eucalyptus regnans): 99.6 m (326.8 ft), south of Hobart, Tasmania, Australia Coast Douglas-fir (Pseudotsuga menziesii): 99.4 m (326.1 ft), Brummit Creek, Coos County, Oregon, United States Sitka Spruce (Picea sitchensis): 96.7 m (317.3 ft), Prairie Creek Redwoods State Park, California, United States Giant Sequoia (Sequoiadendron giganteum): 94.9 m (311.4 ft), Redwood Mountain Grove, Kings Canyon National Park, California, United States Stoutest trees The girth of a tree is much easier to measure than the height, as it is a simple matter of stretching a tape round the trunk, and pulling it taut to find the circumference. Despite this, UK tree author Alan Mitchell made the following comment about measurements of yew trees:

"The aberrations of past measurements of yews are beyond belief. For example, the tree at Tisbury has a well-defined, clean, if irregular bole at least 1.5 m long. It has been found to have a girth which has dilated and shrunk in the following way: 11.28 m (1834 Loudon), 9.3 m (1892 Lowe), 10.67 m (1903 Elwes and Henry), 9.0 m (1924 E. Swanton), 9.45 m (1959 Mitchell) .... Earlier measurements have therefore been omitted."

As a general standard, tree girth is taken at 'breast height'; this is defined differently in different situations, with most forestry measurements taking girth at 1.3 m above ground, while those who measure ornamental trees usually measure at 1.5 m above ground in most cases this makes little difference to the measured girth. On sloping ground, the "above ground" reference point is usually taken as the highest point on the ground touching the trunk, but some use the average between the highest and lowest points of ground. Some of the inflated old measurements may have been taken at ground level. Some past exaggerated measurements also result from measuring the complete next-to-bark measurement, pushing the tape in and out over every crevice and buttress.

Modern trends are to cite the tree's diameter rather than the circumference; this is obtained by dividing the measured circumference by p; it assumes the trunk is circular in cross-section (an oval or irregular cross-section would result in a mean diameter slightly greater than the assumed circle). This is cited as dbh (diameter at breast height) in tree and forestry literature.

One further problem with measuring *Baobabs adansonia* is that these trees store large amounts of water in the very soft wood in their trunks. This leads to marked variation in their girth over the year (though not more than about 2.5% swelling to a maximum at the end of the rainy season, minimum at the end of the dry season.

The stoutest living single-trunk species in diameter are: African Baobab Adansonia digitata: 15 m (49 ft), Big Baobab, Limpopo Province, South Africa Montezuma

Cypress Taxodium mucronatum: 11.62 m (38.1 ft), Árbol del Tule, Santa Maria del Tule, Oaxaca, Mexico. Note though that this diameter includes buttressing; the actual idealised diameter of the area of its wood is 9.38 m (30.8 ft).

Giant Sequoia (*Sequoiadendron giganteum*): 8.85 m (29 ft), General Grant tree, Grant Grove, California, United States Coast Redwood Sequoia sempervirens: 7.44 m (24.4 ft), Prairie Creek Redwoods State Park, California, United States.

Charles Darwin reported finding *Fitzroya cupressoides* with trunk circumferences of up to 40 m (130 ft) implying a diameter of about 12 m (40 ft), but this may be an anomaly as the largest known measurements are about 5 m.

An addition problem lies in cases where multiple trunks (whether from an individual tree or multiple trees) grow together. The Sacred Fig is a notable example of this, forming additional 'trunks' by growing adventitious roots down from the branches, which then thicken up when the root reaches the ground to form new trunks; a single Sacred Fig tree can have hundreds of such trunks Occasionally, errors may occur due to confusion between girth (circumference) and diameter.

Largest Trees

The largest trees in total volume are those which are both tall and of large diameter, and in particular, which hold a large diameter high up the trunk. Measurement is very complex, particularly if branch volume is to be included as well as the trunk volume, so measurements have only been made for a small number of trees, and generally only for the trunk. No attempt has ever been made to include root volume. Measuring standards vary.

The top four species measured so far are: Giant Sequoia (*Sequoiadendron giganteum*): 1,487 m^3 (52,508 cu ft), General Sherman Coast Redwood (*Sequoia sempervirens*):

1,203 m^3 (42,500 cu ft), Lost Monarch Montezuma Cypress (*Taxodium mucronatum*): 750 m^3 (25,000 cu ft), Árbol del Tule Western Redcedar (*Thuja plicata*): 500 m^3 (17,650 cu ft), Quinault Lake Redcedar Kauri (*Agathis australis*): circa 400 m^3 (15,000 cu ft), Tane Mahuta tree (total volume, including branches, 516.7 m^3/18,247 cu ft. However, the Alerce *Fitzroya cupressoides*, as yet un-measured, may well slot in at fourth or fifth place. The largest angiosperm tree is currently a Tasmanian Blue Gum (*Eucalyptus globulus*) in Tasmania, with a volume of 368 m^3.

Oldest Trees

The oldest trees are determined by growth rings, which can be seen if the tree is cut down or in cores taken from the edge to the center of the tree. Accurate determination is only possible for trees which produce growth rings, generally those which occur in seasonal climates; trees in uniform non-seasonal tropical climates grow continuously and do not have distinct growth rings. It is also only possible for trees which are solid to the center of the tree; many very old trees become hollow as the dead heartwood decays away. For some of these species, age estimates have been made on the basis of extrapolating current growth rates, but the results are usually little better than guesswork or wild speculation. White (1998) proposes a method of estimating the age of large and veteran trees in the United Kingdom through the correlation between a tree's stem diameter, growth character and age.

The verified oldest measured ages are: African Baobab, (*Adansonia digitata*): 6,000 years according to carbon dating Great Basin Bristlecone Pine (Methuselah) Pinus longaeva: 4,844 years Alerce (*Fitzroya cupressoides*): 3,622 years.

The oldest reported age for an angiosperm tree after the African Baobab (*A. digitata*) is 2293 years for the Sri Maha Bodhi Sacred Fig (*Ficus religiosa*) planted in 288 BC at Anuradhapura, Sri Lanka; this is also the oldest human-planted tree with a known planting date.

Damage

The two major sources of tree damage are biotic (from living sources) and abiotic (from non-living sources). Biotic sources would include insects which might bore into the tree, deer which might rub bark off the trunk, or fungi, which might attach themselves to the tree.

Abiotic sources include lightning, vehicles impacts, and construction activities. Construction activities can involve a number of damage sources, including grade changes that prevent aeration to roots, spills involving toxic chemicals such as cement or petroleum products, or severing of branches or roots.

Both damage sources can result in trees becoming dangerous, and the term "hazard trees" is commonly used by arborists, and industry groups such as power line operators. Hazard trees are trees which due to disease or other factors are more susceptible to falling during windstorms, or having parts of the tree fall.

The process of evaluating the danger a tree presents is based on a process called the quantified tree risk assessment.

Assessment as to labeling a tree a hazard tree can be based on a field examination. Assessment as a result of construction activities that will damage a tree is based on three factors; severity, extent and duration. Severity relates usually to the degree of intrusion into the TPZ and resultant root loss. Extent is frequently a percentage of a factor such as canopy, roots or bark, and duration is normally based on time. Root severing is considered permanent in time.

Trees are similar to people. Both can withstand massive amounts of some types of damage and survive, but even small amounts of certain types of trauma can result in death. Arborists are very aware that established trees will not tolerate any appreciable disturbance of the root system.

However, lay people and construction professionals are seldom cognizant of how easily a tree can be killed.

One reason for confusion about tree damage from construction involves the dormancy of trees during winter. Another factor is that trees may not show symptoms of damage until 24-months or longer after damage has occurred. For that reason, persons uneducated in arboriculture science may not correlate the actual cause and resultant effect.

Various organizations, such as the International Society of Arboriculture, the British Standards Institute and the National Arborist Association (about 2007 renamed the Tree Industry Association), have long recognized the importance of construction activities that impact tree health. The impacts are important because they can result in monetary losses due to tree damage and resultant remediation or replacement costs, as well as violation of government ordinances or community or subdivision restrictions.

As a result, protocols for tree management prior to, during and after construction activities are well established, tested and refined.

Review of the construction plans 'Development of the related tree inventory' Application of standard construction tree management protocols, Assessment of potential for expected tree damages.

Development of a tree protection plan (providing for concurrent, and post-construction damage prevention and remediation steps), Development of a tree protection plan, Development of a remediation plan, Implementation of tree protection zones (TPZ).

Implementation of the remediation plan, International standards are uniform in analyzing damage potential and sizing TPZs (tree protection zones) to minimize damage. For mature to fully mature trees, the accepted TPZ comprises a

1.5-foot set-off for every 1-inch diameter of trunk. That means for a 10-inch tree, the TPZ would extend 15-feet in all directions from the base of the trunk at ground level.

For young/small trees with minimal crowns (and trunks less than 4-inches in diameter) a TPZ equal to 1-foot for every inch of trunk diameter may suffice. That means for a 3-inch tree, the TPZ would extend 3-feet in all directions from the base of the trunk at ground level. Detailed information on TPZs and related topics is available at minimal cost from organizations like the International Society for Arboriculture.

Trees in Culture

The tree has always been a cultural symbol. Common icons are the World tree and the tree of life. The tree is often used to represent nature or the environment itself. A common misconception is that trees get most of their mass from the ground Actually, 99 % of a tree's mass comes from the air.

These most likely use diameter measured at breast height, 4.5 feet (140 cm) above ground—not the larger base diameter. The right side of this equation can be pasted into a Google search bar to perform the calculation. Extrapolations from any model can cause problems, so tree value estimates for diameters larger than 30 inches might have to be capped so trees do not not exceed 27% of the total appraised property value.

8 LEAF

In botany, a leaf is an above-ground plant organ specialized for photosynthesis. For this purpose, a leaf is typically flat (laminar) and thin, to expose the cells containing chloroplast to light over a broad area, and to allow light to penetrate fully into the tissues. Leaves are also the sites in most plants where transpiration and guttation take place. Leaves can store food and water, and are modified in some plants for other purposes. The comparable structures of ferns are correctly referred to as fronds. Furthermore, leaves are prominent in the human diet as leaf vegetables.

Leaf Anatomy

A structurally complete leaf of an angiosperm consists of a petiole (leaf stem), a lamina (leaf blade), and stipules (small processes located to either side of the base of the petiole). The petiole attaches to the stem at a point called the "leaf axil". Not every species produces leaves with all of the aforementioned structural components. In some species, paired stipules are not obvious or are absent altogether. A petiole may be absent, or the blade may not be laminar (flattened). The tremendous variety shown in leaf structure (anatomy) from species to species is presented in detail below under Leaf morphology. After a period of time (i.e. seasonally, during the autumn), deciduous trees shed their leaves. These leaves then decompose into the soil.

A leaf is considered a plant organ and typically consists of the following tissues:

- An epidermis that covers the upper and lower surfaces.
- An interior chlorenchyma called the mesophyll.
- An arrangement of veins (the vascular tissue).

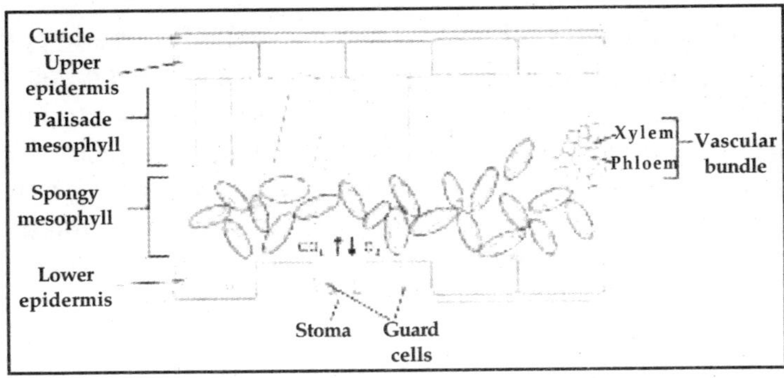

Fig. 8.1

Epidermis

SEM image of Nicotiana alata leaf's epidermis, showing trichomes (hair-like appendages) and stomata (eye-shaped slits, visible at full resolution).The epidermis is the outer multi-layered group of cells covering the leaf. It forms the boundary separating the plant's inner cells from the external world. The epidermis serves several functions: protection against water loss, regulation of gas exchange, secretion of metabolic compounds, and (in some species) absorption of water. Most leaves show dorsoventral anatomy: the upper (adaxial) and lower (abaxial) surfaces have somewhat different construction and may serve different functions.

The epidermis is usually transparent (epidermal cells lack chloroplasts) and coated on the outer side with a waxy cuticle that prevents water loss. The cuticle is in some cases thinner on the lower epidermis than on the upper epidermis, and is thicker on leaves from dry climates as compared with those from wet climates.

The epidermis tissue includes several differentiated cell types: epidermal cells, guard cells, subsidiary cells, and epidermal hairs (trichomes). The epidermal cells are the most numerous, largest, and least specialized. These are typically more elongated in the leaves of monocots than in those of dicots.

The epidermis is covered with pores called stomata, part of a stoma complex consisting of a pore surrounded on each side by chloroplast-containing guard cells, and two to four subsidiary cells that lack chloroplasts. The stoma complex regulates the exchange of gases and water vapor between the outside air and the interior of the leaf. Typically, the stomata are more numerous over the abaxial (lower) epidermis than the adaxial (upper) epidermis.

Mesophyll

Most of the interior of the leaf between the upper and lower layers of epidermis is a parenchyma (ground tissue) or *chlorenchyma* tissue called the mesophyll (Greek for "middle leaf"). This assimilation tissue is the primary location of photosynthesis in the plant. The products of photosynthesis are called "assimilates".

In ferns and most flowering plants the mesophyll is divided into two layers:

- An upper *palisade layer* of tightly packed, vertically elongated cells, one to two cells thick, directly beneath the adaxial epidermis. Its cells contain many more chloroplasts than the spongy layer. These long cylindrical cells are regularly arranged in one to five rows. Cylindrical cells, with the chloroplasts close to the walls of the cell, can take optimal advantage of light. The slight separation of the cells provides maximum absorption of carbon dioxide. This separation must be minimal to afford capillary action for water distribution. In order to adapt to their different environment (such as sun or shade), plants had to adapt this structure to obtain optimal result. Sun leaves have a multi-layered palisade layer, while shade leaves or older leaves closer to the soil, are single-layered.

- Beneath the palisade layer is the *spongy layer*. The cells of the spongy layer are more rounded and not so tightly packed. There are large intercellular air spaces. These cells contain fewer chloroplasts than those of the palisade layer.
- The pores or stomata of the epidermis open into substomatal chambers, connecting to air spaces between the spongy layer cells.

These two different layers of the mesophyll are absent in many aquatic and marsh plants. Even an epidermis and a mesophyll may be lacking. Instead for their gaseous exchanges they use a homogeneous *aerenchyma* (thin-walled cells separated by large gas-filled spaces). Their stomata are situated at the upper surface.

Leaves are normally green in color, which comes from chlorophyll found in plastids in the chlorenchyma cells. Plants that lack chlorophyll cannot photosynthesize.

Leaves in temperate, boreal, and seasonally dry zones may be seasonally deciduous (falling off or dying for the inclement season). This mechanism to shed leaves is called abscission. After the leaf is shed, a leaf scar develops on the twig. In cold autumns they sometimes change color, and turn yellow, bright orange or red as various accessory pigments (carotenoids and xanthophylls) are revealed when the tree responds to cold and reduced sunlight by curtailing chlorophyll production. Red anthocyanin pigments are now thought to be produced in the leaf as it dies, possibly to mask the yellow hue left when the chlorophyll is lost - yellow leaves appear to attract herbivores such as aphids.

Veins

The veins are the vascular tissue of the leaf and are located in the spongy layer of the mesophyll. They are typical examples of pattern formation through ramification. The pattern of the veins is called venation.

The veins are made up of:

- xylem, tubes that brings water and minerals from the roots into the leaf.
- phloem, tubes that usually moves sap, with dissolved sucrose, produced by photosynthesis in the leaf, out of the leaf.

The xylem typically lies over the phloem. Both are embedded in a dense parenchyma tissue, called "pith", with usually some structural collenchyma tissue present.

Leaf Morphology

External leaf characteristics (such as shape, margin, hairs, etc.) are important for identifying plant species, and botanists have developed a rich terminology for describing leaf characteristics. These structures are a part of what makes leaves determinant; they grow and achieve a specific pattern and shape, then stop. Other plant parts like stems or roots are non-determinant, and will usually continue to grow as long as they have the resources to do so.

Classification of leaves can occur through many different designative schema, and the type of leaf is usually characteristic of a species, although some species produce more than one type of leaf. The longest type of leaf is a leaf from palm trees, measuring at nine feet long. The terminology associated with the description of leaf morphology is presented, in illustrated form, at Wikibooks.

Basic Leaf Types

- Ferns have fronds.
- Conifer leaves are typically needle-, awl-, or scale-shaped.
- Angiosperm (flowering plant) leaves: the standard form includes stipules, a petiole and a lamina.
- Lycophytes have microphyll leaves.
- Sheath leaves (type found in most grasses).
- Other specialized leaves (such as those of Nepenthes).

Arrangement on the Stem

Different terms are usually used to describe leaf placement (phyllotaxis):

- *Alternate* — leaf attachments are singular at nodes, and leaves alternate direction, to a greater or lesser degree, along the stem.
- *Opposite* — leaf attachments are paired at each node; decussate if, as typical, each successive pair is rotated 90° progressing along the stem; or distichous if not rotated, but two-ranked (in the same geometric flat-plane).
- *Whorled* — three or more leaves attach at each point or node on the stem. As with opposite leaves, successive whorls may or may not be decussate, rotated by half the angle between the leaves in the whorl (i.e., successive whorls of three rotated 60°, whorls of four rotated 45°, etc). Opposite leaves may appear whorled near the tip of the stem.
- *Rosulate* — Leaves form a Rosette.

As a stem grows, leaves tend to appear arranged around the stem in a way that optimizes yield of light. In essence, leaves form a helix pattern centred around the stem, either clockwise or counterclockwise, with (depending upon the species) the same angle of divergence. There is a regularity in these angles and they follow the numbers in a Fibonacci sequence: 1/2, 2/3, 3/5, 5/8, 8/13, 13/21, 21/34, 34/55, 55/89. This series tends to a limit of 360° × 34/89 = 137.52 or 137° 30', an angle known mathematically as the golden angle. In the series, the numerator indicates the number of complete turns or "gyres" until a leaf arrives at the initial position. The denominator indicates the number of leaves in the arrangement. This can be demonstrated by the following:

- alternate leaves have an angle of 180° (or ½)
- 120° (or 1/3): three leaves in one circle
- 144° (or 2/5): five leaves in two gyres
- 135° (or 3/8): eight leaves in three gyres.

Divisions of the Lamina (Blade)

Two basic forms of leaves can be described considering the way the blade is divided. A simple leaf has an undivided blade. However, the leaf shape may be formed of lobes, but the gaps between lobes do not reach to the main vein. A compound leaf has a fully subdivided blade, each leaflet of the blade separated along a main or secondary vein. Because each leaflet can appear to be a simple leaf, it is important to recognize where the petiole occurs to identify a compound leaf. Compound leaves are a characteristic of some families of higher plants, such as the Fabaceae. The middle vein of a compound leaf or a frond, when it is present, is called a rachis.

- *Palmately compound leaves* have the leaflets radiating from the end of the petiole, like fingers off the palm of a hand, e.g. Cannabis (hemp) and Aesculus (buckeyes).

- *Pinnately compound leaves* have the leaflets arranged along the main or mid-vein.

  Odd pinnate: with a terminal leaflet, e.g. Fraxinus (ash).

  Even pinnate: lacking a terminal leaflet, e.g. Swietenia (mahogany).
- *Bipinnately compound leaves* are twice divided: the leaflets are arranged along a secondary vein that is one of several branching off the rachis. Each leaflet is called a "pinnule". The pinnules on one secondary vein are called "pinna"; e.g. Albizia (silk tree).
- *Trifoliate:* a pinnate leaf with just three leaflets, e.g. Trifolium (clover), Laburnum (laburnum).
- *Pinnatifid:* pinnately dissected to the midrib, but with the leaflets not entirely separate, e.g. Polypodium, some Sorbus (whitebeams).

Characteristics of the Petiole

Petiolated leaves have a petiole. Sessile leaves do not: the blade attaches directly to the stem. In clasping or decurrent leaves, the blade partially or wholly surrounds the stem, often giving the impression that the shoot grows through the leaf. When this is actually the case, the leaves are called "perfoliate", such as in Claytonia perfoliata. In peltate leaves, the petiole attaches to the blade inside from the blade margin.

In some Acacia species, such as the Koa Tree (Acacia koa), the petioles are expanded or broadened and function like leaf blades; these are called phyllodes. There may or may not be normal pinnate leaves at the tip of the phyllode.

A stipule, present on the leaves of many dicotyledons, is an appendage on each side at the base of the petiole resembling a small leaf. Stipules may be lasting and not be shed (a stipulate leaf, such as in roses and beans), or be shed as the leaf expands, leaving a stipule scar on the twig (an exstipulate leaf).

The situation, arrangement, and structure of the stipules is called the "stipulation".

- *Adnate:* fused to the petiole base
- *Ochreate:* provided with ochrea, or sheath-formed stipules, e.g. rhubarb, encircling the petiole base.
- *Interpetiolar:* between the petioles of two opposite leaves.
- *Intrapetiolar:* between the petiole and the subtending stem.

Venation (arrangement of the veins)

There are two subtypes of venation, namely, craspedodromous, where the major veins stretch up to the margin of the leaf, and camptodromous, when major veins extend close to the margin, but bend before they intersect with the margin.

- Feather-veined, reticulate — the veins arise pinnately from a single mid-vein and subdivide into veinlets. These, in turn, form a complicated network. This type of venation is typical for (but by no means limited to) dicotyledons.
- Pinnate-netted, penniribbed, penninerved, penniveined; the leaf has usually one main vein (called the mid-vein), with veinlets, smaller veins branching off laterally, usually somewhat parallel to each other; eg Malus (apples).
- Three main veins branch at the base of the lamina and run essentially parallel subsequently, as in Ceanothus. A similar pattern (with 3-7 veins) is especially conspicuous in Melastomataceae.
- Palmate-netted, palmate-veined, fan-veined; several main veins diverge from near the leaf base where the petiole attaches, and radiate toward the edge of the leaf; e.g. most Acer (maples).

- Parallel-veined, parallel-ribbed, parallel-nerved, penniparallel — veins run parallel for the length of the leaf, from the base to the apex. Commissural veins (small veins) connect the major parallel veins. Typical for most monocotyledons, such as grasses.
- Dichotomous - There are no dominant bundles, with the veins forking regularly by pairs; found in Ginkgo and some pteridophytes.

Note that although it is the more complex pattern, branching veins appear to be plesiomorphic and in some form were present in ancient seed plants as long as 250 million years ago. A pseudo-reticulate venation that is actually a highly modified penniparallel one is an autapomorphy of some Melanthiaceae which are monocots, e.g. Paris quadrifolia (True-lover's Knot).

Leaf Morphology Changes within a Single Plant

- *Homoblasty* - Characteristic in which a plant has small changes in leaf size, shape, and growth habit between juvenile and adult stages.
- *Heteroblasty* - Charactistic in which a plant has marked changes in leaf size, shape, and growth habit between juvenile and adult stages.

Leaf Terminology

Leaf Shape

In botany, leaf shape is characterised with the following terms (botanical Latin terms in brackets):

- Acicular (*acicularis*): Slender and pointed, needle-like
- Acuminate (*acuminata*): Tapering to a long point
- Aristate (*aristata*): Ending in a stiff, bristle-like point
- Bipinnate (*bipinnata*): Each leaflet also pinnate

- Compound: The combination of one leaflet arrangement within an arrangement at a larger level; e.g. " bipinnate, twice-pinnate: the leaflets are themselves pinnately-compound".
- Cordate (*cordata*): Heart-shaped, stem attaches to cleft
- Cuneate (*cuneata*): Triangular, stem attaches to point
- Deltoid (*deltoidea*) or deltate: Triangular, stem attaches to side
- Digitate (*digitata*): Divided into finger-like lobes
- Elliptic (*elliptica*): Oval, with a short or no point
- Falcate (*falcata*): sickle-shaped
- Filiform (*filiformis*): thread- or filament-shaped
- Flabellate (*flabellata*): Semi-circular, or fan-like
- Hastate, spear-shaped (*hastata*): Pointed, with barbs, shaped like a spear point, with flaring pointed lobes at the base.

Margins (edge)

The leaf margin is characteristic for a genus and aids in determining the species.

- *Ciliate:* fringed with hairs.
- *Crenate:* wavy-toothed; dentate with round teeth, such as *Fagus* (beech)
- *Crenulate* finely or shallowly crenate
- *Dentate:* toothed, such as *Castanea* (chestnut)
  - *Coarse-toothed:* with large teeth
  - *Glandular toothed:* with teeth that bear glands.
- *Denticulate:* finely toothed
- *Doubly toothed:* each tooth bearing smaller teeth, such as *Ulmus* (elm)

- *Entire:* even; with a smooth margin; without toothing
- *Lobate:* intended, with the indentations not reaching to the centre, such as many *Quercus* (oaks)
  - *Palmately lobed:* intended with the indentations reaching to the centre, such as *Humulus* (hop).
- *Serrate:* saw-toothed with asymmetrical teeth pointing forward, such as *Urtica* (nettle)
- *Serrulate:* finely serrate
- *Sinuate:* with deep, wave-like indentations; coarsely crenate, such as many *Rumex* (docks)
- *Spiny:* with stiff, sharp points, such as some *Ilex* (hollies) and *Cirsium* (thistles).

Tip of the Leaf

- *Acuminate:* long-pointed, prolonged into a narrow, tapering point in a concave manner.
- *Acute:* ending in a sharp, but not prolonged point
- *Cuspidate:* with a sharp, elongated, rigid tip; tipped with a cusp.
- *Emarginate:* intended, with a shallow notch at the tip.
- *Mucronate:* Abruptly tipped with a small short point, as a continuation of the midrib; tipped with a mucro.
- *Mucronulate:* mucronate, but with a smaller spine.
- *Obcordate:* inversely heart-shaped, deeply notched at the top.
- *Obtuse:* rounded or blunt.
- *Truncate:* ending abruptly with a flat end, that looks cut off.

Base of the Leaf

- *Acuminate:* coming to a sharp, narrow, prolonged point.

- *Acute:* coming to a sharp, but not prolonged point.
- *Auriculate:* ear-shaped.
- *Cordate:* heart-shaped with the notch towards the stalk.
- *Cuneate:* wedge-shaped.
- *Hastate:* shaped like an halberd and with the basal lobes pointing outward.
- *Oblique:* slanting.
- *Reniform:* kidney-shaped but rounder and broader than long.
- *Rounded:* curving shape.
- *Sagittate:* shaped like an arrowhead and with the acute basal lobes pointing downward.
- *Truncate:* ending abruptly with a flat end, that looks cut off.

Surface of the Leaf

The surface of a leaf can be described by several botanical terms:

- *Farinose:* bearing farina; mealy, covered with a waxy, whitish powder.
- *Glabrous:* smooth, not hairy.
- *Glaucous:* with a whitish bloom; covered with a very find, bluish-white powder.
- *Glutinous:* sticky, viscid.
- *Papillate,* or *papillose:* bearing papillae (minute, nipple-shaped protuberances).
- *Pubescent:* covered with erect hairs (especially soft and short ones).
- *Punctate:* marked with dots; dotted with depressions or with translucent glands or colored dots.

- *Rugose:* deeply wrinkled; with veins clearly visible.
- *Scurfy:* covered with tiny, broad scalelike particles.
- *Tuberculate:* covered with tubercles; covered with warty prominences
- *Verrucose:* warted, with warty outgrowths.
- *Viscid*, or *viscous:* covered with thick, sticky secretions.

The leaf surface is also host to a large variety of *microorganisms;* in this context it is referred to as the *phyllosphere*.

Hairiness (Trichomes)

"Hairs" on plants are properly called *trichomes.* Leaves can show several degrees of hairiness. The meaning of several of the following terms can overlap.

- *Arachnoid* or *arachnose:* with many fine, entangled hairs giving a cobwebby appearance.
- *Barbellate:* with finely barbed hairs (barbellae).
- *Bearded:* with long, stiff hairs.
- *Bristly:* with stiff hair-like prickles.
- *Canescent:* hoary with dense grayish-white pubescence.
- *Ciliate:* marginally fringed with short hairs (cilia).
- *Ciliolate:* minutely ciliate.
- *Floccose:* with flocks of soft, woolly hairs, which tend to rub off.
- *Glabrous:* no hairs of any kind present.
- *Glandular:* with a gland at the tip of the hair.
- *Hirsute:* with rather rough or stiff hairs.
- *Hispid:* with rigid, bristly hairs.
- *Hispidulous:* minutely hispid.

- *Hoary:* with a find, close grayish-white pubescence.
- *Lanate*, or *lanose:* with woolly hairs.
- *Pilose:* with soft, clearly separated hairs.
- *Puberulent,* or *puberulous:* with find, minute hairs.
- *Pubescent:* with soft, short and erect hairs.
- *Scabrous,* or *scabrid:* rough to the touch.
- *Sericeous:* silky appearance through find, straight and appressed (lying close and flat) hairs.
- *Silky:* with adpressed, soft and straight pubescence.
- *Stellate,* or *stelliform:* with star-shaped hairs.
- *Strigose:* with appressed, sharp, straight and stiff hairs.
- *Tomentose:* densely pubescent with matted, soft white woolly hairs.
  - *Cano-tomentose:* between canescent and tomentose.
  - *Felted-tomentose:* woolly and matted with curly hairs.
- *Villous:* with long and soft hairs; usually curved.
- *Woolly: with long, soft and tortuous or matted hairs.*

In the course of evolution, leaves have adapted to different environments in the following ways:

- A certain surface structure avoids moistening by rain and contamination (*See Lotus effect)*.
- Sliced leaves reduce wind resistance.
- Hairs on the leaf surface trap humidity in dry climates and create a large boundary layer thereby reducing water loss.
- Waxy leaf surfaces reduce water loss.

- Large surface area of leaf provides large area for sunlight and provides shade for plant to minimize hearing and reduce water loss.
- In more or less opaque or buried in the soil leaves, translucent windows filter the light before the photosynthesis takes place at the inner leaf surfaces (e.g. *Fenestraria).*
- Succulent leaves store water and organic acids for use in CAM photosynthesis.
- Aromatic oils, poisons or pheromones produced by leaf borne glands deter herbivores (e.g. eucalypts).
- Inclusions of crystalline minerals deter herbivores (e.g. silica in grasses).
- A transformation into petals attracts pollinators.
- A transformation into spines protects and plants (*e.g.* cacti).
- A transformation into insect traps helps feeding the plants (carnivorous plants).
- A transformation into bulbs helps storing food and water (*e.g.* onions).
- A transformation into tendrils allows the plant to climb (*e.g.* peas).
- A transformation into bracts and pseudanthia (*false flowers*) replaces normal flower structures if the true flowers are extremely reduced (*e.g.* Spurges).

Interactions with other Organisms

Although not as nutritious as other organs such as fruit, leaves provide a food source for many organisms. Animals which eat leaves are known as folivores. The leaf is one of the most vital parts of the plant, and plants have evolved protection against folivores such as tannins, chemicals which hinder the digestion of proteins and have an unpleasant taste.

Some animals have cryptic adaptations to avoid their own predators. For example, some caterpillars will create a small home in the leaf by folding it over themselves, while other herbivores and their prey mimic and appearance of the leaf. Some insects, such as the katydid, take this even further, moving from side to side much like a leaf does in the wind.

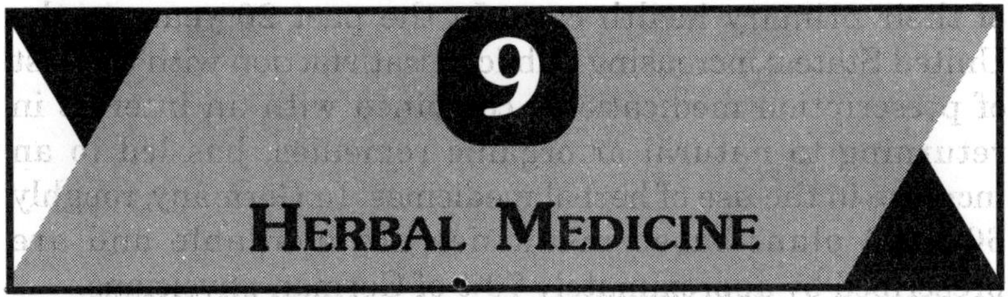

Introduction

Herbal medicine, also called botanical medicine or phytomedicine, refers to the use of a plant's seeds, berries, roots, leaves, bark, or flowers for medicinal purposes. Long practiced outside of conventional medicine, herbalism is becoming more mainstream as improvements in analysis and quality control along with advances in clinical research show their value in the treatment and prevention of disease.

History of Herbal Medicine

Plants had been used for medicinal purposes long before recorded history. For example, ancient Chinese and Egyptian papyrus writings describe medicinal plant uses. Indigenous cultures (such as African and Native American) used herbs in their healing rituals, while others developed traditional medical systems (such as Ayurveda and Traditional Chinese Medicine) in which herbal therapies were used systematically. Scientists found that people in different parts of the globe tended to use the same or similar plants for the same purposes.

In the early 19th century, when methods of chemical analysis first became available, scientists began extracting and modifying the active ingredients from plants. In the U.S. Later, chemists began making their own version of plant compounds, beginning the transition from raw herbs to synthetic pharmaceuticals. Over time, the use of herbal medicines declined in favor of pharmaceuticals.

The World Health Organization estimated that 80% of people worldwide rely on herbal medicines for some aspect of their primary health care. In the past 20 years in the United States, increasing public dissatisfaction with the cost of prescription medications, combined with an interest in returning to natural or organic remedies, has led to an increase in the use of herbal medicines. In Germany, roughly 600-700 plant-based medicines are available and are prescribed by approximately 70% of German physicians.

How do Herbs Work?

For most herbs, the specific ingredient that causes a therapeutic effect is not known. Whole herbs contain many ingredients, and it is likely that they work together to produce the desired medicinal effect. Many factors determine how effective an herb will be. For example, the type of environment (climate, bugs, soil quality) in which a plant grew will affect its components, as will how and when it was harvested and processed.

Uses of Herbs

The use of herbal supplements for medicinal purposes has increased dramatically over the past 30 years. Herbal supplements are classified as dietary supplements by the U.S. Dietary Supplement Health and Education Act (DSHEA) of 1994. The FDA defines a dietary supplement as "...any product taken by mouth that contains a so-called 'dietary ingredient' and its label clearly states that it is a dietary supplement." As per the provisions of DSHEA, herbal supplements — unlike pharmaceutical drugs — can be marketed without undergoing testing to prove their safety and efficacy. However, herbal supplements must be manufactured according to good manufacturing practices.

The most commonly used herbal supplements in the U.S. include echinacea (*Echinacea purpurea* and related species), St. John's wort (*Hypericum perforatum*), ginkgo (*Ginkgo biloba*), garlic (*Allium sativum*), saw palmetto (*Serenoa repens*), ginseng (*Panax ginseng*, or *Asian ginseng*; and *Panax quinquefolius*, or *American ginseng*), goldenseal (*Hydrastis canadensis*), valerian (*Valeriana officinalis*), kava (*Piper methysticum*), chamomile (*Matricaria recutita*), feverfew (*Tanacetum parthenium*), ginger (*Zingiber officinale*), evening primrose (*Oenothera biennis*), and milk thistle (*Silybum marianum*).

Several herbs are often used together to enhance effectiveness and synergistic actions and to reduce toxicity. Health care providers must take many things into account when recommending herbs. For example, the species and variety of the plant, the plant's habitat, how it was stored and processed, and whether or not there are contaminants (including heavy metals and pesticides).

Important Herbal Medicines

Herbal medicine treats many conditions, such as asthma, eczema, premenstrual syndrome, rheumatoid arthritis, migraine, menopausal symptoms, chronic fatigue, and irritable bowel syndrome, among others. Herbal supplements are best taken under the guidance of a trained health care provider. Be sure to consult with your doctor or pharmacist before self-treating.

- *Ginkgo* (*Ginkgo biloba*), particularly a standardized extract known as EGb 761, appears to produce improvements in awareness, judgment, and social function in people with Alzheimer's disease and dementia. Randomized controlled studies assessing the use of ginkgo supplements for Alzheimer's disease in individuals older than 65 years have produced positive results.

- *Kava kava* (*Piper methysticum*) has become popular as a treatment for anxiety, but recent reports have traced liver damage to enough people who have used kava that the U.S. Food and Drug Administration (FDA) issued a warning regarding its use, while other countries, such as Germany, France, and Canada, have taken kava off of the market. However, there is no definitive proof that kava alone is responsible for liver damage in humans. Kava has been used traditionally for thousands of years.
- *Saw palmetto* (*Serenoa repens*) is used by over 2 million men in the United States for the treatment of benign prostatic hyperplasia (BPH). The evidence suggests that saw palmetto provides mild-to-moderate improvement in urinary symptoms and flow measures. Saw palmetto produces similar improvement in urinary symptoms and flow compared to finasteride (Proscar), a pharmaceutical drug used in BPH, and is associated with fewer adverse treatment events.
- *St. John's wort* (*Hypericum perforatum*) is well known for its antidepressant effects. The clinical efficacy of some standardized St. John's wort standardized extracts in the treatment of mild and moderate depression has been demonstrated in about 40 controlled clinical trials.
- *Valerian* (*Valeriana officinalis*) has had a long tradition as a sleep-inducing agent, with the added benefit of producing no hangover feeling the next day.
- *Echinacea preparations* (from *Echinacea purpurea* and other *Echinacea species*) may improve the body's natural immunity. Echinacea is one of the most commonly used herbal products, but controversy exists about its benefit in the prevention and treatment of

the common cold. A meta-analysis of 14 clinical studies evaluating the effect of echinacea on the incidence and duration of the common cold found that echinacea supplements decreased the odds of developing the common cold by 58% and the duration of a cold by 1.4 days.

Standardized herbal supplements are the best way to ensure proper dosages and effects similar to human clinical trials. Ask your doctor or pharmacist about which herbal supplements are the best choice for your health concerns.

Safety

Used correctly, many herbs are considered safer than conventional medications, but because they are unregulated, herbal products are often mislabeled and may contain undeclared additives and adulterants. Some herbs are associated with allergic reactions or interact with conventional drugs. Self-prescribing herbal products will increase your risk, so it is important to consult your doctor or pharmacist before taking herbal medicines. Some examples of adverse reactions from certain popular herbs are described below.

- *St. John's* wort causes sensitivity to the sun's ultraviolet rays, and may cause an allergic reaction, stomach upset, fatigue, and restlessness. Clinical studies report that St. John's wort also interferes with the effectiveness of many drugs, including warfarin (Couamdin, a blood thinner), protease inhibitors for HIV, birth control pills, certain asthma drugs, and many other medications. In addition, St. John's wort should not be taken with prescribed anti-depressant medication. The FDA has issued a public health advisory concerning many of these interactions.
- *Kava kava* has been linked to liver toxicity. Kava has been taken off the market in several countries because of the liver toxicity, although the causes remain controversial.

- *Valerian* may cause oversedation, and in some people it may even have the unexpected effect of overstimulating instead of sedating.
- *Garlic:* Bleeding time may be altered with the use of garlic, ginkgo, feverfew, and ginger, among others.
- *Evening primrose* (Oenothera biennis) may increase the risk of seizures in patients taking drug known to lower seizure threshold, such as anti-convulsants.

Some herbal supplements, especially those imported from Asian countries, may contain high levels of heavy metals, including lead, mercury, and cadmium. It is important to purchase herbal supplements from reputable manufacturers to ensure quality. Talk to your health care provider for more information.

Herbal Medicine

Nearly one-third of Americans use herbs, and it is estimated that in 1998 alone $4 billion was spent on herbal products in this country. Unfortunately, a recent study in the *New England Journal of Medicine* indicated that nearly 70% of individuals taking herbal medicines (the majority of which were well educated and had a higher-than-average income) were reluctant to reveal their use of complementary and alternative medicine to their doctors. Because herbal medicines contain a combination of chemicals, each with a specific action, many are capable of eliciting complex physiological responses — some of which may create unwanted or unexpected results when combined with conventional drugs. Be sure to consult your doctor before trying any herbal products.

Solid of Herbal Medicines in Stores

The herbs available in most stores come in several different forms: teas, syrups, oils, liquid extracts, tinctures, and dry extracts (pills or capsules). Teas are simply dried herbs left to soak for a few minutes in hot water, while other teas are the herbs boiled in water and then strained for consumption. Syrups, made from concentrated extracts and added to sweet-tasting preparations, are frequently used for sore throats and coughs. Oils are extracted from plants and often used as rubs for massage, either alone or as part of an ointment or cream. Tinctures and liquid extracts are solvents (usually water, alcohol, or glycerol) that contain the active ingredients of the herbs. Tinctures are typically a 1:5 or 1:10 concentration, meaning that one part of the herbal material is prepared with five to ten parts (by weight) of the liquid. Liquid extracts are more concentrated than tinctures and are typically a 1:1 concentration. A dry extract form is the most concentrated form of an herbal product (typically 2:1 - 8:1) and is sold as a tablet, capsule, or lozenge.

No organization or government body regulates the manufacture or certifies the labeling of herbal preparations. This means you can't be sure that the amount of the herb contained in the bottle, or even from dose to dose, is the same as what is stated on the label. Some herbal preparations are standardized, meaning that the preparation is guaranteed to contain a specific amount of the active ingredients of the herb. However, it is still important to ask companies that are making standardized herbal products the basis for their product's guarantee. If consumers insist on an answer to this question, manufacturers of these herbal products may begin to implement more quality control processes, like microscopic, chemical, and biological analyses. It is important to talk to your doctor or an expert in herbal medicine for the recommended doses of any herbal products you are considering.

Experts in Herbal Medicine

Herbalists, chiropractors, naturopathic physicians, pharmacists, medical doctors, and practitioners of Traditional Chinese Medicine all may use herbs to treat illness.

Naturopathic physicians believe that the body is continually striving for balance and that natural therapies can be used to support this process. They are trained in 4-year, postgraduate institutions that combine courses in conventional medical science (such as pathology, microbiology, pharmacology, and surgery) with clinical training in herbal medicine, homeopathy, nutrition, and lifestyle counseling.

For additional information, or to locate an experienced herbalist in your area, contact the American Herbalists Guild (AHG). To locate a licensed naturopath in your area, call the American Association of Naturopathic Physicians (AANP).

Although a renaissance is occurring in herbal medicine in the United States, the FDA still classifies herbs as dietary supplements and will not allow manufacturers to claim that their products are able to treat or prevent specific diseases. In some countries in Europe, however, herbs are classified as drugs and are regulated. The German Commission E, an expert medical pan actively researches their safety and effectiveness.

While still not widely accepted, herbal medicine is becoming more available in medical schools and pharmacy schools as a classroom topic. This allows more health care providers to become exposed to positive and potentially negative effects of using herbal medicines as part of treatment for health conditions. Some health care providers, including doctors and pharmacists, are trained in herbal medicine. These professionals can effectively help patients integrate herbs along with lifestyle changes and conventional therapies (including prescription medications and surgery) into the individual's treatment plan.

INDEX

I

J

K

L

M

R

S

❑❑❑